S0-CWR-505

The Kings of the Narrow Gate

The Great Recession
A Journey of Faith and Inequality
in America's Heartland

by T.W. Trenkle

King's Gate Books
Dubuque, Iowa 52001

Copyright@2014 by Tim Trenkle

All rights reserved, including the right of reproduction in whole or in part in any form. No part of this publication may be reproduced or transmitted in any form or by any means without written permission of the publisher.

Designed by TW Trenkle

ISBN 978 0 615 98329 5

Printed in the United States of America.

PRAISE

- *I bought a Sunday Gazette off the newsstand yesterday when I was (in) Cedar Rapids. I enjoyed your piece on the Dubuque mission. That was a nice bit of storytelling.*
  - Jon Walker, Sioux Falls S.D. Argus Leader, Editor

- *We love the piece... It's beautiful.*
  - Ralph Kluseman, Dubuque 365 Inc.

- *Wow. What a beautiful and thought filled essay*
  - Matthew Modine Actor, Director

- *I just finished reading your (article) in the Cedar Rapids Gazette. I thought it was excellent. I also wondered if you had thought of combining your articles in a book. I would be very interested...*
  - Paula Knight (reader)

- *...the politicians crush people all the time and they pretend they're ordinary folks. Where can I read your column?*
  - John Kass, Chicago Tribune, *Columnist*

- *Congrats to you, Tim, for shining light on this.. and getting people to see the light.*
  - Carol Hunter, Des Moines Register, *Editor*

- *Thanks for your participation.*
  - Iowa Writes, University of Iowa

- *This is a lovely piece, evocative and elegiac...*
  - Shane Tritsch, Managing Editor Chicago Magazine

- *Nice word picture that goes a long way to de-mystify a growing segment of the Dubuque population. Look forward to your next effort.*
  - John Martin (reader)

- *Great article – wonderful writing! I felt like I was in the room with both of you.*
  - Sharon (reader)

- *I read your column late in the day yesterday, over dinner in fact, and it was like drinking a fine wine with a meal, or poetry or music. What an incredible gentle, visual piece.*
  - Bei Ruetten (reader)

- *Your article in the Telegraph Herald is amazing … was so touching…so realistic. Your article is wonderful and I do thank you for seeing the need.. and writing the article*
  - Mary Ellyn Jensen (Art and Antiques Dealer)

- *Thank you for your contribution to the ..Des Moines Register. It was beautifully written.*
  - Joan Sutterlin (reader)

- *I found the article to be well written, heartwarming and thought-provoking…*
  - Werner Hellmer, Attorney

- *We love the piece … It's beautiful. Thanks a million*
  – Ellen Kluseman

- *You are, indeed, a good writer and observer of the human condition.*
  – Carol Hunter, Des Moines Register, Editor

- *I am a subscriber to the Cedar Rapids Gazette and read your guest column this morning. I want to take this opportunity to thank you for such an eloquent, meaningful, message …*
  - Jennifer Slife,(reader)

- *What's the blog called?*
  – John Kass, Chicago Tribune, *Columnist*

- *I like your suggestion in the article that we can bridge the divide through community. You are a writer who can touch the heart.*
  – Kelly Larson, City of Dubuque Human Rights Director

- *I was a teacher in Des Moines Public School system for the twenty years I lived there. I taught inner city and working poor kids primarily...I don't know why Dubuque remains so locked in its distaste for outsiders, minorities. ..your piece was well-written.*
  – Ann Bibby , teacher

THE KINGS
OF THE NARROW GATE

The pawn shop sign is lit all day and throughout the night. Some nights it shadows drug addicts strung so far out on crack or meth they're human aliens. Some nights it's a klieg on poverty so deep that the sight of the sidewalk as a mattress, the street a den, the cold rain an air conditioner, shrinks a man's hope. The sign flickers. Pawn. Pawn. Pawn.

The five pawn shops are blocks from city hall. They bail out the multitude of poor who have no credit. How strange it was that Forbes named this place best small city to raise a family. Most poverty is mapped within blocks of city hall. People ask why. "Forbes never stopped here."

Over time, you see the regulars and you understand the pawn philosophy. Make a buck, trade some, sell some, loan some. A bargain in one corner, a tragedy in another. A theme starts at the door and echoes. The song rumbles from the counter, from the aisle, from the man's eyes and his hands, trembling or balanced, con or genuine. What have you got, the broker asks.

A fair question.

It begins inside a pawn where a mission feeds the poor. The Christian sends his prayer. The embattled stand in the cold for a bowl of deer meat.

Here are the kings of that Narrow Gate, a Dubuque mission named for the gate of Biblical Matthew, said to be the words of Jesus:

> *"Enter through the narrow gate. For wide is the gate and broad is the road that leads to destruction, and many enter through it. But small is the gate and narrow the road that leads to life, and only a few find it."*

Thought to be the jacket Burt Reynolds wore during filming of the landmark movie Deliverance. Now, after the mice made a nest of it, the jacket serves the Narrow Gate mission at its entry. Around the corner is the white washed wall where Kevin Costner and Burt Lancaster were filmed in The Field of Dreams.

"What day is it?" Asked Pooh.
"It's today." Squeaked Piglet.
"My favorite day." Said Pooh.

(A.A. Milne)

TABLE OF CONTENTS

Beginnings. 1

I.   The Porcelain Bible 3

II.   Main Street 11

III.   On Liberty Street 17

IV.   Dreamers. 23

V.   Errands. 27

VI.   A Time to Weep 31

VII.   Rattling the Pipes 35

VIII.   The Barber Shop. 41

IX.   Laying of Hands 47

X.   Section Eight. 51

XI.   Hard Times 59

XII.   Covenants 67

XIII.   Rubber Souls. 79

XIV.   Home is a Backpack. 87

XV.   The Old Woman and the Shoe. .95

XVI.   Tonto 99

XVII.   Community Crosses 103

XVIII.   Hoarding 111

XIX.   Dance Like an Invisible Man 117

XX.   Stanley's American Pawn 125

XXI.   The Heartland Campaign 137

XXII.   The Poorhouse 145

XXIII. Standards 157

XXIV.   Pawnbrokers 163

XXV.   Shadows Distort 173

XXVI.   The Camp Town Race 183

XXVII. Dilemma for the Disabled 187

XXVIII. The Dream Denied 191

XXIX.   The Community Church 197

XXX.   Beginning of the End. 203

- - - - - - - -

Photos 209

Frontier Dubuque Survey. 231

News Reports 235

Index. 241

Author Biography . . . . inside back cover

ACKNOWLEDGMENTS

These are my experiences as a journeyman in poverty, stories of events and interviews in the first city of Iowa, called the Key City, from 2007 to 2013. Some of the names in the book have been changed.

The following must be acknowledged: This is for Scott who lived so long without a home; for Jimmy who drank too much and forgot; for Tonto, a Marine who gave his heart to America; for the big man Russ, who gave his last dollar and his best prayers; to Paul and his great family who know the meaning of love and give it wherever they go, his parents Ruth and Bill, whose farm breakfasts made a difference; and Ron and Mike and Jim, who love deeply but sometimes are afraid to show it, and Pat who loves to cuss and who knows more about decency than most of the Christians who came to the mission.

This is for Sister Nancy whose encouragement will not be forgotten.

To Makiah and all those grand and beautiful friends at the first black barber; to Dick McGrane who touts my work regularly on his radio show; to Chris Farber who gave me a weekly radio show to talk about these people.

Thanks to some well known, kind people who corresponded after I wrote them, as I struggled with this book: David Peters at Iowa State who offered me research about poverty and crime; Leonard Pitts the Pulitzer Prize winner who responded with a simple question about race – how can there be only one social spot for blacks; John Kass, always concerned as an observer and as a great, sensitive columnist in Chicago who encouraged me through the years with his interest, who wrote about the strange system of justice in Dubuque, Iowa; Michael Perry, the best selling Wisconsin author who encouraged me to stay with it; and Dale Maharidge, also a Pulitzer Prize winner who kindly responded to my queries and applauded my hands – on work along the main street of Iowa's first city.

Thank you to editors including Carol Hunter at the Des Moines Register who empowered me; Jeff Tecklenburg at the Cedar Rapids Gazette who both encouraged and edited, giving my work such respectful attention; and to Brian

Cooper, a gentleman and ally at the Telegraph Herald, who showed me that to push beyond what he could muster might matter and who allowed me the column Mirrors and Windows, to tell stories of the downtrodden in Dubuque.

To the good people in Dubuque who have welcomed me. What Dubuque makes, makes Dubuque.

And to my encouraging and loving colleagues at Northeast Iowa Community College, who remind me that education matters, that involvement is an ethical obligation and that sometimes, you must trust your sense of rightness, especially when convention pushes back. As President Liang Chee Wee said in an impassioned speech one fall, there are many amputated souls. We need to do something.

FOR
MAGGIE MAE
AND HER CHILDREN

*In loving memory of Lois Mae & F.W. Trenkle, who left lessons
to remember from the great depression, from Hill 400,
from Remagen, from Dachau; who taught me to soldier,
who taught me to keep the faith.*

PREFACE

The Kings of the Narrow Gate begins years earlier when I was homeless, following an anguishing year as a therapist for adolescent boys on a rural two lane outside Dixon, Illinois. I had been a lead social worker at an ancient facility named the Nachusa Lutheran Home, chief of the little Falcon House. I worked with a dozen young men who had been pulled from their homes for various infractions and intractability. Their faults lie in being born to the awful circumstances of poverty.

I was hired because I had experience in the field of domestic violence and in working with families. During my stay, I taught myself as much as possible of the Lakota language and understanding, a view that we are connected to all things, that the creek stone has spirit, a different manner of thought and perception. I cannot say I mastered Lakota but I have tried. I saw a need to leave the city, to help the young people understand power is within and can be found beyond the media, technology and cityscape. Solitude and faith helped me as a counselor and as a man trying to keep his sanity.

Nachusa is a tiny speck on a two lane set behind wide, wonderful pines. It was said to be a translation from the native tongue, meaning 'Place Where the Bald Man Settled'.

The young men were Latino, African American and assorted other mixed inheritances. They had been accused of carrying knives to school, shooting playmates, dealings in drugs and the usual variety of malingering.

Soon, we became Hunka, family, crazy, wild, Ikce (free) men. In that time of the early 1990's when O.J. skirted down the highway with cameras chasing him and Pearl Jam highlighted the new alienation I saw an entire Christian facility turn away while children were abused. It set a tone for me.

After producing a sixty page report for the state of Illinois I walked into the administrator's office and quit. The boys had given me the facts. The last thing I was able to say to the boys of the Falcon house in the hurry of these events was to tell themselves the truth, to be honest with themselves even if they were dishonest with the world. "You will never be real if you don't." It's a hard lesson.

As I quit, the administrator said I was fired, anyway. I responded that he and his fellows had looked the other way while the most serious crimes against humanity had taken place. One of my crew had been sexually assaulted. It was years later, while interviewing for a job in Davenport, Iowa, that I was thanked for the work I did there. The interviewer made me out to be famous for having closed the Nachusa Lutheran Home. He stood up to shake my hand. He said the facility had been cleaned by the state.

The problem with whistle blowing is that you may never go back to that same career, that same life, again. I knew that then and would do what I did again.

Ignorant to the consequence of my actions, I searched for work in social services throughout that part of rural Illinois. No one wanted me. I put an ad in local papers and began to do handyman work. Soon, without enough employment, I embarked on a year long journey, hopping from motel to motel.

I have slept under bridges and know how to steal the toilet roll from camp sites. I know that a few potatoes, some eggs and cheese can keep a man going. I know that hope is necessary to survive. Frankl, a refugee from Dachau, was right - a man dies, slowly, imperceptibly, without enough hope. Or enough meaning.

In writing this story of the rag tag, forgotten, underemployed, unemployed, oppressed, I walked the streets, hung out with the pawns, carried food from the mission and went to the churches where the poor people went. In the six years of recording conversations and becoming a member of the street community I saw that their complaints are substantive.

I stood with young men in bloodied shorts describing a murder. I listened to the sides of a shooting, the white side and the black side, an Iowa Stand Your Ground experience as stark as may be imagined. I listened as a young black mom wept, telling her story of being stripped and left alone in a Dubuque cell; of another young black mom arrested after she attended a Bible study. I worked on the roof of a pawn then spoke to a homeless man who bathed in a plastic, WalMart tub, his wisdom as pure as the Iowa rain. I sang gospel with the evangelicals, saw tired women pawn their rings and children happy with a hard candy, their parents carrying food baskets to a dilapidated car at the curb.

There are ten thousand pawn shops in America, hungry children who will never reach their potential, families who have been torn as if the sky was a meaningless apparition, no one higher than the men who run the banks or dole out the dessert.

This is the Heartland.

I am the son of a meatpacker who went to war. My father was among the first to cross the Rhine, not far from where Caesar's troops had built a fort, millennia earlier. He opened Dachau. His father was a farmer.

When I first walked inside the 17th street pawn shop in the first city in Iowa I was stunned. When I saw the police surround a black tavern each weekend for no reason discernible except the patrons were black or that crime was high in the neighborhood I was mad.

I made lists of debris, inside and outside the pawn shop where we bivouacked after the stabbing murder of 2007: the electrical wires, the boxes, the moldy cheese wrappers, the candy, crushed under the counter, the corrugated boxes of food, overflowing from their weight, supplied by a Farmers' son who sacrificed, and despite raising ten children of his own, used his meager profit from the pawn to create his food mission.

The mission was bare, hardly more than the food boxes and the warmed pizza, the gruel my friend fixed and stirred in a rusty crock pot, but he fed people, each day, he fed the people of the street.

He said he called the place the Narrow Gate. I write and so can take a liberty by adding that the people I met, the tired, hungry, homeless, their children and their families, all of them, are kings of this gate, who have found the lessons of giving to each other, even as the world has turned away from them.

THE KINGS
OF THE NARROW GATE

by T.W. Trenkle

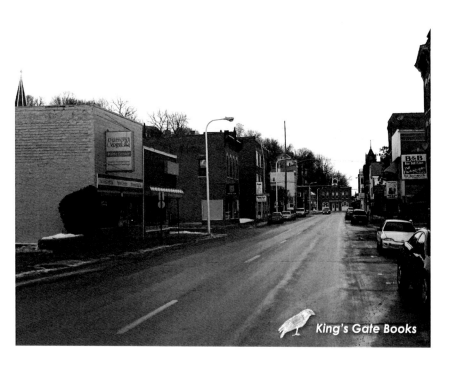

King's Gate Books

BEGINNINGS

To paraphrase Reverend Martin Luther King, I have known hatred and violence, I want no part of it. I have felt the pain of poverty. I wish that we could all walk together, hand in hand.

CITY OF DUBUQUE
HUMAN RIGHTS COMMISSION
MEETING MINUTES OF
SEPTEMBER 14, 2009

Commissioner Rubinstein called the meeting of the Dubuque Human Rights Commission to order at 4:16 p.m. on Monday, September 14, 2009, in Conference Room 2 at the City Hall Annex.

Roll Call:

Present: Jim Allan, Colin Scott, Anthony Allen, Vice-Chair Gretel Winterwood, Marcos Rubinstein, Chair Katrina Wilberding, Absent: Terry Driskell Shane Oswald, Char Eddy

Staff: Kelly Larson Carol Spinoso, Molly Menster

Approval of Minutes

Upon a motion by Commissioner Wilberding and second by Commissioner Winterwood, the minutes of July 13, 2009 were unanimously approved as submitted.

Tim Trenkle Addressed the Commission

Mr. Trenkle teaches psychology at NICC and is a free lance writer who writes about oppressed populations. Mr. Trenkle stated that he gathered data on ethnic relations in Dubuque from a survey he created after reading a book entitled, "White Racism on the Western Urban Frontier: Dynamics of Race and Class in Dubuque," which was written by a University of Dubuque Professor, Mohammad Chaichian.

He stated that 44 out of 100 Dubuque citizens surveyed did not know there was a Human Rights Commission in the city of Dubuque. Results also showed a concern for crime and safety amongst residents, and concerns about race. He encouraged commissioners to get out into the community to get to know the people in the different neighborhoods.

POSTSCRIPT - *Afterward, the city hired Northern Illinois University to look at race, crime and poverty. The people in the neighborhood never received a house call from any members of the Human Rights Commission. Among the most relevant facts summarized, to be used over and over, was the theme that the city's problem was 'perception'.*

I believe George Orwell addressed this very well in essays and books about truth and its spin.

I. THE PORCELAIN BIBLE

While long time ally big Jim busied with his e-bay business, adding videos and viewing possible buys, Scott snuck into Paul's old red bus, curled up in a raggedy seat with a bottle of Beam and fell asleep. The rest didn't help Scott. When Paul found him sprawled across the back seat and stinking like alcohol and ammonia he slapped the door and awoke him. Then Scott did what he always did, he went silent, for his life and his illness, and under his breath damned Paul for his help then asked for a ride. Paul obliged. He spent an hour every day running errands.

Last week Big Steve died. The doctors ordered tests for him after they decided he had kidney trouble. When the nurse entered Big Steve's room, she found him laid out sideways, dead as an empty bottle of Beam.

The Great Recession had begun. The heartland poor would have to hunker down. Their faith would be tested.

The first thing I touched that Saturday morning was the stop and go light. I rode my bicycle to the Narrow Gate and a few feet from the front door the yellow police ribbon was tied to keep people from the scenes of the night. I tugged at the ribbon and slid my bike under it then stood the bike against the fading, white brick of the building.

The big man Roy hugged the alcove of the pawn store. He held a cigarette between his thumb and fingers the way people do on their last drags. He looked into the one way street of Central Avenue. Fifty yards away a fire truck set on four stabilizers in the center of the roped off street. The truck's hydraulic arm raised and lowered as police walked around the vehicle. Plain clothes police walked to and fro with note pads.

"Was a murder," Roy said. They're looking for the weapon."

The fire truck faced the Carpenter's Union hall. Two doors down the regulars were raising their beer at Noonan's. It was 8:45 a.m.

After he opened for business that morning the big man had poured rice into a crock pot, opened cans of beans and then sloshed the ingredients together with a ladle and kept his eye on the door. He added ketchup and other condiments for taste. It would feed the denizens of the street.

"Everyone is welcome," the big man had said. His pot of beans would feed hungry and homeless who looked to the pawn shop's free food mission to fill their bellies.

The full moon washed over the street. The rains of the previous week swept away the diesel and smoke. Butts, debris, paper and leaf littered the gutters.

At nine a.m., red haired Tommy from the American Pawn, walked to 17th Street.

The fire truck was ending its search and drawing up its steel legs like a moon rover preparing to move to another crater.

The big man and the red head talked about the murder for a few minutes, each acknowledged the necessity to take care. Red said he'd been there, heard some screams and watched someone dash across the street during the chaos. He said he was afraid.

He said the man charged with murder had been mad at him that morning. Red had given the police entry to the apartment he shared with the accused then they made the arrest.

Already opinions were forming on the street. The story seemed to move in the wind as if telepathic, crossing the corridors and alleys and into the silences where bar patrons were lifting glasses.

Working people were trolling Central two blocks away at the Farmers' Market by city hall and they too seemed to have heard the story about a native son stabbed by a black out-of-towner.

The story held that the killer was from Chicago. Several people up and down Central said they didn't want more of Chicago. A bartender said he was a cousin and it wasn't racial, it was the Chicago element.

In Red's pawn shop a shaved headed man said he saw bloodshed coming. He said residents had to take a stand against Chicago trouble. It wasn't racism, he said.

The Dubuque Telegraph Herald quoted people who suggested racism. The incident added fuel to the people's accusations that the press was devious. It was about working people, working poor.

In that summer Central Avenue, the main street, had new, expensive street lights erected near city hall.

Two blocks away, where killing poverty stained the street, the same old standards.

The Dubuque Church Of God pasted block letters in its windows, 'Jesus is Lord'.

On the sidewalk of Central, the victim's fiancée built a tribute that grows in the coming days in the late summer of 2007 to include angels and a rosary and a porcelain bible. A portrait of Jesus stares out to the crumbling curb, his Anglo face somber and surreal.

Chaos, fights then a murder…it is said and whispered.

The bright flowers and craft tables and truck beds loaded with corn present arbors for craned necks at the Farmers' Market that Saturday morning but the news is grim.

Some recall the recent debate about Dubuque justice that appeared in the Chicago papers. It had concerned the punishment of a Chicago cop and a fight in town. The columnist John Kass presented the story as a preposterous turn of judicial decision making. Dubuque was made a laughing stock. Now a murderous stabbing.

"Did you hear about last night?"

Residents looking for the ripe tomato, the sweet, ripe melon and the crisp, sweet ear of Iowa corn are whispering about a puddle of blood two blocks from their precious safety.

The police were still searching the rubble in the alleys and climbing to the rooftops for the weapon. The news comes in trickles, if it comes at all.

One man said, "We don't want this criminal element coming here!"

No one seemed to remember the KKK or the national news of cross burnings the decade before. In 2013 HUD will name this a critical, landmark time for Heartland Iowa's first city.

On the Sunday after the stabbing three young women stood at the makeshift tabernacle in front of the tax service on Central. One said "They come from Chicago. They have bulletin boards there to tell them to come here."

At the memorial for the fallen youth a picture of Jesus set on the sidewalk by pipes that protruded from the building. A ceramic elephant stood under the pipes. The young victim's photo was attached to the wall.

Rumor said it had been removed and burned, but his fiancée had replaced it.

Red and white plastic flowers decorated the offering. The memorial was placed on Saturday and soon a ceramic Ecclesiastes 3:1, 'There is an appointed time for everything…"

A home made crucifix and a blue rosary were added to the vigil. The women said his fiancée had been crying all day.

On the Monday night after the violence, a squad car pulled up in front of the 17th Street Pawn and mission at 17th and Central. It was nine p.m.

Paul Downs had placed a chair and a guitar on the sidewalk.

"Waiting for the eclipse?" a passerby asked.

"What eclipse?" Paul asked. He planned to sing Christian songs for peace.

At nine thirty, a goateed man on a bicycle pedaled by. He said he was in the bar two nights before and had a beer with the man charged with the murder. Down the street where the memorial waited for passing traffic, an angel, three candles and a little girl on a turtle were added to the other objects.

At nine fifty a young man speeded by the killing scenes in a sedan with a raised fist and shouted, "White power!"

Twenty four squad cars had passed in the previous two hours. Paul and I had been singing gospel between the pawn shop and barber. We folded the chair up, lifted the guitar and packed Paul's vehicle. No one had ever seen police surveillance like this.

The next day, a dead dove set on the empty lot by the Carpenter's Union, three days after the murder. The lot where the first Narrow Gate mission had once stood. No one reported it. It set a few feet from the grave stones of the monument company. It had been the scene of handshakes and apologies on Saturday when the red head and two blacks involved in the murder stood to make amends for their actions of that early morning Saturday bloodletting.

"I'm sorry," red headed Tommy had said.

"I forgive you," the man known as T-Bone said.

After the contrition they walked their separate ways.

After the funeral the paper again broached race. The street people close to the scene said it was the paper's issue. Except for a handful of complainers, the street allows a balancing act of poor, white and black people to co-exist. Store keeps said privately they worried about the handling of the murder by the press.

On August 31, 2007, Friday, a man with a Lakers shirt and black do rag stood at the opposite corner from our gospel singing on Central at Seventeenth and he flipped a chain of keys, an incessant rhythm of defiance, of anger, for fifteen minutes.

We sang 'The Old Wooden Cross' in front of the pawn shop.

After the man with the do rag, a Chinese woman stooped under the traffic light.

The songs were now warbled by a growing group of people seated in folding chairs. Conversation included stories of China and homelessness. Street people converged to sing.

"Why not peace?" We asked.

By Sunday, September 2, a musical group had formed for street serenades of gospel and repentance.

In the next two years more blood would spill from chaos. The mayor would run unopposed, city council members will tout the safety of the streets. National awards will begin to come. None of the city council will come down for a walk on Central Avenue.

On September 2, 2007 the traffic whirled by and drivers strained their necks to see the gospel singing. The population had been sensitized to the mayhem.

From the shadows where we sang a man with round fish eyes and a hairless face limped toward us. The top of his sandaled foot bled. He said he stumbled and that he did that often since the stroke. Soon, he tells of the time he killed a man in Dubuque.

"I hit him and killed him…"

Singers ask if he'd like them to lay on hands.

"Yes," he said, "That would be good." His story was confirmed. He killed a man over beer.

Friday, September 7. A little girl stood on the corner across from the singers and began to scream like a banshee. Her foul talk, crude for the street, loaded with F-bombs and other primitive words drew a man with a twisted afro and rasta braids in his hair.

"Weren't you loved as a child?"

At 10:48 alarms fired up the street at the gas station a block from city hall. Fire trucks sailed like doves around a church spire. A false alarm. Again the fight or flight syndrome had appeared.

The last full moon of August passed overhead like a scythe and the grime in Dubuque was scoured for evidence. The debris of the murder washed down the drains in the dull, muddy water all the way to the Mississippi.

Police reported a trio of black men at the scene and their report stood like a stone. The newspaper suggested a racial crime and the public reacted.

A knife was found.

In September the police studied the video at the gas station.

In 2008 the conviction came.

What happened? Some of it was told the morning after.

Within hours of the killing red headed Tommy, Chris and Charlie gathered on Central Avenue and each had a view of the death because each had been there. They talked about what had happened and they spoke quickly, filling the space of the American Pawn shop with nerve and doubt.

A fourth man was in the crowd with the accused killer, they said, and still say.

Twelve hours after the stabbing one sat on a frayed stool in a corner, wearing his blood stained clothes. The breeze was fresh as it blew into the store that morning and it cleaned the musty air from the earlier rain.

"I watched him die, right there on the street," Chris said repeatedly.

Chris, the shortest of the three men, stood by a counter with his right hand embracing the shelf like a crutch. His shoulder was stooped and he brushed his crew cut hair as if to brush away the night.

"I drank a bunch of beer but still couldn't sleep."

Each man a point of a triangle. Eyes darted away, to and fro and across to secrets and over shoulders. Red, at the doorway, added to the testimony.

"I was scared. I saw a man run across Central Avenue. I heard a scream, 'You're gonna die…'"

The running man has not been reported and like the fourth man they said they saw, never mentioned, nor the scream before the stabbing.

Tommy says he saw a sedan cross Central: "…about seven or eight blacks inside…" - he says; he wonders about the strange man who made the dash across that poor section of Dubuque street. He says he froze on the sidewalk.

"Yeah," the seated man says, "there were four guys…"

The conversation roamed, voices listening to voices, who saw what and what was heard and felt. The facts tumble from their thoughts like feathers from a nest.

One gave the apartment key to the police. One stood next to the young man as he breathed his last and squinted toward the sky.

"The fourth guy took off," one says.

"They haven't found him yet," the man at the doorway says. Chris shakes his head back and forth, unable to comprehend.

They note the blood stain at the sidewalk.

Cindy, the salon owner from across the street walked into the conversation as the tale unfolded. She carried a 'No Trespassing' sign.

"I need a hammer!"

"You gonna hang that sign?" Tommy asked. "Sure am…" said the black woman who rented the residence of the man accused of the killing.

Silence filled the shadows then as the three friends hung their heads and the pawn shop patrons moved about looking at jewelry. Silence grew. A tired grip of poverty and despair hung like a cloud.

The fourth man has long since vanished into the gutters of time. The news has never been reported about what the three young men saw that night. Their vigil hasn't been completed in any report.

Today, the three friends keep the conversation to themselves, held in that place that haunts them, that time of killing.

Then he was told:

Remember what you have seen,
Because everything forgotten
Returns to the circling winds.

(Navajo chant)

II. MAIN STREET

Central Avenue in Dubuque, Iowa, trespasses beneath ancient Mississippi River bluffs. Every house and storefront for thirty blocks trundles with shadow. Shadow follows every season.

The most recognizable faces on the street are the pawn shops. There are more pawn shops on this main street than any other business. It's where the people dance. They dance and hop and shimmy from one door to the next and finally to city hall and the courthouse. For the poor in Iowa and in America, there is more dependence upon adequate justice. But inequality has changed justice and its meanings.

Within a few blocks of city hall, at 17th Street, the mirage of shadow and sky confound the senses so that a bearded man ambling down the sidewalk appears as if he's Christ, a backpack and a cigarette dangling from his lip. He's a regular at the pawn shops and in the alleys and he drinks as if he had been at the wedding at Canaan. He may speak in tongues and he may claim divinity and he'll go unrecognized not because he's another homeless man in Iowa but because no one believes and that's what it takes in the kingdom of the impoverished.

Faith is precarious. Keeping the faith is a battle.

One of us from the mission may stand at the corner and smoke with Jesus and no one minds. One of the regulars at the mission may even give away a few cigarettes to the man. These are the things that matter on the tired street but history does not have time for vagabonds and it's the deeper meanings that we remember.

For each of the Heartland characters during the great recession, at the journeys to jail, at the laying of hands, at the police tactics of surrounding the only black social gathering place, at the shooting in the back of a black as he left one of the pawns, at the thievery and con and flim flam, at the laughter and eccentric humor – there is the being a part, that sacred or profane or primitive - the street accepts and delivers and becomes its membership so that each soul is a part of the greater whole.

The street has been the object of a great survey commissioned by the city leaders. It has been the focus of the highly publicized Safe Community Task Force. They said more street lights would reduce crime. The lights came and the crime continued.

Such is the American street in heartland Iowa. The newspapers do not report these every day stories of trouble and hardship.

Central may have been the pride of early settlers but pride has grown away from its origins as wealth moved west and the alliances of the working people and the ruling class weakened.

Working class pride has its voice in the taverns and pawn shops, at the gun seller and the tattoo parlor.

The heart is dying on Central Avenue. The arteries harden upon Main Street, Heartland, USA. Christ stumbles down the street but no one sees him except for the guys at the pawn and no one believes them.

The street passes by artists, dumpster divers, hookers, tramps, petty thieves and the general population of poor the city fathers have given up for dead. It could be said that the populace that manages to survive beneath the bluffs was born to different conditions than families whose roosts hang farther up the hillsides, that the great, long shadows looming across the landscape are only illusions.

Of course Jesus comes to shoot pool here.

What society says about you and what you know is at odds.

Christ's parables make good hooks for the working poor. Memories keep people lined up for hope. There is a narrow gate and few pass.

After it was handed a plaque as best small city to raise a family, Iowa's first city mimed the survey experts who called perception the key. As said in the TV show, White Collar, "Perception drives reality." The city manager said so, too.

The poverty grew. Crime grew. The links went unchained.

Playwright Edward Albee asked about reality with 'The Lady from Dubuque.' Poverty and race collide often in the first city of Iowa. As Albee's play ends elegant, black Oscar says, "Therefore, nothing is true." The stylish woman Elizabeth finishes: "Why, I'm the lady from Dubuque. I thought you knew." The great recession is tragic like this, for invisibility and denial.

In June, 2013, both the mayor and city manager were quoted as being shocked that the federal government confronted their management as racist.

From 2000 to 2010 poverty steadily rose in Dubuque County. Crime did, too.

Image improved. America by image, trust in God.

The federal government now says the racism is institutional. Dubuque Human Rights Director Kelly Larson said that in the middle of the recession. No one listened.

The fellas at the pawn shop have a hard time when they have to sleep in the rain. Black babies catch colds when the heat is turned off.

HUD said the numbers show Dubuque has more than one reality.

I asked my friend Scott about his night's sleep under a dripping gutter and he said he'd slept in worse places on Central Avenue. He washed in a green, plastic tub left in the alley and then went to work on a nearby roof. It was his only chance at looking down at anything.

Wealth says it wants for you the role of businessman, mechanic, plumber, millwright, doctor, attorney and teacher. Look sharp.

Has image grown like shadow till it matters more than substance?

People grow restless, feel powerless, get angry when the paths out of poverty are closed. When the dream is unreachable, when they are told that image is real, dream's true, that everyone can have a BMW.

Scott told me he thought there were always poor and that the prosperous look away, they look the other way knowing that by ignoring poverty, it will continue. But then, he said, that's the way it is.

The street watches and the shadows change but what has been real for decades is the loneliness. According to the psychologist Harry Stack Sullivan that is the malaise above all others.

That day in 2006 that I carried a dusty, Black and Decker circular saw to the 17th street pawn shop, I found something I had never seen. A crusty, brown stained crock pot tipped on the counter. The owner offered ten bucks for the saw but offered a bowl of deer meat to warm me. Curious about a pawn shop that gives food away, I stayed.

In time I took notes. In time I saw poverty, I found crime. In time I asked why. I carried food to the poor. I swept dirt from the sidewalk. I held the tired hands of an old man who had become homeless. I hugged a homeless man who became my friend. I saw people look away. I listened to the mayor speak about city greatness. Not a substantive word about poverty. About racism. About crime. His wife scolded me. A man from Premier bank scolded me. I wrote about the street.

On the pebble strewn street of Central, reality comes in many forms and shapes. As many as six pawns look out to the traffic, all within blocks of city hall. Tattoos and metal studs glisten on the faces of the angry young men and women. The elders shuffle back into the darkness, eager to be safe, glad to be quiet.

In the end days the dream of what might have been is said to grow into a contagion. People get nervous that their stuff is still shelved as it should be. Thoughts turn to one last hurrah, a last farewell, a final party to end all. Talk about the end is popular among those who have nothing.

Detroit shines from a fresh reality. The city as a wasteland. Invisible people everywhere.

Everyone at the pawn thinks the poverty, the oppression, will never end. After the years dim the lights in their eyes they begin to see flickering hope but know one reality.

At 17th Street Pawn Shop the food mission will give away food and the pawns will keep coming and all of us would have a place to go were wishes horses. We beggars could ride.

This oldest pawn made a profit for some of its years but inside its bowels it housed a mission that was known as The Narrow Gate. The Gate borrowed till the pawn became decrepit. Irony that a pawn shop would go out of business because it housed a mission.

Debris fell to the floor and no one picked it up.

During the great recession both the pawn and the Narrow Gate were beating hearts and landmarks for the street. The very poor denizens there may be waiting at the gate, at the end, when all will be judged, when the rich will be asked how they treated these, the least among us.

On several late night forays into a nearby tavern Jesus came as a black man but he was hit over the head with a bottle then stripped and tossed into jail. The police let it go and we saw it. Big Jim cried. Roy complained. Of course, Paul had to say that it rains on the good and the wicked alike. Scotty simply drank it into submission. Old Jim and Bambie and others all went about their scavenging.

A day in the heartland concerns dreams, a drift into the rising mists and falling steins, more of a stale beer than of rapture and prophecy, water and wine, but the word of God keeps many of the poor waiting, knee deep in the big, muddy river of time.

Central Avenue is a shadow and a mirage, a dirge, a tug's lonely call, a cop's baton, a cub scout's word, a priest's confession. Steeples dominate the shadows and the horizons. It waits in a half light for the wealthy scions who stashed the chips and paper money in old vaults of the city.

Of all the faces and all the streets, this spiritual space of Central Avenue, a place of thought, a place of dream and desire, crime and heroism, this face says the most and gets the least attention. The other streets and other people that intersect or draft upon the sidewalks of Central are caught between hunger and anger. They say this street is safe. They say it's a dangerous walkway. They say it's clean, it's dirty, it's calm, it's sublime, it's just another street.

The face smiles sometimes and laughs at others, leaves a depth of sadness often and gives insight in the silence when the people are willing to talk. People of the street are from all sections of the city.

The street people have in common a drive to dance upon the walk. They do it in the cold and heat, in the dry and wet. They wear silver and gold, tattoo and scar, sweater and skin. They come to Central like visitors to a zoo and like inmates at a prison; hunger and anger and joy; refuse, debris and donut; pastry and steak and chili and soup and within all the smells of garbage and steam cooked hot dogs lay the tracks of tears and hope, here.

The heartland poverty lives somewhere between the laughter of depression and the laughter of surprise, whether because the people are trying to make it or because they're trying to plant fair play or trying to sneak another round of trouble in before they go; the people here dance to that beat that everyone does. They seem to know that it's not free enterprise or competition. The street here is not about dreams that come true. Some may get lucky at the boat or at the casino. Most strip off their veneer and look straight ahead into the heartland, Iowa street and at the realities that populate it.

III. ON LIBERTY AVENUE

The years have been unkind to the little store where the pawn shop meets the food mission. The phone rings and the responder speaks, "17th Street." Every year is hard for the poor at 17th Street. They die younger. Their children never catch up. Their educational system is less, the justice is less just, medical treatment not as good. Inequality here is greater than any other advanced country. Trust tastes sour. Dreams feel like dysphorias. A revolving door of unemployment and discouragement lines the curb.

Twenty three years of picking at an old phone, pushing away the debris on the shelf, clearing the counter, sipping coffee and answering a call about the value of a poor man's second hand radio, the business wanes. The dirty old shop has ghosts now and dreams that were lost.

The dream began in innocent things, the desire to help others, the conviction that it mattered, the call to the wine, the call to Christ. They decided to put the mission inside the pawn shop.

An old woman crossed the threshold to get bread, an old man stooped to pick at a box of cookies. In the pawn shop, at the mission they felt welcome.

The dreams of these people are mixed up but it's like truth to be mixed up, not knowing if it's that truth from the head or the heart and then if it's about what one of the guys felt or if they all felt the same way.

So tricky the truth that it's hard sometimes, to tell the difference between the dream and the memory. Ever worse is the fact and then throw in how it's understood. These are the ways of the Narrow Gate mission that feeds the hungry from inside the little pawn shop, once a white washed backdrop in the movie The Field of Dreams.

Now, accepting the fire of imagination, smelling the burning wood, accepting that the end is near, and then arguing about the wounds so many have endured, wonder comes. Is it real, this thought, this truth, these pawn shop row peoples of the heartland? Downtown Brown says, "We must be real, otherwise no one exists."

An old customer says he heard the place had burned to the ground.

What can poor men and women mean in the coursing hammers of history?

We see that Ecclesiastics must be true, that both the foolish and the wise will be forgotten.

A three story building in a small town in Iowa, a place no realtor would care about, no newscast would broadcast, no evangelical will send his missionaries to, no one will remember, this was the center. There were times when it felt like spiritual vitality in motion but there were other places in those times, other nows that were there, when we were present at murder and during oppression, when we tried as foolishly as if we fit into the eye of Christ's needle, wanting desperately to help a lost brother, a forlorn sister, another human being.

We accept that it mattered for twenty three years.

Now the dreams came like anesthesia, in waves, in the fire, in the garden.

The cons and flim flams, the itinerate, the ex-felon, the drunk, the thief and bum and no account and the hungry and the thirsty, the guilty and the innocent, they all rolled through this little speck on the map. We're all glad it began but sad it has taken so long, past the point of mercy.

Wasn't it to save a soul? Was it to make a profit? What was it?

February, 2013, and the winter sun tells in shadow time that spring is coming.

In three weeks the pawns will be done. In ten weeks the store will close. Maybe God had insurance, maybe Christ would sit for a game of poker.

"I came down from Chicago. Took the railroad to Galesburg, Sandburg's home don't you know, the favorite spot of presidents, then hitchhiked to Dubuque." Christ said while we were dreaming. He put down a bank roll then said for everybody to ante up.

Pat and Mike sat in. Jim Fill wanted a little of that action. Naturally, Jim the mail guy sauntered in while they were dealing the cards and of course, Jimmy Mitchell, in remembrance, the nearest thing to a man with a death wish anyone knew, but he was a part of the dream, he'd left to rehab and never returned. Roy was in the hospital again and we thought he might not last. Christ offered to bring him in but we had to reject that on account of Roy's penchant for gambling and losing. Scott might have been contacted, but again the sobriety chip mattered. Stanley would have come but his store was prospering and he quit the Bible school years ago, besides he would have wanted to drink in front of the Savior and we all reckoned we couldn't hide the alcohol. The women, Bambie and the ones who pawned their precious heirlooms, Iraq gold, wedding rings and like items, we decided to keep the game among the men. Paul might have wanted to lay a bet. He began the sacred store on a whim and a hunch and his own small bank roll.

Christ said it was time to stop arguing about the truth and ante up. What's everybody to do, or think?

And wouldn't you have guessed? Christ had a story to tell. Seems he met a man on the Burlington route somewhere by the Mississippi River who told him 17th Street was closing. It was Jimmy Mitchell. Everybody loved Jimmy despite the bottle and the living under bridges.

Christ had planned to take his soul but after he heard about the bets the guys had made, the plan to party before Paul tossed in the towel, well Christ changed plans. Go figure, Christ making a change of plans.

Good ol' Jim Fill, he was staying in the empty building and he laughed and said he wanted some of that Christly money. He started an e-bay business and if the others thought they could turn the savior's head, just get him to look the other way, just for a second, big Jim might get a look at the cards and help the store.

Most guys would worry about poker with Christ but how can you think he wasn't a betting man? So he won a few and lost, too. He said he had to get that ride to Rock Island, said he heard Johnny Cash was thinking about coming back, then head back to Galesburg and Chicago, at the end of the dream. He said he would give everybody's regards to Steve, the big guy who was found on the Mercy Hospital bed, dead as a fish. He said he wanted to talk to the poet, the Swede, from Galesburg, Sandburg, about the guys given handouts in one of those poems during the last depression. The stuff about seeing men given handouts when all they need is a job. Maybe Carl had an idea about saving 17th Street. He told the guys, say hey to Roy and thank Downtown Brown for the referral. He'd send regards to the father and all the bums in heaven were praying.

Everybody wished Christ a safe trip, in the dream. Before he left Christ thanked Paul about naming the food mission The Narrow Gate. "Thanks for remembering my stories and don't forget about the rich and the story about the camel in the eye of the needle. You guys need a little hope. Oh, and I knew Jim was watching my cards. That's why I cheated. That flush was straight the first time. Anyone want a miracle, don't look back."

Paul felt compelled to say it wasn't Sodom but Christ smiled and said, forget about it.

The pot was collected then the Shark showed up and he had a good story, his life story. It was in early March, a few days after the robins arrived.

"You guys need some water in the crock. The noodles are drying out. Mind if I go in back and get some cups of water?"

"Thanks, Shark, be my guest," Mikey said as he propped his shoes on the counter. Mike was watching the store for Paul while Paul went on errands, after his success at the Davenport gun show.

No one knew how long Sharkey had been a junker but everybody understood he was a proud man, refusing to take a dollar or a handout unless in emergencies.

Sharkey had some legal paperwork with him and his mind was elsewhere. He asked about the paper coffee cups. He wanted to use one as a bowl for the noodles.

"No problem," Mike responded then sipped his coffee.

The Shark's hair was white as fresh snow but stained by nicotine at his beard and at his neck where it fell down to his shoulder. The bridge of his nose was scarred. The break was clear, a flattened affect and the nose turned to the right. He stood in the aisle spooning his moistened noodles. He smelled like the wood smoke of a bonfire. He asked Mike to look at his paperwork.

"You think it's okay? I'm goin' to court tomorrow."

Mike turned the typed page and studied it. He sipped more coffee. He stared up at the Shark's snarling countenance and he nodded and stammered.

Yeah, yeah, Mikey said, the words look alright. It's good. The junker relaxed then leaned into the counter and wondered aloud if it would work. Then he grew agitated and asked if anyone else would take a look. It was important, he said. The liars in Dubuque had been trying to destroy him. For years, the dirty liars had stolen from him, the corrupt court had taken everything, the dirty bums. It was the mafia only worse and they wanted to get him but now, finally, he had the history and they couldn't get away from history. He was as mad as a hornet in a dream in the fire and the fire started all over.

"Don't know, anymore," Mikey said, "Yeah, there's loads of corruption. Yeah, yeah, seems like nothing ever changes, don't it?"

Now Sharkey the junker was really getting hot. He turned to ask another guy and it was round table and a free for all but Shark knew the score and wouldn't give up.

"See here," he said, "They gave me notice about a building I owned on Liberty Street. They said they had to condemn it. Wasn't the right designation or something. I told them and showed them in the law. I bought that property before, fifteen years before they changed the law and they had to grandfather me in. I showed 'em the law. But no! No! No! So they took my property. Dirty bums. Dirty lying bums."

The junker kept chewing at his ever dried out noodles and he sipped his coffee and became polite, passing around the coffee pot to the other guys. Then he built the fire again with a little gas and a little love. The guys must have thought he was Christ, he was so hot.

"Listen here. Few years ago they come to me and say they got me now. Tell me the ditch weed is marijuana and they're gonna bust me! Says I, you can't come in to my property. That ditch weed is ninety feet away from the property line. Besides the legal limit is fifty feet. So get the hell out!" I tells them, get off my property!"

Sharkey said he's been to the prison in Fort Madison and they held him illegally. He tells the guys he went to the warden and told him the law books showed it. "Let me go," Sharkey told the dirty bums in Fort Madison," And I told em there like I'm gonna tell here. I'll cut your dirty heads off and then I'll shit down your throats before I let you take me again."

So big Jim sees the junker and he says, "Man, I bet that went down well, telling the warden how you're gonna tear his head off and all."

Sharkey glared at Jim and Mike went to his paperwork at the computer. Downtown Brown went to the back of the store. The fire was taking in all the acreage and the guys were bailing.

"That's not the half of my story. I had a trailer on my lot there on Liberty Street. They just drove up and took the trailer. Five days later the bum from city hall sent me a letter and told me they were gonna take the trailer cause it was parked illegally!"

Sharkey was fit to be tied.

"Sons of bitches want to hang me on the cross. Yep, they're gonna just nail me to a cross and forget about me. I'm so tired I might let em do it…"

Everyone was chattering while he rose and the smell of his clothes from his wood fire added to the injurious stories.

"They cited me for a building code violation. Said I had an abandoned building. Who believes that?"

There were no takers.

Outside on the sidewalk the junker's bike stood against the wall. A sleeting snow slanted in the cool air. The smells of ice and metal from the cars blew toward the stop light.

"I gotta go to court tomorrow for a burning code violation. You sure the paperwork looks okay?"

Sharkey stole a glance at Mike and Mikey shifted his gaze from the computer to the wild junker and he nodded and said, yeah, it's good.

Sharkey put down his dirty paper cup and said he had to go, he had some junk to take to the land fill. He left headed north toward his home on Liberty Street.

Most of the guys believe that somewhere, in one of the true dreams, there is a justice and it's not given through merit or capital or by a lottery but by a man hanging on a cross. No one knows where he came from, but it's said that all that's necessary to receive justice is to believe.

IV. DREAMERS

Downtown Brown's hair had been growing for two years and it blew away now, skirting his face then falling on his shoulders. When he wore it forward it had a halo effect, wrapping his face in a sublime ephemera. Last fall he'd begun to use a Wahl clippers to trim his beard so his face had the permanent look of a three day growth. He was becoming an acolyte of the rock and roller, John Mayer, but his neck hair had begun to whiten. His chin already bunched with age as if a sagging pudding drooled there, as if a gizzard had replaced neck and jowl. But Downtown Brown had seen other things in his mirror and no one could accuse him of vanity.

Pat dashed from chair to counter to standing then to cash register. He found Downtown's bag of Snickers and stole a small bar. He had the hair enigma like Downtown, a curling pony tail grew where once he'd had a scalp infection setting on a bald pate.

"I don't care," Pat said but no one was listening and had they been paying attention would have known Pat was talking to himself. His high pitched voice undulated. He sounded like Pat Butram, Gene Autry's sidekick. Butram's WLS radio's National Barn Dance opening line, "…You can dance in the aisles and tear up the place if you want to - it don't belong to us," defined the lives of the impoverished along main street aisles of Dubuque.

Big Jim sauntered in, tried a Snickers but balked when offered a hot dog from the mission crock pot. Someone reminded him that he had been diagnosed with diabetes and he rejected the claim, saying a Snickers bar was good for him.

"I don't care if I die," he said but the group would not cater to his draw and looked away. One said we should take a vote but no one laughed then some smiling arose. Hah hah, Jim will die. Pat said everybody does, so what. None dared to raise their hands to vote for Jim. Jim Fill had what Mike called a lifelong obstinacy.

After Adam suggested that a wall might be constructed halfway into the store the conversation went viral, a virtual epidemic of slang and segues and aphorisms. The principle was simple. Paul had no rights. Sure, he owned the store but it was time.

The first apologist was Mike. He said, you know we've all been coming here for a while and we like it here. Heck, where else would we go? We have to decide. We can't let Paul close the store. Don't matter what he says, we're keeping the place open!

With that the guys all nodded and eyes darted from corner to corner. Sure, Paul owned the place. He was the oldest pawn in Dubuque. Darn right! He started with nothing, had no loan, no cash, nothing. Ol' Paul laid down a payment, carried in some junk and started a pawn shop. God bless him! Here here. Let's hear it for Paul!

Everybody agreed.

"We can't let him do it. Doesn't matter. He's losing money, whatever. We can't close. He'll see our logic."

Scotty shuffled in the door and we remembered how good he was at saving liquor. Heck he practically invented the Smash, that concoction of everything leftover and every stinking, foul smelling drink that stood tall on the bar but had been left by someone with the short term alcohol in his short term memory, an assortment of flavor and age and alcohol percents, sweet anisette, wine, whiskey, gin, vermouth, beer, and five types of soda pop.

An idea began fermenting at a terrible pace, what about that changing water into wine scene. How about Canaan? Maybe there's a way to save the store, to retrieve the dream, to hold off the wolves.

There were some of the other pawns in town who had been talking about 17th Street for years. One said he was sick and darn tired of having vagrants stop in to his pawn store. After all, he said, they want work, fine. I can't give away my stuff, they ask me for sandwiches, for chrissakes.

The well known sidetrack about the 17th Street Pawn shop was that Paul had a street mission inside, that he had given free daily meals and filled cardboard boxes with food for more than twenty years.

"I'm not here to feed the bums!" The man with the pawn a block away had said, his own belly the size of genetically modified watermelon. You'd think someone had proposed walking on water.

Another commented that Paul was losing money, that he was bleeding cash and how could the guy hold on anyway?

The crew at the shop had been there, done that, and, walked away, whether through attrition, time's great pendulum or simple larceny. None worked except as helpers to Paul.

Now the days were numbered.

"Where we gonna go? I say we keep the place open!"

Various ideas were throttled. Time pressed. Paul began to talk of closing shop in the spring of 2012. In November he hung the for sale sign. At February's end, 2013, he taped the note to the front door. The thirty day notice that the law required. Come get your goods. Thirty days. On the thirtieth day, by God, your stuff is mine. Good luck and don't let the bed bugs bite.

Everyone looked around and stared as if lost in the thought of mutiny. Downtown rested on the cloth swivel chair. Mike sat at the bar stool. Jim stood with his hands in his pockets. An old man who was eating the steamed hot dogs but who became a restless cheerleader for the mutiny sipped coffee from a second hand mug. Pat walked to the sidewalk under the pawn logo then returned then went outside again. The idea was becoming too much.

The old names cropped into the conversation. What about Roy? What would he do? John would know, good ol' one legged John, he brought the store back to respectability till Paul's wife kicked him out. Maybe the pastor could pray us a miracle.

"Think about it!" Mike said. "We can't let it go. It's ours, for chrissakes. We put the time in here. We ate the food, drank the joe, spent a portion of our lives here. A guy can't let that go. NO! I say No! We won't go. Hell no, we won't go! To heck with Paul. That's what makes sense. I been turning this over for weeks now and that's it. Who's with me?"

Everybody cheered. Lives were returned from the abyss. Everyone nodded, sure of the direction, positive about the goal, infected with the motive of friendship and camaraderie and, well, it was not debatable. Paul was the owner, that's all. Who knew better, Paul or the guys?

Good ol' Del stopped in for a chat and he agreed, too. A guy spends a part of his life somewhere, he becomes that place, don't he? You sell the place you might as well sell the soul. The guys were the soul and no one, not Paul, not the police, not the archangels if they wanted a piece of it, not a solitary being could say otherwise. The pawn and the mission were staying.

"I tell you guys what. We'll have a party. That ought to do it. We'll show Paul how much we care. We'll have a party and invite everybody. Paul will get it then. We'll find Jimmy and get Scott and maybe good ol' John, too. We can ask Stanley and Russ and even the gals. Yeah! Right? We'll toss the best party Dubuque has ever seen. It'll go down in the books. All of the guys and the gals too, everybody who ever came here. Look at the numbers, thousands of people. Hell, we'll block off the street and we'll toss one great shindig and the whole damn town will know how important Paul is and then he'll stay open. "

And no one could peep. Not one of the men who had spent all day and some nights jabbering about weather, fishing, politics, those lousy liberals and whatnot, what have you and whatever, they all fell into the grand scheme. The pawn and mission would never close. Hey, maybe our grandchildren will be here and salute us with a good stiff drink and poke a hot dog and ask, "Hey what about those crazy fellas back then, those grand, queer, wonderful guys who kept the place open?"

It was the right thing to do.

V. ERRANDS

'The poverty of our century is unlike that of any other. It is not, as it was before, the result of natural scarcity, but of a set of priorities imposed upon the rest of the world by the rich. Consequently, the modern poor are not pitied…but written off as trash.' John Berger

I did not think about it when I placed the two quarters in the parking meter but I had been walking past the for sale sign, the hand written, blue magic marker lettering, for two months.

At the corner of Seventeenth and Central where the first meter stands, the sidewalk pits grow upon the street and sidewalk, tiny, pea sized pits that grow from erosion and rain and ice and summer's anvil of heat. I keep my head down and fumble for change, wary of street people and ignoring the conditions of the street and sidewalk.

Paying the gargoyle is a task like boxing, feigning, slipping the head shot, dropping a right, then waltzing to a far corner.

This space has seen meth deals, murder, assault and theft, chaos and gospel singing. Most of all, it has watched while the poor grow poorer. Looking south, city hall stands like a symbol of miner's fortitude and meatpacker's ferocity. A long look shows the courthouse and the gleaming, golden dome. Between here and there the change in everything comes quickly. Inequality in possession, in real estate, in hygiene.

The stop light standards were painted by hand. New light poles and shining standards were placed near city hall and toward the courthouse. Image is not wasted on the poverty at 17th Street where the Christian and his wife settled, hunkering down like the first miners, to shovel the dirt away.

Gum from years of neglect ravages the cement. Black edged butts scatter. Wrappers drift on windy days. Debris from the aging roofs spills and flows in piles. In the Spring little weeds fight for the sun. Mice scamper between doorways. Old men shuffle into Noonan's tavern. Poor women with rent due carry jewelry boxes into the pawn shops.

Twenty three years, Paul said. Twenty three years of laying on hands, handing out small, corrugated boxes of food, taking in pawns, preparing morning meals and re - warming yesterday's faire - it was ending. Prayer had stitched it together.

This was The Narrow Gate. Named for verses from Matthew. Many will come to the gate but few will pass through. So here it was. Who had passed and who had been left. First city in Iowa. Serving the alley and the stones and the widow and her children and their offspring. Catering to tradesmen and realtors, sales people and homeless. Generations of poor had shuffled through the door.

Now it was ending.

It seems that such a place has been here since the first breath of the first man. Somewhere around Neanderthal caves and from an earlier time, a man with a star attached to his horizon had made a vow. The archeologists tell us the first Neanderthals left pottery and tools and food at the first graves, outside the caves. They saw that there was more here, meanings that matter.

There has to be more. And that is why Paul Downs began his Narrow Gate mission.

A vow is serious. The first man made one.

The vow at the corner is about helping the neighbors. Simple as leaving charred pottery at a grave site. Help a fellow traveler. Relieve the mind of its uncritical conscience and begin to discipline the mind.

Nothing has value but money, this is a lie.

Paul Downs has had ten children, one dying of malaria while helping the poor in Africa. He has forced his will and conscience to see the invisible poor.

A neighbor is a brother. The life blood of all humanity springs from one source. The neighbor is brother and his blood is filled with the first man's blood and it all goes round and comes round and if doing nothing, if whitewashing one pole in the ground but making a new one for money matters, and it must, the first man's vow has been lost.

After I dropped my luminescent quarter rounds into the steel mouth in front of the white building, I sauntered inside. I did not see the heavy door and its smudges, stains, dirt, chips of flaking grey, a grey that was added two years ago, added to improve the street's face, added by caring neighbors, added without charge, added by the city manager and the community activist and their friends and volunteers. It has become worn and tired as the feet of the aged, wrinkled and weakened by the old hands and sorry palms without change.

The door opened for wrinkled, aging hands, thin skinned and luminescent hands. Hands like papyrus, hands like cardboard. Some of the hands are now in graves and some are in hospital beds too weak to lift a quarter and some are working. How many had been struck with arthritis and how many were held out, beseeching the sky for help. Little children's hands and black men's hands. Mexican hands and Indian hands. Fat and thin hands. Hands that hugged and prayed and lifted and carried and brought food to mouths, being fed and feeding.

Inside, I sat on the stool and then the phone rang and I answered. Downtown Ronnie Brown was helping a customer. I was the only pair of free hands.

I'm sorry, I said, but Paul's on his way to Clinton, helping a neighbor. Can I take a message?

Ronnie pulled a sparkling cell phone from a glass box display. Ronnie takes to the magic of tech.

"Well, this here is like that there, the one you used to own, but this here one's the model with that there function. Here."

He wore his favorite cap again today and not counting the end of last summer, he has made a record for consecutive days with the same cap. It's not a well documented record. A few years ago. Downtown had worn one baseball cap for a record year and a half. The grey one he sports like a superstition has seen a full year now. Starter is written on the front but the blue has gone dark and the brim has changed to a mossy, sick color and stains have grown there. Pistol Pete Maravich went long with the same socks, winning the college and NBA scoring titles along the way. Ringworm may have set onto Downtown Brown's scalp but he won the award for Longest Worn Cap.

This here and that there and sitting there, the idiomatic phrase, "Sitting there." Covers everything from a location to a state of mind. It makes Ronnie's dialogues tough to understand. The customers love his Stengelese.

While fixated on Downtown Brown I said goodbye to the caller then the phone rang again. It was Paul's dad, calling from the farm.

"Who's this?" Bill asked. He was looking for coordinates.

"I'm a few klicks from the corner, watching the store." "Oh, you," he said. "So where's Paul?" Then he added, "How are you?"

"Doing fine."

"Haven't seen you for a while." "Yeah, how are you?" I added, listening to his rhythm and staying with his quickness. Bill's cagey and at eighty plus years he's a wise one. He said he thought I should bring my wife to the farm, "Willetta…"

and we'd have a lunch. I said, great, we'll stop sometime, soon. He never gets her name right. He likes to say he's busy, chasing his wife around the house. He prays for America's leaders. He's impossible to dislike. He's the heartland Christian who made his way, like St. Christopher, perhaps, believing these are modern days of persecution.

A few summers ago I built the bridge across the creek that runs through Bill's back yard. I dug and scraped the stone and removed old pieces of the first bridge. I carried bucket after bucket and built the frame for the rebar. Laid the steel and set the gravel and did the pour and after days of breaking my knuckles, after the trucks came with their loads of wet cement, the project was done and Bill could drive his tractor across the water. It's not pretty but it's functional. I gave a cheap estimate but Bill paid well, in the scheme of things, and he was happy with the work. Afterward he gave me the job of painting a barn and a tin roof. Work that employs hands, as he said, is good work.

When Paul called we talked about his Clinton, Iowa, trip. He said the truck had been filled with gas. First time, ever. Maddie the hoarder coughed up one hundred and twenty to fill the tank for the ride to Clinton.

Paul said the gas tank sprang a leak. He said he hoisted it on his industrial lift and played with tubes and added new lines, cobbling it. After a couple gallons leaked out onto the cement Paul said it was fine. He and Maddie tripped down the highway for a hundred and fifty miles, barely thinking that the fix might not work. He said the gas dripped on the exhaust pipe but Maddie insisted.

In Clinton Paul and his son Tommy lifted two pallets of floor tiles from a storage locker that Maddie or her mother Jocelyn had been hoarding. While Paul spoke I saw the time at the clock over my head. I waited till he gave me his pitch for an extra hand, said goodbye and nodded to Downtown Brown. I went to the meter and recognizing the smiling demon as an enemy, got into the truck and drove away.

'You are here to enrich the world, and you impoverish yourself if you forget the errand.' Woodrow Wilson

VI. A TIME TO WEEP

The Rescue Mission on Main Street stands on a corner within listening range of the unfolding wallets at the river by the casino. The bridge over the railroad tracks to the casino is a 10-second dash from the mission but none of the unemployed is running. No one here worries about wallets. The next meal is the concern, set up on that triangle called needs.

In the mornings, the 17th Street Pawn Shop on the other side of town sends an employee to pick up the day's hot meals. A few years ago, the city made an arrangement with the 17th Street Pawn: "You can stay open with your food mission but the rescue mission will do the cooking." The thorn was hygiene. The pawn agreed.

"It was a blessing from God," the pawn said.

If you don't know Dubuque, check Dick Tracy and Dubuque on Google. A panel includes one man's comment to another: "Hard times in Dubuque."

This year the rescue mission announced plans to expand. Its history dates back to 1932, the big one in the black time. Locals from that age talk about being children, waiting at the switch tracks, waiting when the coal trains slowed, tossing coal onto the grass, keeping their family furnaces going.

Today, wedding rings are pawned, families shuffle in and out, taking heirlooms to the pawn counter so often that the clerk just says, "What did we give you last time?"

Each week, someone will waltz into the pawn to ask for work. If the owner Paul Downs is around, the query comes to him. He'll ask about the person's need, look at his clothes, his eyes, his hands, then he'll tell the store employees, "This guy can clean up the basement." Or, "This guy can sweep and vacuum." Or, "This guy can arrange the videos." The list of jobs holds up to a mirror and if you've been hungry, you can see yourself.

New arrivals to Dubuque will know within a day that the Narrow Gate, has food.

One morning, a clerk moves a big-screen television away from the door. Another early morning, videos are splayed across the counter. Each day is different at the pawn but the sameness of the unemployed, the hunger on the dirty faces, remains.

In front of the counter, boxes of bread wait for the day's poor and tired. The wretched souls without paychecks wobble, sometimes limp, as if the despair has begun a paralyzing job to limbs. After time, the men quit shaving, the women stop combing, give up the makeup.

The first thing said, before scanning the important space by the counter: "Got any bread today?"

The owner will nod, for the day brings many of these scenes, and he will try to smile. The poor unemployed will effect a smile but the pain never seems to dissolve.

And this pain is unlike all others. It's a gnawing pain, a deep in-the-gut burning of acids, watching in the mirror of dreams as death smiles, the soul slowly seeps away, in the pit of your own stomach.

In time, you lose sight, in time you can only remember to keep moving.

One morning after the old woman with the turned up, white collar and the black sweater left the Narrow Gate Mission the fellas were in an unusually giving mood. Maybe the woman was a reminder of church, the white collar and the black sweater were cues; maybe someone up there was looking out for us.

Downtown Brown sat on the hard seated bar stool, his dirty grey cap tilted like a river boat captain and he affected a howdy smile. It was an imp's grin that set upon his grizzled features and toothless upper gum and if not a beam of light, his attitude was a lesson to abide charity and good company.

A working man's hard life is given less credit, his risks less acknowledged and his rewards more diminished. Joy seemed to root in simple things.

A young man appeared as if by fate on the rainy morning in the little store in Dubuque and he limped and pain seemed to radiate from his right heel and echoed from his spine. He asked if the mission food was in place and Paul the owner said, yeah, help yourself, I think it's warm now.

The man wore a blue hand towel around his neck. A red, wool cap covered his head and ears. A black, long coat hung to his knees and his shoes were tan work boots that were wet and stained. The men at the mission know not to ask personal queries of a poor soul come in from the rain and cold. The man sat on a box and greedily devoured his stew.

"Anyone mind if I take a cup of that soda?" He asked and was given, lifting the two liter Pepsi and pouring the contents into a paper cup.

His nose was red at the end and his eyes were red around the lids. Scars of acne set at his cheeks. His eagle shaped face was set with an angular jaw.

He talked about caves south of town along the river where the railroad tracks rumble, beyond the recreation area, The Mines of Spain. Mark Twain had sailed by a hundred years earlier. At first he seemed to be talking about camping.

He said he'd walked for miles till he had blisters then found an overhang on the limestone bluffs. He settled there.

"I built a little fire and was okay," he said.

After a while, the man said the rain came and the sweater he wore was drenched and hung so low, so filled with rain, that he took it off.

"Last night my feet hurt bad. I thought I'd get frost bite, you know, they were wet and blistered and I lost some feeling but slipped closer to the bluff and kept warm that way."

How did he come to be that way?

He said he came to Dubuque from Woodstock, Illinois, a town north of Chicago. He said his employer went out of business then his landlord declared bankruptcy. He was homeless very soon thereafter.

A chill came across him. He shivered. He stared and spoke clearly, neither shifting his gaze nor making himself out to be unduly victimized.

He wiped at his nose. He nodded. He said he'd only like to get back home, back to his family in South Carolina. He'd tried to find work without success.

He was without everything we take for granted.

"Myrtle Beach, you say?" An employee asked him and thumbed down a web page looking for a bus schedule and ticket cost. One of us hazarded that maybe the bus ticket would be affordable, maybe we could chip in and help him get home.

He wasn't thirty years old. His voice was strong, his speech unimpeded. He was coherent. He was unemployed, homeless and dirty, neither a cent in his pocket nor a friend he could call to warm his spirit.

The young man shuffled away within the hour.

We reflected about another man who drove to the new parking ramp the first week in April, parked his vehicle on the top floor, then walked to the railing and jumped to his death on the sidewalk.

Now the young man without work or hope had come looking for a little mercy. One man at the mission said the times were hard and another said it was a time to weep.

VII. RATTLING THE PIPES

Paul walked thirty paces to the back of the store where the upstairs water pipes crawled down the wall by the basement door. He picked up a hammer. He began to pound the pipe and it echoed through the long room like an oriental gong. Then he began to scream, "Yahhhhhh….yahhhhhhhh…yahhhhhhhh"

Downtown Brown slept upstairs in a little nest of debris above the pawn shop and he was late for work. Paul smirked as he walked back to the front counter.

Swinging his arms as he walked, he stumbled as he moved. A VHS tape set in a corner behind the cash register. Like a palmetto bug on its last legs, the tape was hung up, balanced on an edge. It had been there for a month, stuck between cash register tape and a torn corner of a corrugated box, nestled by a hard piece of week old pizza.

The smells of steamed sausage brewed from the cooker to the counter and the stacks of pizza slices formed hands laid one over the next.

The pawn shop was ready and the mission was ready and now all that was necessary were customers.

Paul said he spoke with his accountant.

The two month old for-sale sign rippled in the window.

Twenty six wire ends scurried in an aisle behind the glass display of jewelry like millipedes. Wires from a dozen different repair jobs were strewn at angles on the floor. Talking to his accountant seemed an optimistic break for Paul's despair. It was nine fifteen and he'd been open for business since nine .

He began the day with the food preparation and his stomach growled. The toaster stood over the crock and next to the toaster oven he had filled a yellow covered warming plate with dry pizza.

A clean cut, white haired man asked Paul if he was selling. For the first time, he said, yeah, I am, but if we can't get anyone interested, I don't know. I'd like to sell the building, but, we'll see.

Paul's fat fingers strummed the paperwork at the counter. He looked around at decades of memories. Twenty year old televisions with their tiny VHS mouths hung above a shelf at the stained ceiling tiles, the aging computers, the twenty year old radios and stereos, all the things he'd purchased at garage sales to keep it going.

"Oh yeah," he said and brushed the bad haircut at his neck, "I talked to the accountant. He said we can begin taking donations. If those people you know are still interested."

'Have you seen men handed refusals till they began to laugh…?' Carl Sandburg

The owner of the Narrow Gate was getting in shape. For the fifth day in a row he had arisen early. He had brought his Bible to the exercise gym. He had ridden the stationary bike. He had done sit-ups. A diet had begun. Paul Down's once hefty two hundred seventy five was getting tight. Yes sir, money could be coming, now.

He said he had a busy weekend. He had rented a table at the gun show. On Sunday he was going to Joe Carter's benefit in Sherrill at the Barn. Joe has been the only black man in Sherrill, Iowa. He hunted on Bill Down's farm.

"I've rented a table at the gun show. I'll be there all three days. You have to stop."

A super size bottle of Heinz ketchup set by his left elbow. The sausage smells drove out the smell of the icy street. Paul plopped a fat, grey sausage on his paper plate. He poured ketchup into a mound and then he lifted the sausage between his right thumb and index finger and stuffed it in his mouth.

A man with a red cap walked into the store. He turned to Paul. He was stooped, head down, eyes to the floor, hands hidden, jaw pulled back. He wore a black coat. Paul asked him what he wanted.

Paul stared at the bottle of Diet A&W root beer on the counter and popped the top and started to drink. The man said he had come for his DVD's and DVD player. Paul asked him if it had been bagged. The man said yes. Business conducted in a deeper region of the brain stem, Paul feeding and a sad faced, rubbery necked man standing in catatonia. Neither seemed alert.

Now, Paul raised from his swivel chair and turned and pushed at the steel door that led to his store room, the one old man Marvin had died chiseling. He held the sausage in his meaty fingers and chewed as he went.

"Okay, bagged," he said. When he returned he held the man's things. The man said, yeah, that's the stuff and he placed his cash on the counter. Paul put the square bag filled with the orange, blue, green, yellow and black DVD's and the thin DVD player on the counter. The coffee from the coffee maker smelled robust and clean and Paul walked to the crock pot and knifed another sausage. Its casing was crisp and its color was mahogany.

"Thank you," the man said and he carried his entertainment away. When he had gone Paul turned and grinned. He began a story about the man in the red cap.

"Years ago we owned an apartment building. He rented from us. He's not very smart but his girlfriend was. After a while, he came to me and asked if I would co-sign a loan. He wanted to get the money to pay the rent for his apartment. I signed. It made sense."

Paul hesitated and smiled. He said the man stopped paying rent. The bank called him and told him the payment was overdue. They wanted the money. He was ashamed about being made a fool.

"You know the Bible makes it clear that we should never co-sign loans. I won't do that again." The binding shame still gripped him.

Paul added that he and the man made amends and that they got along fine, anymore.

Paul uses movies to impart wisdom and he began to tell about the movie Soylent Green. When he started, another white haired man sauntered in and asked about tools. Paul interrupted himself and pointed to the back. The man wore a white pony tail and it stuck out from a baseball cap of blue stars on the skull and red stripes on the brim. He looked like Custer.

Paul has been a doppelganger for Benjamin Franklin for most of his adult life. His often dour face and wide cheeks, the neck and bald pate with the hedges of stringy hair curling at his ears were signals of American independence. He even pulled it back against the balding pate in the fashion of a long ago America. Custer just walked by. A sitcom had begun.

"So Soylent Green was about the environment and there were all these types of Soylent products. Blue, red, orange, whatever. Soylent was a company and you didn't find out till the end that the little square, green cubes were people. They were turning people into meals."

I asked him if that wasn't one of Charlton Heston's sci-fi movies and he said yeah, a good one, I should see it.

Movies as parables. The store was closing.

I started to harp to him about getting a grant. He said it seemed okay if there weren't strings attached. Two years ago, the city manager helped to paint his store. He offered a contact with the city but Paul was vehement. He didn't want to be told what to do. He felt the city would only make demands. Now, he was open to help. Rumor was that his church was helping to pay his bills. One of the church goers complained about loaning the decrepit store money that circled the drain.

While we spoke about grants there was a constant banging sound, like nails rattling in boxes and the man with the American flag cap yelled about wrenches.

"I found one. Thanks!" He said. I looked over my shoulder for Crazy Horse.

The pawn shop is a treasure chest of old toys, new technology and very odd and unique products. At the ceiling edge behind my stool I saw an old Rocky album cover and as I looked down the ceiling trim, another album cover, this one The Man with the Golden Gun with Roger Moore. On the counter the jewelry case had not changed in months, except that several worn half dollars now set where rings had been.

"An old Robert Mitchum movie. Mitchum and George Kennedy. They were enemies then worked together. Mitchum had to see a guy named Grundy and he went up a mountain and found old man Grundy laying on the ground. The old geezer slept outside. Mitchum asked him why he didn't use his house, why did he build it if he wouldn't use it and the old man told him the house was for appearances, for city folk. He didn't need it." Appearances as double message.

We laughed but another subtle tale wrapped around him. Who needs money when Jesus answers? Don't judge a book by its cover.

Paul quit with that and as he does, let the story and its metaphor become the more concrete point about wants and needs.

The morning rolled along like a well oiled train, curve grease applied, no trouble ahead. Paul started to tell a story about big Jim and his trip to Pecatonica and the auction where he bought a button autographed by Shirley Temple he later sold for a few hundred dollars.

"Did you hear about the asteroid hit in Russia?" He asked.

"Not a thing." I answered.

"They said it was big and it could have done damage. You know what I think? I think it's a matter of perspective. For example, let's say the world is six billion years old. That's important, right? Now what if it were six thousand years old, say a Biblical age. Then the whole idea about an asteroid takes on a different meaning, doesn't it? There's thousands of examples of some big asteroids hitting earth. What if the world were thousands of years old and the asteroids, well, they're coming and…"

If time were folded then astronomers would be wrong. Asteroids might be coming next week.

Maybe the world was ending with a ricochet. Too bad good times didn't boomerang.

Paul was on his A game now with the myriad possibilities of reality.

Pat the Poke walked inside and he went to a chair in the corner.

"So in the movie Trinity, Trinity comes into town and he walks into this bar and he pulls his boot off and out falls a scorpion…."

Pat interjected that he didn't care, never would. Life sucks, he said, get used to it.

Suddenly a gravelly voice repeated over and over, from Pat's cell phone – "Die! Die! Die!"

Paul looked at Pat and he frowned. He laid in more ketchup on a pair of stacked sausages and wiggled his fingers.

Downtown Ronnie Brown arrived and stood at the counter and he yawned. The rattling of the pipes had done its handiwork and Downtown was ready for the incoming rocks. Del entered, his three foot long beard tied with twisty ties, his eyes on fire.

"What's goin on?" He said.

The fellas looked around as if someone might have an answer but no one did. There wasn't anything going on except the stories, the friends and the day ahead.

"Mind if I take some sausages?" Del said.

"Help yourself," Paul said.

"We're all goin to hell," Pat said.

Everyone returned to what they'd been doing, unconcerned about the trip to hell, believers in that Narrow Gate, believers in that fortune that lays in a valley beyond Custer, beyond poverty, beyond the debris. Everyone still standing was born a king. Maybe we would be the judges at the gate at the end of time.

VIII. THE BARBER SHOP

The newspaper quoted city officials who said that the local economy was rolling along, but the great recession had begun in Iowa's first city.

Sure, the working man said, sixty new jobs each week in the Iowa registry but they pay minimum and will kill you as fast as standing on the railroad trestle in the neighborhood.

An ominous national story described a man who will call himself the Bishop Bomber. He's sending incomplete bomb devices to Wall Street, demanding that they send him money. The FBI says he's so savvy they might not ever catch him. The fellas said he was a customer at the pawn shops on Central Avenue. Bombs from the main street of America.

Working men without work come to the pawn shop. They complain about Chicago blacks taking jobs.

The first black barber in Dubuque is on the outside, referred to as if he's an alien, often said to be from Chicago, a shadow to the people who call themselves Dubuquers. Makiah Cooper laughs.

"People gonna talk," he says. I sent a story to the local paper about him and the comments were all positive.

During January, 2010, the Telegraph Herald had a front page about Section Eight, the program that helps poor people with housing. The association was clear to the street - Chicago.

At the task force the city created, the lone black man asks if their phrase about Section Eight is a cover-up for the N word. In one city document people are referred to as 'dregs.'

People are angry. The message from the city development offices to the neighborhood has been understood to mean the city does not care. The opposite of love is not hate, it's apathy or silence.

Shirley sat in the chair next to Ray and Makiah pushed his whirling razor across Ray's scalp in tight rows and short, rolling stops, up the temple then back and up again. The first short cuts the barber applied from a line running from Ray's eyes around his head left an impression of hip hop cool. Soon the razor swept higher and higher till the entire scalp was short and neat, tight to the man's head yet with a darker shadow of longer hair across the top.

Cadillac Cutz has been the only black barber in Dubuque. Makiah is its owner and he's proud and hard working.

"This is what it used to be about for us, for blacks in the barber shop. We'd sit and talk about whatever we wanted, talk about race, weather, church, work, you name it and we covered it. And it's a part of us, an important part. And we can't forget this, we've got to keep it. It's about us and community and it matters."

Ray frowns when he speaks. Shirley watches him and adjusts her grey sweatshirt and shifts in her seat. She mentions church and Ray says that's the foundation, that's the black community, the foundation.

"It's like this," he says, "You may fall five feet or you may fall fifty feet, but you better have a foundation. We need that if we're going to make it."

He talks about reality. The shop turns electric, with static in the voices.

The red, white and blue lamp at the wall outside turns and the traffic rushes across the vista of the Elm Street windows. The leafless trees and morning shadows sway in the breeze. The music from the CD on the nearby shelf turns the words into wisps of old wisdom. Ray notes the old slave songs, the master and the house boy. The shop is filled with African Americans and the lyrics are old and the words ring out like the hammer of a smith.

"I was in K-Mart and a white woman and black woman were walking through that aisle, you know, that thing that checks you on your way out.

The white woman went through and the buzzer goes off and the clerk just shoos her through, but when the black went through and the siren rang the clerk stopped and checked it out."

Shirley wears two round, silver ear rings and she raises her hands for emphasis and she frowns and watches for reaction and the others nod and sense the truth. She goes on.

"Nobody does anything here. They all have committees and talk but it doesn't go beyond that. The NAACP does nothing here. The only time you see the NAACP, the only time they come out of their offices is when it's Martin Luther King's day and they step into the parade.

They just anger me."

Shirley speaks for race and class.

Shirley squares her fingers to signal the meanings, shaping meaning with her hands.

"I see the blood in the lady's yard, I knocked on her door. Somebody's got to help." Shirley's reference concerns the fall chaos in a stabbing in 2009. She refers again to the NAACP and to the city and its organizations, committees and clubs. She says, "They're all sort of dismissing."

The conversation picks up now, Makiah applies a spray then a talc across Ray's head. The smell of cologne sifts into the talk about justice, denial, avoidance and activism.

"As long as it's blacks, as long as it's in the flats, no one pays attention.

The Telegraph Herald looks for a black story every February when it's black history month. Otherwise, they don't pay attention, they can't be bothered. If a white man was shot in the back three times, shot three times in the back, shot then beat on and kicked, do you think he'd be arrested? Come on now, who's the victim?

We don't know what happened but a man is shot and he's the only bad guy there is…he's black, that we understand…"

The recent news is considered here. A black youth was shot in the back as he left the Dubuque Pawn. No charges were filed. Later, the pawn owner was sent to prison for running prostitution and drugs. He was known as a racist who had been a part of cross burnings in the city, events that brought Oprah and the 20/20 news magazine. The police information officer said that the city was safer, that he expected less crime because the pawn owner was a major ringleader of crime. Despite the pawn owner's arrest and imprisonment, no one ever asks how it could have happened that an unarmed, innocent man was shot three times in the back. This is about everyone and it's about truth and caring for the truth.

Shirley says, "Our children deal with that…we deal with that."

"Another focus on that is, what could you be thinking, walking into a pawn shop, we know they have guns, walk into a white man's store and just a few days after you've been in it with his daughter. Are you high, what?" A tall man named James, a social worker, adds to the reframed picture each is considering.

"I mean, man, what are you thinking?"

The next customer comes to the barber chair as Ray leaves but before he goes he embellishes. Deft and warm, his words have an echo. He's a twenty two year Army vet and the group pays attention.

"We need to do more," he says and their eyes follow him as he ambles out the door toward the crusty mounds of dirty white ice and snow.

"Good to see you…"

Street Voices

The sidewalk vibrates with a living voice and the voice attends to the street. It is a voice of the common man and it's unrecorded. The subjects the voice articulates concern things only the street people know and they know these things before all others.

One sunny day, the blue sky stretched out an arm in the tiny port of Dubuque. The voice tired of the topics of weather and attempted robberies and it brought the conversation from far away Chicago and Milwaukee.

"Where you from?" The six foot five inch man asked. He was white shirted, clean shaven and with a long chain dangling to his waist, a tiny silver cross affixed.

"Chicago," the other said. He wore a taqiyah, a Muslim cap.

They stood on Central Avenue outside a pawn shop. Both had been customers of Cadillac Cutz.

"Chicago, where from?"

"I been all over, Cabrini, Robert Holmes…" He referred to the failed projects, high rise slums that became gang infested hostels of violence.

"I'm from fifth and the neighborhood. West side. Know…" The tall man said, now curious.

"Well, brother, I know Chicago," the shorter man said, his taqiyah now balanced between worlds, his string tied hair looped behind him.

"Huh uh. I was an athlete, did basketball and football. Kept me out of trouble."

"I got into it. They marked me. Man, them disciples chased us from one end of the city to the next."

They were two old men now and from urban reckonings and their conversation has been upon the street and its corridors for five years but the news hasn't heard enough to report and in Dubuque there are no investigations and the police don't say anything. The talk was friendly and the men seemed to have a camaraderie.

"You get marked?" The shorter, older man said.

"No, man I didn't get marked. They watched out for me cause I was an athlete."

"All the dead brothers, maaaaan…"

"Everybody I knew is dead or in prison."

"Three hundred sixty five years of prison time…know that…" the one said as if each day became a year.

"You know Willie?" The tall man asked.

"Willie? Willie Fields?"

"No man…"

"Brother, I am from Milwaukee, I mean I know Chicago and could take you around but my home base was Milwaukee."

"You said Robert Taylor Holmes, Cabrini…"

"Yeah, brother, them by the expressway…"

The bigger man shook his head and smiled and the other did the same and they parted their conversation by wishing each other well, see you again and be good. The elder man stayed on the street for a while and a twenty something man put out his hand as he walked by and the elder with the taqiyah, the white Muslim cap, pulled a pack of menthol Marlboros and opened the box, separating the foil at the top and picking out a cigarette then pushing it to the hand of the young man.

The young man pulled two coins from his pocket and as he did he strained his neck and the black tattoos stretched at the sides and front of his neck like snakes. His close cropped hair and the skin of his head shone.

"Now brother, I don't want that. Put your money away."

The young man smiled now and doffed the cigarette on his lip then saluted the old black man and waltzed away. In his wake, little smoke rings sent a new voice skyward.

Inside the pawn shop another fellow harkened a friend to discuss race and the white friend smiled, oblivious to the prompt. The dark skinned man wore a green corduroy cap with a blue t-shirt that hung around his waist and he was chewing a toothpick but he was articulate and spoke with clarity. He resembled Snoop Dog.

"I've been here five years. This is just a small town. When I arrived it was safe, yeah, it was safe. Now it's dangerous. I know white guys and black guys who've been mugged and assaulted. It's the people who come here."

As the man spoke he finished with his thought and then walked to the door. Outside at the curb he stood with his friend among a small gathering who smoked and stared at the traffic as it rushed along Central Avenue.

"Once they started to come here, it got bad. Integrated the city. This here's a small town. It's not LA or Chicago or New York. Lots of people coming here and they don't get along. There's eight, nine gangs here now. Some wear the cap to the left, some wear it to the right, or they wear white shirts or whatever. You have to be careful in Dubuque, now. It's just getting worse."

With that he switched his toothpick from the left corner to the right then he finished.

"All the people, they come here. It's not safe here now."

In the past week the paper counted a crime spree emanating from a pawn shop and a stabbing among its stories, this day's headlines revealing murders in nearby Manchester, Iowa, but it missed the other story, the one this man and the others reviewed. It's not safe in the tiny little port, called the Masterpiece on the Mississippi. The age old alliance of the people of the street and Central Avenue, the aged and unspoken voice that said you would be safe here, it was dissolving.

The fellas at the Narrow Gate were right about the Bishop Bomber - he was from Dubuque. The FBI had said once they didn't think they would catch him, he was that good. One of the guys said, yeah, we have a few smart ones here, don't believe everything they tell you. With a bottle of ketchup on the counter, Downtown Brown said as he pointed, "Maybe they'll catch up..."

I should ask a choir what do you require to sing a song
that acquire me and to have faith
The streets sure to release the worst side of my best
Don't mind, cause now you ever in debt
To good kid, mA.A.d city.

Good kid mA.A.d city (Kendrick Lamar)

IX. LAYING OF HANDS

In Downtown Dubuque, there are dozens of people who comb the sidewalks for moments of alliance the street offers. Even the sounds of leaves are better than loneliness. There are moments of freedom, flights of connection. Some moments seem weightless, some frozen, some only passing breaths of time.

Most people of the street are poor by any standard. They are poor in appearance with rag tag clothing, second hand borrowings, with unkempt faces, rough beards, bad complexions, rotten teeth, uncombed hair just awoken with mats to one side or frozen skull cap hair like rug segments mashed upon their heads.

It was a Friday in the Fall when the little group of gospel singers assembled on the corner for song. High time to dance, to spread the good word, to sing songs of sixpence for the tired eyed poverty that washes upon the street. Winter is coming but Jesus is lord.

"Hey Robert! How are you doing?"

The Central Avenue sidewalk in Dubuque was clean for the group of believers. Friday night brought them to sing about peace. They had been lobbing gospel songs to the street. The tanned face of Robert, a familiar face in downtown Dubuque, drew one singer's attention.

"Hey, "Robert said.

The little chorus was singing songs of joy in praise of scripture, crying to the savior, looking for affiliation with street trolls like Robert.

"Hey you," another singer added.

The slow walking man hobbled toward them. Rusty, tin chairs were pushed against a gray brick wall for sitting, guitars were unboxed, sweatshirts were donned.

"Okay, how are all of you?" Robert asked. He dragged his foot. A trickle of blood stained his sandal.

"Good to see you," a gray haired guitar player said.

Now an echo pushed out from the street where the cars passed and it's ghostly breeze mimicked a voice. Robert looked over his shoulder.

"Are you okay? What's with the blood on your foot?"

Facelessness in the dark night of a Friday, evangelicals filling the sidewalks with tavern tripping bar hops, weaving and stinking of whiskey and blasphemy, made the night a Halloween parade.

"I'm doing okay. I've been going to Iowa City for treatments. I'm walking a lot. I tripped a little ways back, that's all."

Robert is a kind of Orc who lives across from the Central Avenue McDonald's. He walks restlessly, tirelessly, relentlessly. He used to drag his foot but that's improved. Tonight the tough skinned soldier of Central tells the believers he's overcome the stroke. He sports a tanned face, his hygiene is meticulous, his hair combed, face shaved. Just few years ago, people said that he would be lucky to live a month after his circulatory system ruptured.

"How about we lay hands, Robert?"

Within a moment, the group crowded the thin, red eyed man. They prayed aloud for mercy, asking Robert be shown the way. They lifted a group voice to heaven. They asked that he be given help with his sorrows. Twelve hands lay upon brother Robert. He began to cry, whimpering softly, fighting the tears and wiping at his eyes.

Now most people think it's for Halloween or a tall tale, but the street has a spirit. If you're there often enough, you feel it. Tonight the feeling of a dark man alone on a dark street, walking to nowhere, touched by no one and touching none. The vibe, the juju, the smells of stale mufflers, the scents of day old cooking, potato and onion smells and day's end garbage draft the street. It's as if a ghost seems to abide. Words cannot describe or show the apparition.

Some know the breath of a foul voice hangs upon the street. It doesn't show in the statistics.

The story about Robert is that he killed a man in the alley behind the singers on Central Avenue a few years ago. It's said the killing began with a fight over a six pack of beer. Robert drew a big fist and uncoiled it, rammed his paw into a face and sent a man to his grave.

Robert says it happened.

As they finish the laying of hands, the gospel singers look for direction. Heads turn, one to the other. "Where's everyone going? When do we do this again?"

 Robert wobbled like a box of bricks fell from the sky on top of his head.

"Okay, let's sing a last song."

Robert smiled but his handicap from the shady back street where the smoke thickened one night long ago is still remembered.

He reminisced briefly, whispering with the gray haired guitar player who leveled his pick to his guitar, then he shuffled back into the dark. As he sauntered away, he left them with a soft mouthing of a word.

"Thanks…"

X. SECTION 8

Paul called me from his store and said a young woman needed help moving some things.

I helped in the moving and saw the barren life of a zipper thin, black mother and her beautiful child. This was a prison without walls, freedom denied through poverty. A two flat on Jackson Street.

The young, black woman lived alone with her twenty month old daughter and the steps to her porch were cracked and the gray paint peeled away from the steps onto the walk. The green house next door flew old glory. The flag ripped in the wind. The young woman was wary, isolated.

A knock at the door and she looked through the window.

"Oh, okay," she said from behind the door.

"Come in."

On the bare living room floor were blue and gray blankets, sheets and pillows and they were spread out under a second floor banister. Blankets strewn about the raggedy, worn out carpeting. I wondered about Dubuque's inspections, their complicity and shame on them and how a young mom and her child can be sleeping on this corrupt surface. The elfish, brown eyed little girl sprung from the bedding toward me with her arms raised. The musty taste of stale air filled the room.

"Let me get ready," the young woman said.

"I can wait," I tell her.

I stand as anonymous as I can, wanting to make their world cleaner, safer, brighter, but the little girl has raised her stick thin arms and wants to be picked up.

The woman's black hair is streaked in swirling browns wrapped around a bun that rises from the center of her head. She's wearing earrings that flash in the light and her little girl wears butterfly shaped barrettes of yellow and blue and red. The butterflies are twisted in the tot's dark hair as if they rested upon a flower.

"Would you get me her shoes, right behind you?"

Everything here is civil, behaved and feels warm, the family warm feeling one has at a Thanksgiving, to me, but the poverty tastes like dirt and the sadness that stands next to all of us seems ready to jump down our throats. I feel like the young mother is a giant who has learned how to compartmentalize this despair until tomorrow or the day after or any day that may bring relief, whether realistic or defensive, holding on for the psyche and the day when life becomes fair and good, when it will brighten.

I held the little girl in my arms while mom tied the yellow laces. Mother then tossed a black leather jacket on and the day began. The open sky and daylight at the sidewalk felt social and refreshing.

As we walked to the moving van a barrel chested neighbor stood silently under the American flag, then looked over his shoulder then turned his back.

"Can you take me to Family Dollar?"

"Yeah, we can go to Family Dollar," I said about the out of the way request.

A bed and dresser, a night stand, a child's scooter and plastic bags of clothes wait in storage.

"Can we go to K-mart, too?"

"I don't know if we'll have time for another stop."

"Okay, then," the woman said.

How sad it felt to conserve time when helping her.

The woman talked when prompted. A grandparent died the day before Thanksgiving.

"Where you from?" I asked.

"Chicago."

"What brought you to Dubuque?"

"Section 8."

"What's that?"

"Well they give me help with rent. If you can put up the deposit they pay the rent. Then they'll pay half or all of it, depending…"

"Do they have that in Illinois?"

"Yeah, they do. But it takes like years to get it so I came here."

"How long you been here?"

A hesitation, then a slow response.

"I've been here four years."

Once we arrived at Dubuqueland Storage, the young mother told me to stop.

"I have to pay to get the lock pulled. I'll be right back."

Day to day, the next meal, the home, safety, the stares in white spaces at their clothes, their demeanor, driven by poverty, this has been a part of mother and child and it's endless. The young woman cloaks herself with invisibility, an impassive, uncluttered, emotionless face, she watches her surroundings without blinking.

"Okay," she says, after paying charges to remove the lock on her belongings, "down the hill and to the left."

The little girl licks a blue lollipop and is behaved, content, quiet and curious. The warmth of the human touch is changing and diffuse, sometimes unresponsive.

When the furniture has been moved to the home, and the bed set up, bags of clothes, a few pots and pans, several white, plastic sacks with flour, beans and honey move from truck to the barren, ancient kitchen. A yellow manila envelope with x-rays peaks up from a black, plastic bag.

I don't ask.

Thank you," the young mother says as we finish.

"It's not a safe neighborhood," the big man under the flag says as I walk back to the truck. He tells me it's not safe to leave keys in a vehicle.

"I was watching," he says.

As I leave, I look back, then walk quickly to the blue truck, looking forward to the empty street and the cold silence.

According to a study published in Human Organization in 2010 little is known about why Chicago African American families choose Eastern Iowa as a destination. Demolition of urban housing, violence, poor schools and few opportunities appear to motivate the search for a better life.

In a Dubuque community meeting attended by the mayor, city manager and human rights director, the lone black and an emigrant from Chicago,

Jonathan Cheatham said, "You all sit here and have nice jobs but what about the rest of us?"

Dubuque eventually reduced the number of vouchers for Section 8. The street voices said it was a racial issue. In 2013 HUD accused Dubuque of racism. They noted the percentage of blacks who had been affected by the reduced vouchers as evidence.

"Most people who come here are aware of what's going on," the owner of Players bar in Dubuque said in 2010. The bleak light of the tavern sputtered to the walls and circled the rectangular bar as he spoke and I felt the metaphors of a thousand conversations about light and shadow. The conversation about racism floated like a cloud. The issue he addressed was about profiling in Dubuque, specifically blacks from Chicago.

"Section 8 is so transparent in Dubuque," the bar owner said, "I'd like to see the percentage of Chicago blacks they threw out."

According to Iowa Public Radio's Joyce Russell, the voucher system changed from forty percent African American to four percent during the reign of city manager Mike VanMilligen.

For the bar he called Players the issue of policing became such a volatile front page story in Dubuque that after the city refused an alcohol license, claiming his tavern had a significantly greater number of incidents, he took it to court in Des Moines where the judge granted him his license, stating the incident numbers were afoul of the truth.

According to Jonathan Narcisse, editor in chief at the Iowa Bystander, things have gotten significantly worse for African Americans in Iowa over the years, from home ownership to poverty to academic declines to health, "We are in serious decline."

Narcisse notes that the incarceration rate is double the national average. He says both political parties are ignoring black Iowans.

According to Player's owner, the police told him to close at midnight. That would end his 'problem.'

The curious issue of the old Sundown laws is focused – laws that Iowa cities once had to prevent blacks from being on the street after sundown.

Dubuque had a special strategy for Players.

On weekends when the music reflected a whiter taste, before 10 p.m., no police were seen. Then the Players bar put on hip hop and a decidedly changed crowd slipped inside, a patronage almost entirely black. The black customers said it was the only tavern in town where they could socialize.

Sometime after midnight, four squads rolled across the perimeters of the bar, each parking at a quadrant corner and several uniformed officers stood vigil till the tavern closed.

No other place received this treatment. I stood on the sidewalk as cops brandished batons.

The weekly magazine The Black Commentator says that Iowa is the second worst state in the U.S. to be an African American.

In October of 2009 the owner of Players said he spoke with a Dubuque policeman and he asked, "Why are you citing my patrons for jaywalking?" This said at closing time at 2 a.m.

"Because of the traffic," the officer said.

James Loewen, professor emeritus at the University of Vermont, wrote the first book to chronicle the sundown towns, places where blacks were pushed away, using the law.

"Most Americans think ethnic cleansing means killing everybody. It's not. It's driving people out."

After honors student and widowed mother, Denise Hall, a former Chicagoan, watched her neighbor urinate on her mailbox, she left Dubuque. The story I sent to Des Moines prompted the city to invite me to speak. I told the Human Rights group they should be ashamed.

After the police told Player's they worried about traffic, the tavern owner responded that there's no traffic at that 2 a.m. hour. Why the jaywalking?

"The cop told me to shut my mouth."

That kind of police agenda encourages a poverty of thinking. I found a young, black mom at the 17th Street Pawn. Sister Boo reflected a mind in turmoil and it hurt to listen to her.

Downtown Brown nodded to the corner where she was working. Her face lit the alcove as if wild wolves had threatened her. Her arms were herky jerky, her body caught in another place.

The baby stroller set by the crock pot and the warmed meal for the day was a spaghetti concoction of noodles, tomato, onion, Parmesan cheese and beans. No mission meal at 17th Street seems complete without beans. Paul says that's where the protein is. Hungry, toothless people eat from their Styrofoam bowls till they're full, rubbing their bellies, appreciating the nutrition and glad for the chance to soothe the nagging ache. Hunger does not go away. Once you've been hungry, you never forget that. "When did we see you hungry?" The righteous said to Jesus. For Aristotle the justice system tumbles in the wake of this poverty.

The black mom and her child, like hundreds of others, had eaten the mission food, against a backdrop of a ragged but once profitable pawn shop.

A bundled, thick blanket, patched in places by blues, reds, white, orange, pink and green and sewn in strands of circling clouds and little boxes with clown faces spilled on the infant in the seat of the carriage. The baby gurgled underneath the blanket. At the wall, working the shelves behind the crock pot his thin, petite but mannish mother picked at her short, burr style haircut. She pushed at a decades old stereo and shoved it two feet down the shelf to an empty space.

This was the work of a vampire librarian. The neatness of her approach was worthy of an audience. She looked over her shoulder toward the baby stroller and past the baby to Paul and she screamed but he didn't hear her. She picked up a stereo receiver and lifted it toward another space to her left and she wiped away the dust. She seemed shamed.

When the baby began to cry the woman strutted to him and yelled into the blanket, "Shut your pie hole!"

It was an odd thing to say to a baby and peculiar that she thought the infant would listen and understand. He quieted at the harsh command.

Two weeks before Christmas and the great recession had been ended by experts but economists like Paul Krugman wrote that the economy was depressed. The great papers of the nation collided with main street.

Cold hands grab at bowls, bearded waifs shuffle and shoulder inside the store. They carry the cold winds when the front door opens.

The woman stared but minded the task she'd set for herself, paying in guilt and effort for the free food my friend had given.

The woman wore a pink billed cap and she might have been in her thirties and her frame was frightfully lean, her faded blue jeans pasted to celery shaped legs. After she finished with the baby she shuffled to the shelves and walked down the aisle as if she was imprisoned and pacing back and forth inside an eight foot cell. The tomato smells passed in the air and another woman walked through the bulkhead door of the pawn shop accompanied by a middle aged man and two boys, one about twelve and the other six.

A family stood at the door of the mission.

Lonely people, people who need attention, the mom with the infant, confound the rules of family. They start impromptu conversation with anyone available, despite propriety and manners. The eminent family theorist Minuchin suggested the rules and boundaries provide space and health but these, the poorest of the poor, cannot afford therapy. They're glad to have second hand winter coats. They surprise strangers frozen by the odd familiarity they will take as a matter of course.

"Hey," said the mannish woman. The little family ignored the greeting.

The older boy skipped down the aisle and as he hopped the woman who appeared to be his mom rebuked his motion, telling him that he'd just had the cast removed and that he should slow down.

"Yes momma," the boy said as his brother began to dance like a marionette while watching the television. A frantic energy descended upon the aisle.

From the stereo shelves came the scream.

"Ya'll can't be jumpin round here now. Listen to your momma!" The woman highlighted by pink had now decried the scene. Her mannish declaration a contrast, a wedge in the family system but the impoverished understand broken rules. The screaming command fell to the torn rug.

The baby began to cry but everyone in the store ignored that, the mannish woman inviting shock as she walked into the tiny space of the family, there for a meal and maybe a fifty cent VHS movie.

"I said, shut your pie hole!" The pink brimmed woman said again but her infant was unimpressed with words. A certain fear arose in the shop.

"You best listen to your momma," the mannish, pink capped woman said as she redirected her newly minted role to the older boy, "My boy had a cast on and he wouldn't listen. No. He had no ears for me. That's the way boys is…"

She said her son had a car accident.

"Uh huh," the second woman said and turned to talk to the man about getting a movie. She wore a blue Chicago Bears sweatshirt. Maybe she ignored the other out of fear.

Chicago is a three hour drive and the fresh infusion of poor immigrants from the projects of the great city has given Dubuque an emotional imbalance that prompted the city manager to take away hundreds of HUD housing vouchers, claiming the city mistakenly allowed the large figures of welfare housing. Then he reckoned they lacked the socials service net. That was curious. The uptick of violence among the poor made front page news, a time when the local machinist sent threats to Wall Street and was given the name 'The Bishop Bomber'. The association of crime and skin color. Violence plagued Dubuque.

HUD took a couple of years to review. Finally, they said, "No! No! No! Dubuque, pay greater attention to your poor and your tired."

At a corner on Highway 61, the famous route immortalized by Bob Dylan, where the thousand telephones won't ring, an eight foot statue of Liberty stands as if a welcoming hand to newcomers.

The people were clouds, and the river of time reflected the clouds and the animation of their energy stifled but no one was headed anywhere and everyone knew it. It felt like they were towing a barge heavy with coal that could never burn, laden by sorrow and darkness that would never see light.

The man who seemed to be the Bear woman's spouse asked about the record collection in the basement. Paul encouraged him to look there among shelves. The basement walls are aged, giant limestone rocks carved a century ago by immigrants who tore the nearby Mississippi River into shards, some dying there in the process, leaving their bones among the falling river rocks.

When the man finished his search in the ancient bowels of the 17th Street Pawn and Narrow Gate he had found gemstone.

"Look here! I found Papillion and Billy Jack! I'm so happy!" He beamed.

"How much?" He asked as his boys danced and shook to the rhythm of a hip hop commercial on the ever present TV.

"Two dollars," Paul told them and they smiled.

The little boy scooted to the water cooler and the pink bill of the mannish woman flapped at him and she screamed to his mother that he was thirsty. She would never let go. The African American mom who had begun to clean shelves was trying to fill a shame she had endured that wouldn't leave her alone.

The boy's mother agreed he could drink and when he was done and the transaction was complete, after they had supped on the spaghetti and bread, they left the store.

At the intersection of 17th Street and Central Avenue, after their purchase, the man turned again to the woman and yelled so other walkers could hear: "I'm so happy!" He lifted the movies like they were newborn infants and he momentarily looked to the skies.

XI. HARD TIMES

The epoch poverty may become important in history but it may become like a jack lost at the curb, strewn and spun until it's forgotten, even as lost souls will not find a place in history. The soul of poverty is discarded. If it's not spoken it doesn't exist. The sad eyed people know this.

It may be that we are all a part of one great thing, one whole that lives and breathes and each is a microcosm, being a tree and a leaf at the same time, starting as seed then splitting and reaching to the sky and for seasons dropping leaves, but finally, cowering from the wind and falling to become earth again.

On Central Avenue the losers and the raggedy were once children and some still are children but most grow into youth then fall. They have the same lifeblood that flows in everyone's veins, we see them and smell them but look away from the despair.

These are hard times.

Eventually it washes over even great empires just as it covers the little children of the street, be they aged or youthful. This is the heartland, the agricultural foundation of prosperity in the greatest nation in history. In the first city of Iowa. Ragged poor. Dry skinned children. Hungry elders. People living under bridges.

The story of Narrow Gate finds a sharp beginning on big Roy's hospital bed and we talked stories there as we like to do, sharing the feast of friendship with the burden of riddles. Our conversation lingered and we wanted to stay longer, speaking goodbye but meaning hello.

We spoke of the bluffs of the great Mississippi River where the shadows fall upon the pawn shop and the mission. The weather changes because of the bluffs and the buildings are slanted because of them. Business profits from the bluffs. Roy and I stood in the rain there. This is where the smart and touched, the ill smelling and the hustler, the segregated and the free, everyone worth knowing in Iowa's heartland, comes, finally, like the last breaths of wind before the season changes.

We thought about the bluffs that hang over the city and shadow the little, thin streets and tall brick curbs built for horses and the alleys and ancient stables turned into garages that house the poorest of those we have known. It's these people who have strolled and shuffled into the pawn shop and the mission that we were concerned about.

The sweet, polished brown and burnt orange colors of the hospital room and hall warmed us in the soothing, amber lights. We held onto the epoch of a little mission we knew and that house of trade where hungry mothers pushed gold wedding bands across the counter and in their tears, children next to them, would ask for mercy.

Roy sat up tall in the bed. His near four hundred pound girth balanced upon the point of time. He held on and we talked. Above his head a silver chain hung and was connected to a pull up bar. Three, soft grey, wheeled walkers waited in the corners of the room. The ever present silver tray set in front of him.

His ankle was purplish, red and swollen. It was Roy's birthday, December 31, 2012. He was going home in the afternoon.

His black dotted gown looped over his shoulders and the tiny mice footprint of the gown's patterns made the mystery of his near death more real. Noting his thinner face he responded that he'd lost sixty pounds.

From a thousand memories I saw him; standing with a pinched, hand rolled cigarette, staring south down Central Avenue, watching the police truck weave its heavy hydraulic arm over rooftops, searching for a murder weapon, shaded by the ancient sandstone bluffs of the river; then sitting in a broken, wobbling chair behind the pawn counter, comforting an old woman who had been homeless. About 640,000 people were without a home on any given night this year. I see him opening his wallet to share his last ten with a hungry, street person; sharing gospel talk and booming with his deep voice a memorable gospel tune with a local minister. He's as big as a bear and as good at laughter as any man but better with story.

It's a riddle why we laugh but we agreed it's sacred. We stayed with the ritual of pawn shop talk and mission talk, who was alive or dead and who had changed or not.

The rituals of the 17th Street Pawn Shop, with its Narrow Gate Mission, like wafers at communion but repeated in Styrofoam bowls that friends and the destitute (Sometimes these lines blur) share over prayer and laying of hands, the sharing of deer meat and noodles, of pasta and tomato and beans, always beans; ritual conversation about justice and how people fail; ritual meanings of prodigals and Samaritans; norms and values that begin and end in the Bible though sometimes include native America, these are the birthing and legitimacy of the stories.

The big man said he'd been given a CD of The Baptism of Jesse Taylor, an Oak Ridge song that won the Grammy in 73. He was happy.

In the song a drunken man who has consorted with the devil has now given his soul to God. Once the right arm of Satan, Jesse transforms into the warrior and Christian all know he was meant to be. Roy doesn't shed a tear but he seems to identify with it, something of his own soul sings through the baptism of Jesse Taylor, in the lyrics and rhythm of Jesse Taylor.

Above the pawn shop the street rises and a church building sets high above on a bluff. Its red brick cornice and steeple are eternally silent but the edifice sings and looks down on the impoverished that come through the doors of the pawn and mission. These shadows cast a hand everywhere in the area called the flats.

The flats consists of more taverns and pawns, tattoo parlors and gun sellers than anywhere within fifty miles. Roy and I used to stand on the sidewalk under the pillars and rising bluffs, inside shadows of the city, and wonder how life could have treated so many so unfairly.

Those we remember have left something of themselves and that is a remarkable thing, a palatable thing, a meaningful note that's hanging from a top pocket like a rose where we can retrieve it and if we're lucky, we can remember the love and so remember who we have been.

Jimmy

Jimmy had stayed with Roy in that little apartment that Paul had that wedged in between his warehouse and the back yard where his children played. Jimmy stayed the sober route for years. He did his best. He played guitar at the back of the store. He lifted the food boxes for the poor as they tip toed into the mission space at the pawn shop, begging for food. Finally, he began the drinking again. At first he was subtle about it and no one minded the extra mouthwash he slurped. Then he became blatant. He forgot the ruse and went to the rubbing alcohol as if no one could imagine he'd try that. Then he went AWOL from the daily wars of helping the poor move ahead. The crew at the shop searched. When he was found it was after weeks of searching and he had had a heart attack. After all of that slow decline he'd begun years before he reached the Narrow Gate and the pawn counter, he slid fast and hard into mortality. The last anyone saw him, he was strumming a guitar on a newscast from Iowa City. Everybody loved Jimmy.

Jimmy was gone.

Scott

Scott was the alcoholic who fell in and out of the years as if his being had turned specter and in a spectral light, a twilight time, had left his spirit behind after a last drink and had never looked back. He was the gentle ghost who ambled in without a sound and said hello, made his wide armed hugs, then left the store as he'd found it, like an Indian, a man who cared and maybe cared too much. He drank and then went to Jesus and came to Paul. Paul fed him, housed him and brought him to church. In the opponent process theory the author notes that good feelings are followed by bad feelings and that is the paradox, that pattern that people become addicted to. Scott went on long benders then returned for absolution and the taste of redemption that everyone at the shop gladly passed on to him. Then he went back to the great ferris wheel that for   him turned and turned and brought him high and low. After Scott received disability he stopped hanging out at the pawn shop.

Scott was gone.

Down Town

Ronnie Brown liked the nickname 'Downtown'. A few of the customers called him that. The down on their luck men called him that. Ronnie liked it. He worked at the packing house for a dozen years then he went to a Radio Shack store in Dubuque after the meat packing business went away. He lived upstairs, above the pawn shop. Each day he took twenty five dollars from the cash register. Each day he walked to the gas station three blocks away for his Marlboro cigarettes. Each day he sipped diet Pepsi and helped with store sales. In the years of his employment with Paul he came to be trusted. Downtown Brown learned the pawn shop could be an excellent reference for him and he made a living with the pawn as his address, installing remote starters and stereos at the curb. Downtown did alright. After Roy and Jimmy left, it was Ronnie all by himself.

The whole of the emerald city ambience will be gone, soon. The streets were changing and we reflected.

Kevin

Many others worked at the 17th Street store. Kevin worked one summer until he found a job at IBM. He stopped back once in a while, to say hello, always his new girlfriend on his arm. That made everybody feel good. Someone had made it and it was normal. Normal being a relative term.

John

John worked the store for months and he turned business around after Roy had left but Paul's wife decided he had a problem. One legged John didn't like that. He and Paul had been friends for twenty years but after the accusation, John left and did not return.

We all loved John.

Roy said that he and John had issues but he added, "We know each other, we come from the same clay."

Pat

Pat lived upstairs for a while until Paul's son Danny wanted the apartment. Pat moved to Iowa City for a spell while he worked out his rehabilitation. He did return as everyone hoped he would and he worked hard to help. He loved the heavy metal and the negative sounds of noise. The grinding gear sound that scratches most people somehow empowered Pat. He liked to wear black and among his favorite lines was, "Life sucks. Get over it."

Pat has stayed on, sure to be there when the last items are carried away and a sad man among them all will say something to remember the place.

Mike

Mike has been a long time ally of the shop who has stepped up to keep things moving, in perspective, much as Crusoe did when he met his own footsteps coming and going. He had experiences with Paul and they had been friends for years. Mikey helped out. When he quit his job at Lowes he became a fixture. He sometimes cussed till Paul asked him to leave but those were extraneous matters and not manners to remember for in the days of counting he has said the prayers and lifted the boxes and asked to help and done so without asking. Mikey was a razor thin, middle aged man who tried. The trying may be a last testament to all of them. Mikey's dad came from Ireland for opportunity. To say Mikey tried, that is to say something more profound than the sounds of words allow, meanings mankind has not been able to find symbols for. His face was battered by age, creased in worries, hounded by doubts and economy and faithlessness. When he became still, when a small parcel of peace fell to him, he was as good as anyone there.

Big Jim

Some days Jim said he hated everyone but I never believed that. He had been hurt, somewhere, a deep grievous hurt. He was in his forties. He was happy when he had enough beer and cigarettes and someone's attention. He was a permanent fixture but usually disallowed from working the store. Roy had barred him for more than a year. As he said, "I'm a bum, a maggot." Still, as time has its ways, he was loved. He was also loyal and decent and he cared, too.

Others came and went.

Del the painter who talked of covering the Dubuque bridges and who wanted to talk about the Bible. Del had a longer beard than both of the guys from ZZ Top and he braided it with twist ties.

Sharkey the junker who seemed mad most of the time. Another man filled with love if you had patience to listen.

Of course, Roy and I remembered the man we called Tonto who had seen too much as a soldier and drank so much he wobbled when he walked.

Sue was a regular who smiled like an angel. Bambie was a con who begged for cigarette money but who seemed to understand that life is about trade offs. Her layers of facial masks a mirage, a dream within the dream of all, a nightmare if a person is seen as a means rather than ends unto themselves. Sister Boo stayed for a few months, hawking as much for a handout as for attention, her baby in tow. The women regulars nourished everyone, even as sadness can show where the light glows.

Jeff

For years the man from across the street stopped and shared his lunch over conversation. He quit a few years ago when the quality of the customers dropped. Roy inquired about Jeff and reckoned that if Jeff didn't eat lunch at the mission then the whole and its meaning was dissolving.

Through the years all borrowed, all gave, all traded, all saw and felt and touched. Each accepted bread and comfort. Each in their own way tried to return to what

had been given in the garden so long ago. Each tried to pass something along in that right way of giving and giving without reward. For each lonesome brother losing his way on that lonely path home, each was an answer for the other.

Roy liked a taste and sometimes the taste turned into more than one and some of his friends said it may be he's ending the ride on these terms, letting the mercies that people invariably offer while you're headed down, be a comfort to him.

The big man asked about how things were going at the store. He saw inside its battleship doors and he touched some foundational rhythm of street life there; riddles of life that brought the old stories and the days before and during the great recession into a paint by number focus. He liked to say that life is simple but no one allows it to be that way too long.

In the scant hour we talked of the heartland campaign of a small group of people who populate the stories and shed their tears and light on the meanings of grit and invisibility. Faith always intersected.

"Jeff still come by?" He asked a second time and we reviewed again.

We remembered Jeff worked across the street at Welu Printing. A nice guy, Jeff had been a regular at lunch, sitting on the chewed up stool, talking and listening about neighborhood, religion and politics. Orwell would have liked the pawn shop then, when Jeff stopped. It had the politics of heart that Orwell preached.

"Haven't seen Jeff there in a year or more."

"Then it has changed," Roy said. "Conversation's not much, heh?"

"Still homeless people, still serving food. Woman dropped in before Christmas and she stole a Red Velvet cake. Paul told her to put it back, she had three others, but she set it down then as soon as he left for the back of the store, she stuffed it under her arm and slid out the door. Never seen anything like that, in the last seven years or so –"

"Was bad during the recession but it started to go down before then, you remember…" Roy said and indeed , I did, having written an essay for the Des Moines Register about the subject of great poverty before the official recession, an essay that seemed to prompt the city to help re-open the Narrow Gate.

"Not much better now.," I added, "Paul says there's less money out there now. You know he's got a for sale sign in the window. Renee made it. A blue and white, printed sign with Paul's number and the fact of sale noted."

"Goin down a long time, "Roy said.

It seemed like we were talking about another thing, the country or ethics or justice, maybe faith.

Paul Downs and his wife Renee had begun their little mission twenty five feet from the current property, in an old building where now sets a parking lot.

The big man worked for Paul for eight years and his steady presence promised success but near the end of his tenure there were questions of what the meaning of success was and he finally agreed to leave. It was a story of betrayal, I had said to Paul but Roy said to let it be.

New Year's Eve and Roy was leaving the hospital after a month's stay and Paul was guarding the door of his futile endeavor, once a money making business, now ending a decades long run.

Paul had laughed that week, saying, "The fall of the house of pawn!" As if Poe could have seen the beating heart and had carved it out himself.

Roy mentioned that there had been talk of a meth lab upstairs, that Paul had looked the other way too many times.

Roy and I held onto one of those brotherhoods you get in life, whether by great misery, by war, by tragedy or by simply the hard edged years that mean more to you and a little group of tried and true pals than to anyone else.

We said, finally, the stories made a difference and they're universal. These things that happen while we're on our way somewhere else.

Roy said he might smoke again but we shook our heads though he didn't see that. He thought he'd sort it out after he got home. He planned to take a nap then maybe head out to the Canfield Hotel, do a little Karaoke with friends.

XII. COVENANTS

People in the unwritten systems of Dubuque trust Paul Downs. When Sam's Club wanted to give 700 pies away one Thanksgiving, they found his number.

To Paul, the message of giving is stirred by the internal voice that drove his namesake to Damascus. He's a man who hesitates with confrontation but who kindly pays back someone who bought a shaving razor, even a month earlier, accepting that the razor blade had been defective.

Paul had been giving to the hungry and homeless for years. This particular Thanksgiving, at the beginning of the great recession, the great retailer called him. They had pies, lots of pies. They had boxes of cookies and desserts. Would he help get the food distributed? Was he interested?

Paul had the place and the will. If ever a will made the tired world of the streets come alive, it was his.

A round faced, balding man who limped at the end of a long day, Paul had offered to anyone entering his store the bread to fill a belly and the smile to keep them going. Some will say that he's a strange man but the world should have more strange men like the owner of Narrow Gate, the man Downtown Ronnie Brown called Mister Paul. He spent his life as if he were the richest of all men and he gave the very little he had to the poorest of the people his savior had spoken of.

Dubuque's super retailer had sent forth a word. They had set aside the bakery from their massive shelves within the warehouse, in spaces bigger than small towns.

Paul gathered four of his nine children, his wife Renee and friend Jimmy Mitchell, sober and light hearted this holiday week. They piled into the old, red bus and drove toward Asbury, Iowa, with a mission.

Paul's family bus smelled of oil and damp clothes. Rust clung to its doors. On its last miles, it appeared to be a Sesame Street van, children hanging from its windows.

Paul called friends and church members and each then alerted to the gift, prepared to pass the message. People in concert, led by a middle aged man with a penchant for helping.

In a Sesame Street parade.

It took three days of lifting, three days of carrying, three days of passing pies and bakery, hand over hand, to the next person in line.

"We piled those pies on seats in the bus till they touched the roof. We put them wherever we had room," Jimmy said.

The bus dropped low on its axles and wobbled as it revved and chugged down the hills. Seven hundred of the large pies, each weighing several pounds.

"They had to get a pickup truck after they loaded the bus," a man from Sam's said.

Sam's manager said he didn't want any attention. It was an anonymous, charitable gift without thanks necessary.

"We rode low on the axle. It was packed...I thought we might have trouble with the weight," Paul said.

The red bus bumped along the Mississippi River bluffs. The children laughed.

The hungry and less fortunate had to be helped. The word had to be passed.

Love didn't wait.

A small bus loaded with pie from floorboard to ceiling, each huge pie wrapped in cellophane, each measuring between three and five pounds rolling down the streets of Dubuque like an ancient mariner.

No strings attached, no plans to advertise. No advance publicity. The directive a simple one: get out the pies.

Chad Parker of Sam's said, "We just wanted to help. We do what we can."

Somewhere within the creaking noise and the clatter of the rusting vehicle a song had begun, a song about giving.

More than two thousand pounds of pie filled the rickety old bus.

At 17th Street the white haired, raggedy old men and women touched their childhoods. The children skipped and yelped and laughed. The toothless and the tired. Eyes creased in smiles, perhaps for the first time in years. Apple, cherry, pumpkin and rhubarb pies there for the taking, for the asking. Wonder back in life after a long hiatus.

More than five thousand dollars of pie given to those without a dollar to spend on dessert.

Apple pie with thick cobs of crust streaming crosswise in quilt patterns. Pumpkin pie wide as baseball gloves and cherry pie thick with a tangy goodness and festive in glowing red. Pecan pie with swirls of walnut cream and frill running at the edges of mouth watering, belly filling, smile making pie for the holiday.

Paul drove through trailer parks where he knocked on doors. He passed pies out in his store, gave to the church and the neighbors who then gave to their neighbors.

Seven hundred pies given out from Wednesday night to Friday.

Afterward, the parking lot at Paul's home filled with debris. The wind blew at the willow under the rocky ledge where the tire swing hung. After giving a ton of dessert away to the most grateful but the least among us all, everyone was tired. The wind blew down from a higher place on the ridge. Paper and toys and garbage were strewn across the big lot.

Paul rolled in with a wide turn and his tires screeched as he covered the cattle crossing between the road and his home. The wind dropped branches as he turned off his engine and he strode away from the car like a bandit hurrying from a robbery.

He opened his front door with a push. A step beyond the door his infant daughter Faith waddled toward him with grapes in her little hand and a smile. Paul stared down to his baby and grinned.

"What are you doing? Come here!"

The baby squirmed when Paul lifted her and then settled into his arms. She set her chubby arms around his neck and watched the rooms glide by like a sailor holding to the mast. In the dining room Paul's son Tommy waited for him.

"Dad! Want to see a trick?"

"Sure."

The bakery was delivered. The economy's great retailer had shown us magic.

The boy lifted a silver dollar and said, "This is a dollar. Correct?"

"Yes, it is, son."

"Okay," the boy said, "Now watch."

Paul's son then placed the coin under a napkin and waved his hand over it. He whipped the napkin away from the hidden coin and said, "Wallah!"

The coin had disappeared.

"That's good, son."

The family's frugality paid for the meals given to the poor. Their efforts filled bellies and brought dessert. Everyone felt reborn in hope.

It was a Thanksgiving to end them all.

Thanksgiving Auction

A Friday auction drew the cortisol into his blood stream, his heart raced. His eye began to glare into distant bargains. He had worked at that dead eye look for years so that he could turn to a spot in the distance, stare at the spot as if the bid was irrelevant, then wait. Waiting is not an easy thing. If ever a master walked this earth it was the bidder from Dubuque. Paul was without peer.

"The stuff on the far wagon is junk but that pile of scrap metal, that's gonna go low."

The master had traveled to hundreds of auctions and the auctioneers knew him, cultivated his eye, waited on his command, waited for his bid.

It was time for Paul to make money on bargains he would sell at his store.

"Get some coffee for yourself, Paul" they'd tell him, "Try those cookies, my wife made em and she knows how you like that extra batch of chocolate chips in the mix. Go on, you've got time."

The master was made from the Iowa soil of implement and gravis, sentiment and wisdom. He could smell a burned clutch, see a dark capacitor, envision the profit from an unweighed box of iron. He knew the going price of scrap and the dollar value of an ounce of gold. If ever a man understood the glint of a bargain, this king of country sales, the master from Dubuque, the boss of bids was he.

The somber man attended most public auctions. He often liked to peruse his quarry before grabbing his cash but if he hadn't seen the thousands of items at the Fall school district sale it didn't matter. When he strode on the asphalt off Chaney Road the eye scanned, his almost mystical understanding leapt toward the four directions like prayer. He moved with stealth, shading his face, drinking bottled water, scowling down the competition.

"Lots of stuff," was Paul Down's Spartan comment. A mission, a pawn shop and nine children depended upon him.

In the beginning, he whipped his long neck hair away from his neck. A hundred buyers stood in the sun, coveting the bargains, hunching over their prey.

The schools of Dubuque had accumulated and stored and now piled high, hundreds of school room accessories necessary to teach the children. Televisions, security equipment, microscopes, desks, book cases. The master would have at it.

"If I had unlimited funds," he said, "Boy! I could have done some damage." He could have filled the Acropolis at Athens.

Others in the auction world were glad that day he left a few items on the tables. Once the blood smell engulfed the bidders, only one would take home the spoils. Ever buy a box without knowing its contents, then finding a rare book worth thousands? Ever latch onto silver dinnerware, worth a fortune, bought for pennies? The master was one of a kind.

Friday, the blue step van, polished and maintained by school district maintenance department personnel, hauled and supported the master's boxes of computers, stereos, chairs and cameras and that funky carnival money machine, the one that blew cash around inside a plexiglass booth. The master also bought the van for a cool $625.

"I would have bought the scoreboard if I had the funds. You could sell it to an alumnus some day, a rich one…"

The master had an insatiable appetite for auctions. He had a genetic servo valve that prompted bargain hunting, an evolutionary gene, mutated for the industrial, consumer economy. What he bought, he sold or stored. If the world ceased to turn, the master had a gear to supplant the earth's demise. The fact that he always kept unopened boxes of bargains hidden from himself, ready to locate and open during down times touched his need for purchase. He was the grand champion, the Bobby Fischer of auctions, the unparalleled, undisputed master.

"Can't eat today," he'd say, "Too many bids, not enough time."

Seven garages serve the compound where he lives. A warehouse hides beneath his home. Hidden rooms adorn the hallways of his home, places where he stacks books, videos, televisions and cans of food. If ever the big one falls onto Iowa skies, the master will be safe, equipped with unlimited videos, food stuffs, water and transport for when the radioactivity draws down.

After the school auction that day he attended the rural auctions. He bought garage sized fans, industrial heaters and furnaces. These items, worth many thousands, were had for hundreds. If he didn't have a buyer, he would, one day. The master had time and time was what he understood, what he relished, how he excelled.

Be there, wait, stare down. Analyze, understand, cry bid and time it.

"I wait till the other guy gives me a figure, mostly. I buy as long as I know it's right. "

If you're ever at an auction, he's the one with the key, the one who resembles Benjamin Franklin, an ancestor of Prometheus, the one who stole fire from the Gods.

The Nashville Ride

A Winter's day in a deep and dark December. It was 26 degrees with a clear sky, 504 miles to Nashville from Dubuque, December 28, 2009. The destination, 2572 Music Valley Drive. It was three PM. The steering column was repaired, leaks noted, sounds considered, tie downs observed and belongings, with children, dutifully packed. A vow made and a journey readied.

The old Frito truck, white and yellow, a broad stripe running down its middle, wide and flat bottomed as ever a river boat was, had been refurbished with cots, a cabinet, a table, music system and a portable heater. Cabinets filled with bread, oranges, canned vegetables, boxes of pancakes and rolls. Under cots the coolers held cheese, meat, oranges, bread, apples, soda and juice. Snacks of chips, crackers, cookies and candies completed the grocery list.

As the brontosaurus set in the parking lot by the stop sign near the restaurant Happy's Place, the children, nestled in blankets and sitting on the cots, whispered and chattered like squirrels. Paul peered into the engine compartment under the prop of the hood. His bald pate shone in the reflected sunlight burning off the drive. Diesel smells and exhaust smoke hung in the calm. Stern as a badger, his breath billowing in the cold wind, he said the radiator seemed okay. He noted that other engine components would have to abide. God's will be done.

"Mom, can I have an orange?" The eldest child Tommy was hungry.

The frigid air stung faces and hands, humidity was dropping, little noses dried like dates in a freeze drier; the rapping chill hit all hands like a hard edged ruler. The cold tapped with intermittent stings across bare knuckles.

Paul rubbed his hands together. He added oil to the crankcase then announced the ark ready to enter the water.

"Everybody here?"

"Yes Paul. Everyone's here." His wife Renee said.

"Okay. Let's go."

The engine smells poured inside, bit nostrils then moved away through the door shim. Breathing was visible everywhere. A north pole caravan. The kids had games, dolls, music, little computer puzzles and snacks. The gauntlet began.

Eight children, Paul's wife Renee, me and my spouse, we took our seats on the space craft's various platforms. The Dubuque to Nashville run, dead winter, Christian zeal.

"Faith will see us through."

Paul had assigned his son Daniel and Downtown Brown to watch the mission and store. We were heading to a Christian conference.

The space by the door extended three feet from the driver. Wind whipped into the space through a long, thin crack line where the door refused its lock. The cold moved like a meat locker chill, swept into the silver lined door and rose at the step. It was ever present, smelling of fuel, oil, smoke and soot and with humorless intent. Behind driver and arm chair pulled from a garage sale to make a co-pilots loft, passengers armed themselves for the long, laborious, arctic journey to the southland.

"Everybody okay?"

The message behind the message being: "Anyone in danger of freezing?"

Each child and adult behind the arm chair and the driver, the two women and eight children, held a small place like a carrot seed holds a tiny dot of earth, like swallow tails at tree tops in a south American forest. A constant fog of breath rose to the ceiling where wires hung in a scattered cloud. Heat was planned. It would grow from a propane tank and a wick mesh. Safety was based in faith.

The children were dressed in a colorful array of neon, blue, yellow, green and orange; caps, jackets, boots and gloves. The rainbow army of Paul and Renee. Dubuque Christians driving to the Mecca where the Overland Mission Company would pitch African missions.

Cots stood to the ceiling and leveled under each other like bunks in a barracks. A swath of mesh screen and mattress had been built with drill and screw, sleeping quarters for the unbridled disciples of Christ.

"Everyone okay?" Paul shouted as the beast lurched upward and onward to the Dubuque airport just four miles from the liftoff.

Yards from the airport entrance a thwack a thwack a thwack rumbled into the cabin. Jules Verne would have been pleased.

"Let's get on with this adventure gentlemen... where's the sea creatures, the space monsters, the squid, whale, dragon?"

Paul pulled over to the shoulder with stone spitting up into the step at the door's crack. Once he shut off the engine he opened the inside hatch as if the old submarine were taking on water. Peering inside for the source of the racket like a midwife veering into birth Paul announced a possible change of direction.

"I don't know..."

Compression had died. The uphill rise was impossible.

"I think if we screw this piece on tighter it'll hold…I don't know."

If the beast had broken its leg the Nashville skyline and the entreaties of Christ would never be gained.

After the tight, tight, tight, ratcheting of the brown and rusty boot part, Paul restarted the gutsy old ark.

"Here we go!"

Within a nautical mile of the pit stop the tratt tratt tratt and grunk grunk grunk revisited.

"What do you think?"

The word and promise for this voyage lay in spirit. The destination: Nashville. The mystery, Overland Missions. A covenant as true as a rainbow.

The culprit of clanging fates was a red boot attached to a port by the manifold.

"What do you think?"

"I think we could try the hardware store," I said.

Paul drove back to Dubuque to the True Value Hardware in Key West where he bought three clamps. He stood in the parking lot with the hood again raised. Surgery seemed necessary.

"Get a screwdriver!"

"You're good at orders, try some patience." I said.

Burnt smells entered the cabin of the vessel. Worry piled as high as a snow drift.

"I think this will work." We turned the bolt.

As the sun set, the chill began to seep into everyone's bones. Tempers were melting like the wax hands of prayer on a Christmas stand.

The boot worked with an extra turn. Step by step success. It didn't bulge nor break. Paul cranked the engine. GGGRRRRR.

The great beast, the whale to their episode of Jonah, spit and sputtered and returned their faith in providence. The caravan regrouped and began again. On the road again. White dust swept up from the road and the shoulders of the road.

"Can't hear much up here!" Paul yelled. The engine rattled and spurt noise. Paul pulled the rod at the dash. The headlights flared up and the road began to turn as if Newton's theory about constant motion had been given proof on Highway 61.

This was 61 as it rumbles through and beyond Dubuque.

"Next time you see me you better run, God said to Abraham…out on Highway 61…" Dylan followed the ark, his song Highway 61 Revisited.

"Tommy, fix the GPS." Paul yelled to his son.

"Tommy, put in WalMart." His mother wanted a stop.

A rhythm soon grew with a confidence.

Harmony and Tommy sat together. Bonnie sat by me. The little boy Willie sat in a yellow hoodie by himself. The little girl Gracie spun like a top every few minutes, gathering attention like a prairie dog gathers burrs, hair winding and flashing in the other's faces, then Gracie laughing and jumping away into the back of the truck. Joy was with Faith. The baby Andrew sat on his mother's lap.

Once at the conference center in Nashville, a wealthy church where the missionaries told their stories, the stage took precedence to thought, to deed, to people. The pamphlet handout read, "In these last days…" and "Living in the last stretch…"

"What a place!"

"Glad we made it!"

Behind the crowd near the stage the graphics lit every eye. An old man knelt, his dark black face, the face of the wandering horde of biblical psalm. 'One Tribe' a mantra that repeated in hypnotic percussions of song and speech was written above the old black, weathered man. It might have been my old friend Makiah Cooper from Dubuque but it was a tribesman.

"Did you see the pamphlet?" Paul's wife asked.

A nod.

Message simple, clear. Humanity now shrunk, all of history shrunk, into the words of a handful of Christian men who spoke in tongues and reveled in their vision of the holy life. In their humility they intoned scripture as their own, speech was God inspired as sure as the video graphics behind the charcoal face was a photo of an African. This was white Christianity. And a version of 'I'm okay and you're not' straight from the introduction to Psychology class.

Awesome a word like none other, showcased each speaker who by turns grew more humble, more possessed than the next. Each wore designer jeans, open necks, gold. Each pounded the podium, paced and cried.

"I remember when it was so bad…"

Stories of modern miracle, of modern possession, of walks on water.

"And we don't want anyone who's less than the best to accompany us, no sir…"

"The name of Jesus….the name…"

"We just worship God. Give him praise. Can I hear you say amen?" Testimony, revelation.

The man on stage carried a big bible in hand.

"The lord walked into the room and his eyes were ablaze…"

"If you're not engaged in building his church you're opposing it.

"Jesus is your elder brother and his DNA is your DNA."

10:10 p.m. Tuesday. Nashville's weather was frigid. Sleep had been postponed. Sleepy eyed children, tugging at parents. Parents wandering, ambling, unsure. In the parking lot were large rocks with speakers set within that broadcast Christian music.

"It won't turn over…"

Nashville, the temperature is forty degrees and cooling. Paul and I walk back to the church to place our hats in hand. Faces down into the line of fire of pastor, disciple and stage manager.

Jonah would not complain. The ministers saw. I hoped they didn't sense my incredulity.

"You were staying in the truck. You're planning to sleep in the truck this week?"

"Alright," said one minister to the other, "The first step is to get their truck started. Then we put them in a motel. They can stay where I'm staying."

"Oh, no! No! No!"

Paul wouldn't have charity.

"All we really need is to get the truck going."

"No! You're going to stay in a warm motel. You have a baby. How old? Twelve months? No! In the motel. We'll find you a place while you're here in Nashville."

"What do you think?" Paul asked me .

"I think you need to accept this as a gift from God and keep your family safe and warm." The image of Jellystone Park in twenty degrees, Nashville in a sleeping bag, cold truck , raw wind…not a Night Before Christmas poem.

Paul would say he'd been humbled.

"I think it was alright…"

On the ride home Paul pulled over.. Always an obstacle in this journey. The diesel fuel was slushing.

"I think we can make if we pour this additive in every hour or so."

The propane tank used as a heat source catapulted across the truck interior. It could have become a bomb.

The propane hose almost burned through.

Yet we rode the mule, rode it with wind chills at forty below zero slapping the inside of our little caboose, the windshield so cold inside, we wiped it to maintain visibility.

"Everyone's okay? Right?"

Each child was wrapped inside a cocoon of rags and clothes and blankets. Adults wrapped in blankets and scarves, huddled inside deep parkas and hoodies. Red noses and parched throats, numb hands and ears, everyone persevered while the Frito truck crawled up hills and plowed through the dusting snows, riveted to the purpose; chugged and rocked and rode each wave, each current of dangerously cold wind till at last, having heard the word and the promise, the oath had been kept.

'If a man vow a vow unto the lord, or swear an oath to bind his soul with a bond; he shall not break his word, he shall do according to all that proceedeth out of his mouth.' Numbers 30:1

Everywhere upon pawn shop row the rumors were passed about the Nashville caravan but the gossip was good, they said, and everyone kept the faith.

XIII. RUBBER SOULS

In the late summer of 2009 Paul said that the roof was sagging. We climbed to the third story then mounted a creaking ladder to assess the tired, aged roof. The ancient tin, rusted and torn like a ship under water, and the tears and sags seemed ready to fall into the second floor.

The hot sky filled with dark blue and the brown, tar soaked poles rose into the sky and held dozens of wires like spindly little white threads of yarn and were covered with dust. Squirrels ran on the wires above the alley. The roof was as impoverished as the people of the alley below.

The peeling brick walls of the century old building, the boxed, crumbling, jagged stairs that attached to the walls, and the flaking age of the alley drew old crows and hungry squirrels, old men and forlorn women.

Roof tin shone in the sunlight. The bent lips of the garbage cans on the alley floor smiled like the mouths of old hoboes. Some opened in rusty creases. We were in the midst of Ezekiel, in a story of a broken landscape. Like Elijah, crows had come to feed us.

Sometimes, a homeless man will drop a sheet from an iron rail off one of the staircases, place cardboard on the alley floor and sleep.

"Do you know a third of the world sleeps on the ground?" He'd say, as if his accommodations were as dignified and honorable as the mayor's.

In the beginning of the roof rehabilitation, we surveyed.

"What do you want to do with the tar paper?"

"I'm worried about the roof. We have to peel everything off to see what we have here."

The roof was degraded. In the next two days Paul asked an itinerant roofer who was passing through town if he might help us. He asked the man what he thought.

"I don't know," the man with the pony tail said. He called himself Cat.

"It's spongy. There's rot here. I only hope there's not too much," I said.

He wore a red, white and blue handkerchief bandana tied about his head, the hair curling like a rough weed around his neck. I kicked at the tar paper then bent down to pull it up.

"Look here," I said, "This plank is a mess. Don't walk here."

"Oh god," he said dramatically, "This is gonna be a job."

"We'll patch and fix it then cover it."

The man who called himself Cat knew the ancient art of flim flam. He fit in.

He pretended he knew about roofing work.

We planned to add a rubber roof after removing a tin roof. The shop and the mission would be out of business without a rehabilitation. Paul was adamant. So while the hungry converged three stories below us, we bore down on an ancient appendage of roofing and cobbled planks.

The dimension was fifty by twenty. A local man with a stubble of beard and a vacant eye said the building was raised during the civil war. Once, it had been a stable. It was a relic.

Smells of rotting food rose above the dumpsters from the firmament. A dog barked and pigeons flew in circles around the steeple of nearby St Mary's, flights deep in the blue spaces of the horizon that ran east to the Mississippi River.

The morning we began a drunk limped out of Noonan's Bar and the traffic on Central Avenue in Dubuque was surly and hurried. The traffic quieted as the Labor Day parade assembled west of the alley on Iowa Street.

"Hey, you see those old tractors?" Jimmy Mitchell yelled.

John Deere builds its vehicles north of the city and the old timers and the children run to see the tractors as they march down the streets each year. Jimmy Mitchell was a fan. These days on the roof he held to sobriety and we thanked him for that. A jewel who seemed too sensitive to life's turns and crossroads, a guitar player and once a concrete laborer, Jimmy was a vestige of baby boom gone bust. He was a beautiful guy too deep in the pit of discouragement.

We pulled several sections of the roof down. The wood had been hewn from trees, each board a wide, thick slab made for this battleship artifice more than a hundred years ago. We laid down underlayment sheathing then began to unroll the rubber sheets. Starting at the roof edge closest to the parade we rolled rubber till we had two sheets even and measured.

The man with the pony tail who called himself Cat tip toed in the third story breezes. He had come as a referral from an army vet who had been eating the stew of the mission. Cat arrived in town on his way to somewhere West and he'd told Paul he knew roofs and needed some money. He said he once roofed the mile long John Deere roof and he knew about rubber. Cat cut the first sheet of thick, gray rubber to end at a chimney top but his unnecessary cutting hinted at his inexperience - jagged and uneven.

At the street level the mayor rode and waved and his smile never dimmed. He waved like a general after a battle as if he'd conquered the city. The news of the month about two stabbings in Dubuque seemed remote. The paper reported sustainability. The paper choreographed.

We placed two rubber sheets end to end, the two sheets lined against each other with one tucked under the other. Cat put the adhesive tape on top of both sheets at the edge where they met. Before the tape had been tucked, the sheets stuck and adhered. It was a mistake that could not be undone.

"Why did you put the tape on top of the sheets. Doesn't it stick on both sides…. Don't you place it under both so they form a single barrier with each sheet seamed to the other?"

Cat stared glossy eyed. "No. We do it this way all the time. Oh, sure, I mean, you can do it the way you said but this here, this here's easier and works as good."

"Why did you put that tape on top of the rubber sheets?" Paul asked.

"We done it this way at John Deere. The company I worked for does it every year."

"So…" I said under my breath, "You done it this way… like good ol' Waylon done it or like good ol' Hank or who, 'cause I'm damn sure they never did it that way."

On break, I climbed down the wobbling ladder and visited the store and talked to Tonto, the hungry man with the wispy white beard who looked years older than he was but who was kind and calm.

How do you look at a toothless man and not feel something?

The leaves turned up in the breeze and the bluffs were brown with dying grass. On the roof tops the deep, old curbs and the newer sidewalks and the hand brushed white paint on the standards gleamed. The old curbs had been set with deep templates. The parade swirled the dust as it settled on the cars.

The Cat said, "Heck, I'll do it whatever way you want."

A crow cried over our heads like Lenore's lost soul and the Cat smiled.

"I think I'll do just that," Cat said, "What I'll do is, I'll lay these here ol' rubber sheets down and tape 'em from underneath, like you said. It'll work just as well."

He needed a paycheck.

We finished the roof the week of the parade. Good, old Jimmy helped carry large sheets of plywood as did the others, all except Cat, who blustered, picking at the tin and red brick of the walls.

Cat took off his shirt and 'The Cat Man' was tattooed on his left forearm.

"I raised lions and tigers," he said, "Oh yeah, lions and tigers. Look here," he said as he raised his right arm and scar tissue, gray welts of a deep tear stretched from his ribs. "My daddy said I might have been killed. Not me. They was just playin'." The scar looked like the ragged rubber.

That week the roof was tested with a terrific downpour and the rain could not sneak under that rubber roof. The roof section Cat did was layered with adhesive and caulk.

Paul said, "I'm giving you veto power so whatever is done here, it's your say."

"I'm giving Tim the veto on this job, so you know. Not offense, two heads work better, understand?" He said to Cat.

Cat smiled a cat smile and he did not hide his sneer. I smiled. At the next chimney top I cut an elegant little hole, by our standards, with the right dimensions.

"That's what we call corn country work." I said and the other guys drifted toward me.

I wanted to point out to Cat that though he came from Arkansas and had bragged it up, about being an outlaw hillbilly and all, we did the right thing in Iowa and no one was taking that away from us. None of us like being conned. None of us like being looked down on.

"What can I do?" Jimmy asked and I was glad he hadn't been drinking. Later I watched him and Cat make a tin edge round the back chimney top and though they told me they knew what they were doing, they applied duck tape to keep the tin from unfolding.

Throughout the job, Pat helped to carry materials. Alliances make a difference in the pawn shop and the streets. Pat Polkinghorn was a pawn shop regular and he lived in an apartment on the second floor. He'd complained about leaks. He became a feature story I wrote in Dubuque's Telegraph Herald and, a friend.

Pat Polkinghorn and I carried the rubber rolls, the four by eight sheets of plywood, the adhesive, tools, studs and miscellaneous materials up the three roof lines, past a rickety, rotting makeshift ladder with rails that fell off as we held them, past and over a bending ladder. The carrying was the worst of the job.

One day during the rehab of the roof I carried bags of books to the rusty, green dumpster. Even Colleen the local bookseller a block away was disinterested, even the library.

The garbage can is a steel truck that appears like a dinosaur, like a hungry gargoyle, a cavernous trap on wheels that has dug riveted holes in the asphalt. The monster stands by a telephone pole burdened with many wires hung too low to the ground that traverse the parking lot. I carried five bags of books and fed them into the waiting mouth. Books that no one wants.

It feels wrong to throw books away like trash. It feels distant, as if the luggage were from a prison yard or a sanitarium. Who throws away books? Aren't these voices that someone might listen to?

I thought of the people at the mission and the pawn shops. I thought about Cadillac Cutz and the street.

But many books were worthless and listed on the web at one thin, red cent. A penny isn't worth a penny, either, anymore. Does anyone read? Is reading tied to democracy?

Each ruffled, crumpled part of America, each parcel, each plastic minnow, sack by sack, the top like a hobo's handkerchief wrap of leftovers, it ends its existence in a metallic can. I carried the bags to the iron clad monster.

One day during the roof work I drove through an alley in Dubuque where I saw a gray bearded, anorexic man with dark circles at his eyes. He bent over a garbage can. He held a plastic Wal Mart bag at his side while he rifled through the debris, leftovers, paper, gruel and cat litter. I drove around the block, later finding the gaunt man with the jacket many sizes too big for him, bending over another shriveled, tin can.

I entered the next junction of alley and street following the turn around at the pawn shop and I spied the man standing under a stairwell. I pulled away from a stop sign while the tired old man reached his hands into the dark, crumpled can. I think he had a route that he followed like a sales vendor of potato chips or a bakery vendor who moves from big box to big box store arranging the shelves for his employer. The old man's employer is we who toss out what we don't want.

He began at an end of Central Avenue in Dubuque then strode through the alleys till he was done. There must be another old man that has a territory that meets the thin old man I saw and I wondered how they create their routes and spaces. I wondered if anyone else sees them.

The old men who run the street at the garbage bins are the souls of sadness. The local institutions manage to help through social services after the economy drowns them or a tragedy confounds them. They're invisible and their economy depends upon the wealth of others. Their lives are strung together by the power of free market. They can't compete anymore in the job market, maybe never could. They're marginalized, without an advocate. Millions of them abide by the warmth of a heating duct in the freezing winters and the providence of the refuse and throw away things that show up near every corner and close to each city, everywhere.

After I finished an errand I drove back through the same streets then headed along a line that notches a corner where the Central Avenue stabbing took place. A young white man without a shirt, his baggy pants slung to his knees and green and red, patch quilt underwear lifted to the lower back. He sat at the curb then dove for a football that he tossed across the street. I turned to follow the ball as I drove through the intersection and saw a young black man catch it on the curb.

The paper says racism is the issue in Dubuque but they never send any reporters out and whenever they quote a resident the resident says racism isn't the trouble, money and opportunity, tension and justice are the issues.

A 100 respondent survey I did showed eighty percent of the people thought both that a power elite exists and that diversity is being opposed. It suggested powerlessness fills many lives.

It feels like powerlessness down on the street.

I scolded the Human Rights Commission about this. The director said she wanted my phone number because some of the members would be calling. No one called. I had more than one hundred surveys completed. I learned to do surveys in graduate school. Maybe they didn't like my attitude.

That day I brought garbage to the dumpster a fat man wearing a dirty, faded t-shirt stood over his bicycle while rummaging in the garbage.

"I'm just looking for cans," he said. "That's okay, buddy…" He added.

"That's okay," I said as I turned away. We validate each other. It matters.

The roofing work mattered but the garbage seemed to be a constant rain, pouring down everywhere I went.

I planned to do the pawn shop roof in two stages. I'd lay the plywood, add the rubber sheet and fasten it. I'd coat wall areas with tar.

One morning as I poured coffee a reed thin man with a Chicago Black Hawk jersey hanging over his jeans stood in the middle of a tight group of people waiting at the cash register. Tremors moved about his neck. His legs were like the legs of a blue heron, whisper like sticks, toothpicks stuck on the floor. A sadness gripped his face, his black hair appeared like a fresh tar. The eyes cast a spell of otherworldly fog. His right eye was red at the center, covered by a contact lens.

A chubby faced man with a few day's growth of beard wearing a Minnesota Vikings shirt stood by the red eyed man. The two were pawning a television and when the deal was done they smiled and the tension rose away.

Outside the door on the sidewalk one questioned how the thin man had a red eye.

"Oh, that's Marilyn Manson. He's trying to look like Marilyn Manson. Did you know that guy had breast implants? He has a red eye. You've heard about him haven't you?"

"That guy had breast implants?" Someone asked.

"Not the guy in the store. Manson. He goes to church every week. It's Satan worship. He worships Satan every week."

"Weird," said the one attentive listener and he passed back into the store, leaving the two men in the cloth beach chairs at the sidewalk's edge. This wasn't Cancun.

Later in the morning a young man with a white cap followed a fresh faced, clean shaven, middle aged man who spooned a large bowl of saucy spaghetti, took a few big, tan napkins then waited quietly at the door. The middle aged man might have been a banker. The younger man sauntered to the glass display where the X-Boxes filled up several boxes.

When other customers turned away from the middle aged man he opened the door and walked outside. The clean cut man who looked like he'd been prosperous, an insurance man, a middle class office life, sat on the dirty, white stoop spooning spaghetti and hunching, hidden behind the railing.

"Dude this is definitely the place for Nintendo 64. I got a great deal here." The young dude said.

"I bought a guitar here the other day," the youth added, "… and man am I happy with it. Bought it for twenty five dollars." His wispy, brown goatee fluttered like tragedy.

Transactions were hurried in the heat. An obese, foul mouthed and dirty man walked inside the store, looked at the spaghetti, then left.

I waited and helped with a pawn.

A few days later we put the finishing touches to the rubber roof that none of us understood, except for Paul, who knew that its economy mattered. He could feed a few extra souls with the savings.

When we did a last review after all the sheets had been laid, the roof seemed fit. Paul complained about the costs but treated us all to a Pizza Hut dinner. We talked about fat wallets and good food.

"...I feel that my country has gotten a bad name, and I want it to have a good name; it used to have a good name; and I sit sometimes and wonder who it is that has given it a bad name."

Tatanka Yotanka, (Sitting Bull)

XIV. HOME IS A BACKPACK

Scott's life beams from his eyes. His eyes have seen souls as they rise and fall in the throes of a monster.

"I'm going to Maquoketa to see my mom. She's moving and I'm going to help her move."

His thin, brown hair is combed straight now and flows down his back and is parted. The pony tail has been undone, the ties and wedge at the end now gone. He wears a white baseball cap with the word, Bass, printed across the center of the brim. His ever present backpack is wrapped through his arms and slung across his back.

Scott does not work. He lives with friends, weather permitting, outdoors, under a stairwell, in an alley. He lacks insurance, savings, security.

"How are you?" he asks and hugs. His eyes mean each word. His feelings wait right there, obliged by loyalty, compelled to be truthful, a black and white address of affection: "Accept me or reject me, I'm here and alive."

Whenever he greets a friend he opens his arms as wide as the sky. He never shirks from fear of rejection. Rejections have passed this way, but Scott sees the forty days in the desert and he cares even if you do not.

"She's moving and I'm going to help her. She's moving from one side of town to the other."

Here he raises and lowers his head, a sort of prescient understanding of the listener. It's a sensitivity that obligates wonder, and you want to ask, "Are you hurting because you feel these things others of us don't?"

And, you feel more deeply because he does and you will do whatever you can to find that place of solidarity that is between you and him.

"I'll take a little of that pain, yes. Thank you, I'm feeling better. I needed to feel alive, too. I won't let my friend here feel all of that. Life has to be shared, right. I'll take some of that hurt from my friend here. Yes, give me as much as he needs to be rid of…that's right. Whatever helps him."

When he hugs he pulls in close. He hugs hard. If that was all you knew about Scott, that would be enough, that is, if love is enough. Jung says that where love rules there is no will to power.

The angels have been calling. He hears things we don't. He says the drink is a monster. Years of wrestling with…what…pain. "Make me blind, take my hands, cut off my feet, just hide me from the that, that…do you know…?"

He has seen full years of intoxication. A year is a long time. A child is born then walking and talking in one year.

Whole years gone to empty, left in alleys, lost in hallways, thrown up in dumpsters along crumbling brick streets. Whole years living under bridge, under stairwell, against dirty walls in rain and snow and freezing cold. Years when his name was pressed against his tongue with a pliers grip of pain and he couldn't speak it. Years when his tongue was as broken as his heart.

"I talked to a friend in Maquoketa and he's glad I'll be there. They have a meeting there but it's not the same. They don't get as many people in a small town. He's glad. I'll be one more person at the meetings. I usually go four times, maybe every day here but it's just a couple times, maybe once a week or more, whatever. But I'm going."

And then the smile comes and it hurts, in its loneliness, in its depth and turmoil. One could be looking into a pool of water and the water would be going muddy and deep and getting darker then as you saw his eyes again you'd watch the long light continue toward a deep place without an end, like you were being covered and pulled in and it went so far when you looked that you got scared and turned away.

"I'm going to sing 'Thank you.' At church. It's the song, 'Thank you'. It's a Christian song. I sang it at my friend Wilbur's funeral."

He's standing now somewhere between life and death. In his eyes are sights of the beyond. He cannot describe what he's looking at but you and he know. And you don't want to.

Here he drops the backpack and lifts the rolled smoke and we walk outside. Again we hug and he says he'll see me in a couple of weeks. I say, "Sure. I'll see you soon. You take care. I'll think about you."

There's a phantom hovering next to us and his name is beyond, this the specter of all the things you don't know in this life. It happens with Scott. Something he's carrying around with him, in the backpack, upon his person, in his eyes.

"Don't forget to pray for him," you tell yourself.

Scott says, "Thank you…"

We stand near the door of the pawn shop. We stand in the silence. It feels like we're going to be there again, and forever.

Years ago, when he was a much younger man and the drag of the brown bottle had not yet slowed his pace, he climbed a wall in Dubuque and somehow fell from two stories up. The wounds were never enough to switch on the internal light that the rest of us have. His switch was recircuited somewhere but it doesn't matter anymore. The matter is not about height or if he has a genetic disorder, an inherited disease or the pull from a bottle of scotch, gin, vodka, any… or is environmental. The issue is life.

"God and my relationship with NA saved me. I've had relapses but this time, whatever, I'm not giving up…"

Scott kneels on the hard, gritty gray sidewalk of Central Avenue. His knees take on the unyielding rock of old concrete like it's his living room floor. He's opened his wallet and strewn receipts, business cards, Eagle Grocery discounts and scraps of paper with phone numbers against a brick wall. A Hillcrest business card falls to the cement and he pushes it to the wall where he kneels.

"I used the inside paper from a cigarette pack for this note."

A one sided note is made of aluminum foil and paper like the lining Crackerjacks once had. He pulls his pony tail over his left shoulder and smiles like a sober clergy man with a sermon. The black residue of old gum, many wads melted onto the cement, are his carpet. Butts litter the curb. He shifts his knees against the pitted, stony sidewalk and when he rises he's slowed by arthritis. Drizzle grows with the drops increasingly larger.

"Me and him were doing siding in Muscatine and we went to this church service. It was really a cool church. That's where he started to change. I think Jim found his faith there. But then…"

He speaks about a friend who's finishing a stage of the illness. The space between faith and living is crucial. The primitive truth about meanings greater than the pleasure of being high is an ever present need.

"Church is important."

He's been to many churches and during the sober times he's spun into songs about Jesus and resurrection, working so hard at sobriety that he's isolated himself from spontaneity, and, from himself. Times are when sobriety is painful.

"How you doing, Uncle Jim?"

A man with a white mustache strolls across the path. He's wearing a Hawkeye cap and black suspenders and a frown. Scott raises his volume of greeting to a joy.

"How've you been?"

Uncle Jim mumbles and walks with a quicker pace as he returns from a stop at the store one door down.

"He's mad at me. I have to suck up."

Scott says that his uncle loves him and is mad that Scott hasn't stopped to socialize. Scott's eyes take on a shadow like a dark force has briefly crossed his path and he turns to the sidewalk.

A man walks by who's talking without anyone near him.

"I thought he was talking to me." Scott refers to the man with the Blue phone at his ear lobe. The tattoo of a cross on Scott's right thumb seems to redirect now, though, and he changes subject smoothly. He says his phone had been stolen and wonders about the Sim card and then the conversation rolls away like the sunshine turning away from dusk.

Scott knows so many people in Dubuque that walking the street just about anywhere means finding a kindred soul, a greeting about what's been and a silence about what will be and the hug, then ambling farther down the street. He sprinkles his conversation with stories of friends and the size of the disease.

"I was at the IRCNA at the Holiday Inn on July fourth."

A blue wrist band is the proof of his attendance at The Iowa Regional Convention of Narcotics Anonymous. As he talks about the IRCNA the tattoo of a heart above his wrist, the one with the arrow sliced through it, moves back and forth. The tattoo seams a story of unrequited love and, without Scott elaborating, an unspoken tragedy of love lost and found. Maybe a form of justice has been imprinted upon him. The heart adds to the cross tattoo on the thumb and forms a loop of energy.

A half hour after the rain drops began to fall Scott climbed the stairs of the Mission on Main Street.

"You seen Jimmy?"

"I saw him this morning. Don't know where he is now."

"Okay, thanks."

Friend Jim Mitchell has had numerous heart attacks this Spring and survived open heart surgery in Iowa City. When he was retrieved from the hospital he stood on a curb with a cigarette dangling from his lip. When he came home to Dubuque he began to drink again.

A steady, light rain falls on the sidewalk as Scott again moves into the street. He shifts his shoulders against the weight of his back pack and the keys on his belt loop jingle with an ever present chime. He's like an island in the river that's been covered by silt and now the weather has rerouted the island and Scott is shuffling under the swift moving current

----

Scott is a man who has been without a home for years. Yesterday he slept in a closed store with rain water dripping down from the ceiling, drop after drop, into small, clear plastic ice cream buckets. I woke him at nine a.m. to ask if he wanted to help carry roofing materials up an iron stairs to a first floor roof in Dubuque.

My friend lives in a closed up store in Dubuque where the gray paint falls from the ceilings and the ceiling tiles hang like broken limbs and the shelves are filled with bugs. As the cold frost dances in the early dawn mice flicker from corner to corner, prepared to fight for warmth in the tatters of carpet and paper strewn upon the floor. My friend huddles in the dark, waits for the season to become ugly and prays.

"Yeah," he says, "It's better than some. It's not too bad."

The carpet smells of must, a broken radio sets above a broken chair. The cold wind drapes the back door, a gray steel ship door. A three foot by three foot bathroom sets to his right a few feet from his mattress.

My friend shares the cold howling songs of wind from the back yard with the silences of the store that play like sand upon a desert hill, shifting and laughing. The yard fills with tin sheets, broken bottles, newspaper, fast food bags, cigarette packages amid food deposits in the dying, brown weeds. His neighbor's yard shows shining and polished stones, the smooth and cold colors of eternity, cold black, deep gray, purple, smooth as silk and hard as death, where the ends are carved for everyone. The Lenz Monument Company ignores Scott as he comes and goes into his secret hideaway.

"It's always been that way," my friend told me. "The rich have always been at the poor. No, it's not about race as much as it is about wealth and poverty."

I had the gall to tell him I'd been thinking that classes, the wealthy and the poor, had been the main theme of civilization.

"Every society, since the beginning has been that way," my friend said.

"I wish you could get out of this." I said.

He sports a goatee. A single, homemade, silver cross dangles at his neck. He touches his face, rubs his goatee and cheeks as he speaks. Sometimes his eyes cast to the floor as if he were on a hook, eyes walled and struck to a permanent glaze. I woke him the other day to ask if he could help me carry caulking, tar and plywood to the roof of Paul's store. He rose from the stained mattress like I'd startled him.

"I'm sorry, I didn't know you were sleeping. I thought you'd be awake." I opened the store's front door, not knowing he had made the room into a home. Later, I remembered he'd expressed pride last summer about making a bath from a WalMart tub, filled with a garden hose.

"It's okay," he said, "I was just thinking. Have a lot of time for that. What's up?"

"I wonder if you could help me. It's only a ten minute job, carrying some plywood to the first roof."

"Let me tie my hair and wash my face. I'll be right there." As he spoke he lifted the raggedy mattress to its side and propped it upon a tight corner where the glass counter showed a water mark from a cash register. He smiled and pulled at his hair and pushed at his trousers, tucking in the patched, faded blue shirt.

"Okay, then, I'll see you at the stairs, in the back," I said and let the door close behind me.

Several months ago I asked about my friend's whereabouts and Paul said the location was a secret.

"Clandestine," he said, as if it were a government facility and my friend had been undercover. I laughed to think a man was living in an abandoned store and this home was classified as clandestine.

When I left him I turned back to see his sleeping quarters. The front glass windows measure five feet by six feet. They're covered with sheets and dirty carpeting. The display floor shows an old planter. Flaking paint rests upon the sidewalk.

Within the discussion of wealth and poverty, the rich and the main street of the community we call America, hides a morality. As Kant explains, nothing is greater than good will. Kant argued a morality, and I heard it in that loneliness I see with my friend and that poverty he breathes. Kant says the duty is to sustain his life.

Duty here in this rank smelling store where my friend sleeps in the cold and wet, has moral worth; a moral worth, in fact, of dignity and necessity.

Paul Krugman argues in his New York Times column of August third 2009 that Citigroup, a case we subsidized, does what is bad for America: that speculation based on information unavailable to the public often combines private profitability with social uselessness. He refers to a Citigroup employee now owed 100 million dollars. Recipients of federal aid now making astronomical sums.

"Always the rich have had it and it's always been them against us," my friend says. My friend works odd jobs. He does not get subsidies.

When he climbed the outdoor, rusting staircase to visit with me as I took measures of the roof, he wore a bandana, and his clothes were many hands down the line from store bought. Yet he wore a smile.

"How can I help?" He asked as the wind whipped across the rooftop. I told him and he agreed to help with whatever he could as soon as he finished an errand.

Two days later I opened his door and said hello.

"Hey, how are you doing today?" He said.

"You seem like you're getting stronger," I told him, "You've got more energy in your face, you're clear."

"Well," he said, "I'm staying with it. I did fall off, but I'm doing good."

As I left him he started into a song. He doesn't own a thing but the clothes on his back.

XV. THE OLD WOMAN AND THE SHOE

{ She gave them some broth, without any bread, then whipped them all soundly and sent them to bed }

The bright sunshine waffled into the store and as it roamed through the debris and the displays the old, red haired woman followed it. She pushed a wire cart that held two tattered pillows and a little dog sat on the ivory pillows. The sparrow faced dog stuck his pointed nose into the air.

The old woman appeared stoned. She stuck her face onto the plane of the counter, an invasion of ruby lips, red, red rouge and splattered eye liner. Her purple dress was chiffon and it whisked and wobbled. She primped her dyed hair as she invaded Paul's space.

"You boys want any of that egg salad I make. You know the salad I've been bringing to you for the last five years now."

The egg salad was a cue to Paul. He noted her needy energy and having experienced the three day old, gray egg mush, given like an offering after she received loan money, he waited for the punch line.

Bambie bent as she stuffed her profile on the counter top and, ignoring etiquette, she let her bosom drop. Her wrinkled arms sagged and she gave her best seductive smile, repeating her question to the twenty something clerk, Paul's son Daniel, who was now fidgeting and squirming at the thought that she left on the plane of the counter.

The summer dress was sleeveless and low cut. The old woman's backside seemed to hang a bustle. The clerk tried to look away. He tried to stay calm but his shivers showed and his eyes blinked. His best game face, his ruse that he had been focused on a computer, that he was not betwixt a hard place and a cliff, was dissolving. Bambie saw that.

The sweet smell of tomato paste and toasted pizza crust fingered the sunshine and stood everyone's nose on end. The mission crock was steaming yesterday's pizza but it marinated the air with sweet basil and tomatoes and so the trap was setting, a breeze accompanying the old woman's temptation, a gravy to the train she rode.

The cool May breeze freshened the air but the action had turned south. The usual cues the young Daniel expected were not forthcoming. The dog behaved and the red haired woman stared. The stringy haired clerk looked to another man for confidence but the other looked away as if to say, "It's your deal kid. Good luck."

As the transaction grew in proportion to the stiff silence, a delivery came and the delivery man smiled and said howdy. Now everyone seemed comfortable with redirection. If the clerk had read Brando's lines from On the Waterfront and he knew to tend the pigeons, the moment would have changed. Somewhere, the balance of give and take shifted and the only one in the know was the old, red faced woman.

"My pay's coming in two days," she said, nonchalantly, and facing to the side, as though she was sharing inner thoughts but in this place she was setting her hook and the prize would be forthcoming.

"Do you have any radios. I only have the one radio and I'd like to put another one in the kitchen. What about a radio?"

She twinkled her eyes and grinned like she was letting the young man help her. This was seduction done as well as seduction is ever done. She had opened her hand and heart, became vulnerable and now, asking for the kindness of youth, she had only to pull in the line and then the grappling hook to haul aboard her mighty catch.

Such is the way of the poor. When the sharks have come to feed on the lone marlin at the side of your boat, you will see that the club has many uses. At first the hand is offered and as the predator glances off the wave, the club waits, resolute and steady.

"I don't know," young Daniel said, a waif in the den of a lioness, and he brushed his stringy, greasy hair across his forehead. His long, fanged teeth shown in the sunlight.

"Is that a radio up there, at the corner, yes, on that shelf..."

A cylinder shaped, silver chalice hung on a corner edge. Daniel reached. He tugged at it then dropped it to her eye. He didn't know he was in her bed.

He said, "No. Sorry. It's a karaoke machine."

"Don't you have any radios?" She mewed.

"What's that over there? On the shelf, halfway down, Yes, there..."

A long, black, rectangular radio with the two cassette faces came down and she asked how much.

"Fifteen," the young clerk said, now showing a drowsy face to distract her and to defend himself. His eye lids were half open.

"Fifteen is perfect. I'll take it!" She was excited. "Would you put that away so no one else buys it. Yes, set it aside for me. I'll come for it in two days."

Now the old gal turned like a ballerina but the youth did not see the energy as it grew from her conquest. He stood and stared at her, waiting for her departure. Her stoned energy had grown like a gale and engulfed the store.

Again, she employed the bent over apparition of a hungry woman and she smiled and whispered-

"Can I have two cigarettes, from you. Just a couple of cigarettes…"

The young man shook his bangs then and his hands worked quickly, opening the red Marlboro box and stabbing the top for two cigarettes. He pulled them, turned his hand over and handed them across the counter. The old woman sashayed now as she moved back into the swift and bright sunshine while the young man trembled in the shadow.

Aged Bambie peered inside when the door opened, the sunshine struck the alcove at the door and shone on the old woman's face and dress and it held a reddish glow. Color splattered across the dirty floor and her smile was at once grandmotherly and girlish. Every appearance she made struck coup, begged and tempted for hers an agenda with the "Nothing up my sleeve, fellas…" The rouge at her cheek a remnant of 1955 but her hoop earrings swung low and brought her attire toward the 2010 accoutrements.

"Hey fellas," Bambie said and gripped her stroller.

The wire stroller added to the woman's act and she seemed to understand the stroller as a gimmick, much like the old professional wrestler Jesse Ventura's ostrich feathers. She tipped her dark sunglasses back on her ears and slid them back to set on her head. Her red hair gleamed. The attack of colors grew but her voice was slight and she whispered to the clerk at the counter.

"How do you like the shoe I left?"

The shoe was a prize. Paul could not assert himself when she first left it and so the psychedelic shoe waited on the shelf behind the counter.

"Well, I can't say. It's colorful," Paul said and smiled as demurely as she had. The two were playing a long standing repartee that had grown from a first meeting when she needed a few dollars and one of the store employees had opened his wallet.

"You like it, don't you?" The red cheeks glowed ever brighter but her confidence ebbed. She frowned suddenly.

"You want to keep it, don't you?"

Here Paul lifted the high heel shoe from the shelf above his head and turned as if he were handing a bomb to a specialist in explosive devices. The shoe had been painted with a day glow series of bright colors and it would have blended into a rainbow had the rain been obliging. The running length of the high heel had a robin's egg blue that had been delicately laid across the curves. The heels were a banana yellow and the yellow hummed about sensual New Orleans nights and long hot, humid summer days. The old woman affected a grand, southern drawl.

"I thought you liked the shoe, it was a gift."

"I don't think we can sell it, now…" The wide faced, Ben Franklin - like Paul responded.

In the back of the store the sweet scents of marinara sauce ruffled and now pervaded the front door space.

Sweetness.

"We have pizza on, if you want some," Paul bandied small talk tete-a-tete but the old woman was certain about her shoe and not to be discouraged.

"Well, if that's what you think," she said.

Along the sea blue drifts that she had left upon the toes and the smooth surfaces on the curves where the bottom of the foot rolled away, were little red hearts. The two hundred seventy five pound farmer blushed when she pulled the high heel from his counter.

"Okay then, I'll take it back…"

As sure as the sun rose up that bright morning, swiftly stealing the darkness, not a soul in the store knew what she was up to as she lifted the fine, polished, red, yellow and blue high heel, only that it meant something to her and that poverty plays strange tricks.

XVI. TONTO

I first met him at the Narrow Gate and as he stood by the Rival crock pot near the front door I wondered about him but was afraid to ask before I listened and watched. He ate methodically as if he was hungry and the food usually caught at his mouth, staining his cheek whiskers. He always carried a napkin to clean after he finished a meal. Odd, eccentric, wizened, victimized, suffering, sad, funny, smart, tired and civil, he was all these things. As Kristofferson sings, a walking contradiction.

He shuffled when he moved and his arms dangled at his sides. His thin, white beard straggled everywhere across his pale face and his hair had been tied at his neck into a pony tail. The silver tone of his hair made him appear almost ancient, a mummified presence among the living denizens of the mean streets.

Whenever we met he was sure to greet me and he was upbeat like seeing me mattered and it always made me feel good.

He often wore a spackled, camouflage cap. His smile was an infant's grin and his manner both gentle and serious. During the six years that I was acquainted with him he seemed intelligent and even studious and I wondered how much I would write about him because it felt like an invasion if I took to story without telling him or showing him the work before I sent it to be published.

In many notes I took, in both written and mental hooks, I used his name until today. Today he asked that if ever I did a story, I should not allow enough of him in that essay to tell. No detail ought give my friend away.

A few years ago I saw him at the library.

His elbows stretched across the table like wings. His hair cascaded down his neck in white waves. He wore an army cap with camouflage greens and browns spackled upon it. His jacket flecked in brown grease stains and as he stared through the spectacles with the missing left lens he bent to the page and table as if his reading made communion with the angels. He smiled.

"What's the news, today, man?"

"There's hungry people on the front page."

"They're everywhere. Homeless, hungry. Sad, isn't it?"

"Yeah. I don't understand."

"Not much can be done. We can help ourselves, that's about it."

"Story here about a fella living in a dumpster outside a McDonald's. Sad faced man. This here's Iowa. We grow more corn than anywhere. Think folks could help. I do what I can."

"I'd like to give away my possessions like the man says in the good book, but how do you know where your charity goes?"

"Yeah. Says here he gets his meals and has a roof, says he's better off than a lot of people."

"Shame on us for not doing more. Know what I mean?"

"Have a great day."

"Good to see you."

The white haired man rose from his perch at the table and shuffled then limped as he walked across the carpeted library floor. At the entrance he pulled a paper from a pack and with the bag of leaves, dropped the tobacco then turned the paper and rolled and pulled it to his lips. After he ran it across his tongue he waved it then snapped the match. Out the door he ambled.

At the corner, turning toward the highway and climbing a hill across from the library, he dragged deeply from his cigarette and blew a cloud of smoke into the dry air. He doffed little rings with his habit, rings that circled around his wrinkled face. He dragged his feet as he walked. When he reached the alleyway he turned, looked both ways for traffic and walked, then followed a path in the stones that girded the buildings and led to his home.

Once home, he pulled his pallet up to hide himself, grabbed the mattress under the stairwell and laid his head down. He slept till morning when the crows came screeching through the alley and the dogs came looking for scraps.

I saw him again after a year hiatus in which he'd been diagnosed with a brain ailment. Most of what he shared with me was new and that fresh information made him sadder. I felt like hugging him and protecting him, like wiping away his pain and burying it then carrying him to some place closer to the sun so he could always feel warm and his path would always be lit.

"I was diagnosed," he said but I barely heard that and within the space of urging him to be louder and wondering what he'd said I failed to feel the first pain of recognition.

We stood under the shadow of the famous clock tower in Dubuque and the blue sky pretended it would go on forever.

"Cerebral," he pointed to his head and looked across the street at the clock tower. The people with wallets enough to sun themselves stroked fresh haircuts and pulled on polo shirts and smiled. The anecdotes about secure lives penetrated the breezes like deodorant. This is what Dubuque wants.

I saw some big bellied newspaper guys, never turning down another roast beef sandwich with computer geeks who luxuriated in the steel seats by the food vendor. There were two staring at a local hipster musician that everyone seems to want to know. The musician had arrived on his motorcycle but as his habit, made it appear he was indifferent, a step outside the usual history of common farthings and workings, his the poetry for the upwardly mobile. He'd worked himself into the crowd, the original vagabond, making money at being cool.

Cool daddy, me and my friend, a summer day in the heartland.

"The vets diagnosed me. It was the drinkin. Twenty five years, every day. That's why I lose my balance. It's getting worse."

Here was a many layered pain. It wiggled in his eyes and tightened in his voice. It hunkered down till he shriveled and seemed paralyzed.

"How old are you?" I asked.

"I'm fifty five but the doctors said my body and brain are in the eighties."

I nodded and saw he understood what that meant. And he was getting worse.

"They gave me disability."

"You okay with that. Feel secure. You alright…"

"I'll be okay. I got my house and the payments are set up and all…"

"You from Dubuque?" I asked.

"All my life except when I was in the service."

"I didn't know you were in the service. What branch?"

"In San Diego."

"You were a Marine?"

"Yep."

Time splits off in those steps we take from talk to silence, when the pain can't be held and you have to let it go. I stared off to the fat gutted newspaper guy. I wondered why a fat bellied guy would wear a red polo shirt but then thought, his business. He's doing well and seems happy. When I wrote for him he didn't pay but that was okay. He didn't understand I wanted to write about white haired, homeless guys with long, Fu Manchu beards who were once Marines and served the rest of us slackers.

"I'm kinda down."

"Can I help?" As if I could repay or find the kind of funds he needed to get him his life back.

"I stay by myself. Always have. I don't have any friends, Just acquaintances. Only acquaintances. That's it. Would bother most people. Don't bother me. I only want acquaintances."

Running down his cross tie path, over the stink of tar and creosote of a railroad that rumbled inside him, I changed subjects.

"What about your house, you said…"

"Yeah, my sister and mom lived there until 1984. I own it. It's where I'm gonna stay."

"That seems good, real good."

He pointed at me and said, "Now if you write this stuff you make sure that no one would recognize me. I don't want anyone to know."

We shook hands. He said he was okay. I said I'd see him again soon. I told him to go down to 17th Street, the guys would be glad to see him.

XVII. COMMUNITY CROSSES

An upheaval of ten million lost jobs in the great recession, the finding of great beaches of bones where the waves of prosperity ebbed, the cliff jumps of banks all over the globe added fuel to Dubuque Iowa's image making machinery as the recession stole food from the plates of the working poor.

If bragging worked, more bragging overshadowed the despair of isolated streets where the crime grew. As council woman Joyce Connors said, "Awards are important because they help us with grants." So they built their dream on a field of images. But as a neighbor said about allowing Connors election sign in his yard, "She's a nice woman but I probably won't vote for her."

Lost jobs were not discussed at city council at length. The homelessness grew. At the mayor's annual city address he turned away from talk about murder and race, poverty and agony and insisted the little city of Dubuque was growing into "…an international brand." Can you believe a lie and the truth at the same time?

Poverty and crime grew from 2000 to 2010 but awards became the focus for a city hungry to be recognized after an All America city award in 2007.

When IBM came to town through very little marketing from city administrators it seemed someone in heaven had taken a liking to the city advertised as 'The Masterpiece on the Mississippi'. When Forbes named it the best small city to raise a family in 2010 the impoverished people of the street came to call the profusion of awards and the newspaper's lack of investigation of crime and poverty on the streets a lie, a propaganda, a great con job.

The year 2010 would be referred to as a watershed. The federal government would refer to the great recession and various race crimes and the first city's impoverished main street as an affront to civil rights. The mayor and city manager would express surprise.

"Our intent was not to harm anyone." City manager Mike VanMilligen would say.

"Shocked." The headline of the newspaper referring to the mayor's reaction about being called a racist.

There was chaos on Central Avenue near 22nd Street and it fit the times. Iowa's stand your ground law. Unlike Trayvon Martin's case, no one paid attention to this main street calamity and a man shot in the back. The shots could be heard at city hall.

The raucous voices had pitched to the dirty sidewalk that day from the Dubuque Pawn. The foul smell of hatred sifted to the street. For two and a half years the Dubuque mind had been black and white. Middle ground had been lost. Now, gun shots and the poverty of despair and racism erupted as if a dormant wasp nest fell.

Two and a half years earlier the Central Avenue stabbing ignited obsession with race and poverty. Soon crime and race will prompt the city manager to void many HUD vouchers that assist the poor, black families in Dubuque. HUD will confront these events and decisions.

People take to the trench, digging in about right and wrong and the Dubuque way. John Kass' description of the Chicago Way, half truths and image shifting, spins, seemed to mark the first city of Iowa. The Chicago Tribune's Kass wrote about Dubuque justice as an oddity of ethics.

People at the gas station on Central at 22nd , across the street from the pawn, looked for exits that winter day. Gun shots echoed. Three hundred pound men poured from the pawn shop. The street turned into a bar fight.

The newspaper had been reporting good news, happy small town, anecdotal stories. Word on the impoverished main street was that the paper had been renamed from the very old Telegraph Herald to the Tell Half Herald.

The story was the violence of the poor, working street. The white violence from the Dubuque Pawn was well known to the national stage.

Seven men, three middle aged white men and four African Americans with baby faces yet remembered by their mommas, let fists fly. They bloodied the tiny pawn shop next to the used car lot. They wrestled to the counters and walls of the Dubuque Pawn, screaming "nigger" and "fuck you," slamming bodies to the shop floor then to the dirty sidewalk near the corner of 22nd . Blood spewed from a young, round faced, dark skinned child of hip hop who'd been shot in the back.

Traffic coursed around the men as they fell from the red brick store. The mechanics at the Meineke muffler shop across the street stopped their wrenches and stood to watch the violence.

A witness said shop owner Mike Vandermillen tried to kick the youth in the back where the bullet lodged, to force the bullet into the spine.

Cameras across the street had footage but the cameras at the pawn shop were said to be down. Only owner Mike Vandermillen knew for sure.

The scene at the Dubuque Pawn didn't have any video despite Mike's consistent story line in daily chats with his customers about having it on all the time. He was giving away an ice scraper that suggested he was watching everything. I remember Mike talking about the security, the video, the foolproof nature of his anti theft agenda. He'd complained about thievery in 2009. The video was lost. No video feed about what happened. Geromey Gilliand shot in the back.

The violence became their word against ours. The white 'our side' concerned Mike's cousin shooting a man as he fled the store, bullets pounding into the black man's backside. The gun Mike's dad owned.

When Mike had burned KKK crosses and the national media came running he found celebrity invigorating. The incident with Geromey grew into a Grimm's tale. Two hundred forty pound Mike said he was afraid, said he thought the baby faced black boys were carrying guns, said he believed he needed to defend his life. The blacks had no weapons yet the county okayed the bullets of the Vandermillen crew, using a stand your ground law, defending the home grown's side.

Alliances weeded from a community used to crosses.

It began when the four blacks had begun a conversation at the long counter. The first, black Geromey, asked, where's Mike?

Tools and electronics set under glass where the hands of cousin Moe moved along the left periphery. Movement in a mirror and a rage. A sword hung from the ceiling. Mike had finished a smoke. Mike's friend Rollie stood by the front door. WWE wrestling did not write better scripts.

Geromey Gilliand said he was looking for Mike Vandermillen. He asked Mike like Renfeld asking Dracula. What are you doing out in the daytime? Mike said he wasn't there.

Perhaps he was remembering the KKK he'd etched into his first cross twenty years earlier. Perhaps he recalled the feel of prison, the dank and the grey, the mesh and steel and cement.

After young Geromey asked him, Mike picked up the phone and called the police. He planned to ask for Mike's location…as if he were not Mike.

"…I was doing the right thing…" he told me after the shooting.

Art Portfolio Series VOL. 1, No. 16, MAY 14, 1894.

PART XIV.

ISSUED WEEKLY, BY SUBSCRIPTION $25.00 PER ANNUM.

BEAUTIFUL SCENES OF THE WHITE CITY

A Portfolio of Original Copper-Plate Half-Tones of the

WORLD'S FAIR

COPYRIGHT 1894 BY L.U. BENSON

ITS MARVELOUS ARCHITECTURAL GROUPS, STATUARY, INTERIORS, LAGOONS AND VIVID SCENES FROM THE FAMOUS

MIDWAY PLAISANCE

CHICAGO: LYON & LEE, PUBLISHERS

He'd asked his father and gained that gun, then passed it to his cousin.

The four black youths said they saw him pass it. They said they had heard it cock. Did Mike see the national media drive up his lawn?

Mike had a plan and it fit into Dubuque's group thinking as sweet as chocolate from the local Betty Jane's candies.

On Monday, two days after his daughter told him that she fought off a rape, Mike had waited. He waited in a seething memory of twenty years earlier when he said a black man insulted his girlfriend. He waited while his daughter's story boiled in his ears. He waited while his wife cursed the f-ing niggers.

His daughter alerted him that she had heard the blacks were going to his pawn shop that day.

He expected them and laid a plan.

Mike's daughter had walked into the black party that Saturday night.

By Monday the police knew the story, knew the landscape like they were a part of writing the script. Now, daughter had been unleashed, raised to understand the racism that prevailed along the satin white Iowa street.

The youthful African Americans said they were scared after she confronted them in the Senior High School hallway. Sunday after the party a brick had been tossed through the apartment window where the party had been. They said footprints were left in the snow.

By all accounts hell cracked through the facade that heartland Iowa had built. Mike was a favorite son of a working class family.

A code of ethics in each head of every native born Dubuque resident that the government in 2013 said had been a creed of "Go away" to the black population.

The role had been set by the rule – stay out, if you're black, if you're Chicagoan. Stay out!

The rules were televised on 20/20 to a national audience – Nigger written on street walls, get out scribbled across alleyways. Dubuque Iowa as the whitest place in America. The white city.

According to some the police scandals of Chicago were being repeated. Working class fingers pointed to black Chicagoans - they would regret their intrusion; they'd pay, some day, they would pay.

A fury unleashed across that pawn shop floor. It poured into the street. Where that amount of energy came from was never reviewed. Newton was not consulted. For every motion the equal and opposite comes to play, a bouncing, red ball on Central Avenue, the first city of Iowa's main street. It was leaving little splashes of blood.

It concerned the poorer classes and the pawn shop trades, the races and the crime. It hung upon that cross of inequality, first carried by the Christ, according to the regulars at the Narrow Gate.

The county attorney said Mike had been appropriate. No charges. A mile away at Cadillac Cutz, the first and only black barber, the script had been seen for hundreds of years. In the spring a brick would be thrown through the front window. No one would mention the fire started at the black church.

The newspaper does not report the shooting for three days. Waiting, they say, till they have the story. Yet the bloodshed and the chaos seeps into the neighborhood where it still sets, waiting. In 2012 a young black was killed blocks away. No one arrested.

A black man had assaulted Mike's daughter. What was Mike to do? Self defense.

Mike's dad Joe told me so. Friends said so. Neighbors and family and even strangers given the script and the story agreed.

Ralph Potter, the county attorney wrote a press release that exonerated the three white men. He said he was using Iowa code, said there would be no charges filed. Man defends himself.

"Yeah man, we showed em. We taught em. They know not to fool with us."

In 2011 Ralph Potter refers to a local black woman in a letter as a 'posse commitas loon.' KKK was recruiting again.

After the shooting Mike was set free. The story about how police had investigated him for several years during that time was not reviewed. Why didn't they prevent the violence?

On the street it's said he had a get out of jail free card.

A white cross burner not indicted for shooting a black man in the back.

David Dukes never saw a more welcoming community or better press for his white hooded adventures.

A Chicago African American in Dubuque named Phil would tell me, '...despite what you think of the history... - you should look at the phone call and the times, the police were in on that shooting....they okay it.'

Upon returning home from the gun range Mike's wife said that she never felt better. When I reported the black side of the story on Cumulus radio, she called the station. "F you Tim. F and F and more F.

I remember her carrying the punched, gun posters, holes nicely filling center rings. "I hit that fu_ _in target like I owned it." She said.

Mike and Rollie and cousin would laugh at her. The target was another 'Nigger'.

Not a tinge of light would break the narrative.

Mike would only say, to me, that the cops knew and he knew.

The newspaper wrote that Mike's stories and language was "saucy…"

Since that Monday in 2010, Mike has been sent to prison. Rollie is dead, rumored to have overdosed. Mike's children have been arrested. His wife is gone.

Geromey Gilliand carries scars and loose pieces of a bullet lodge by his spinal column.

That day four young men were bludgeoned and one was shot will be a storied memory that never sees the light of any day.

XVIII. HOARDING

After he picked up the fifty bags of Chili Cheese Fritos, boxing the sacks haphazardly, he boxed the other foods strewn about his van: the wrapped chocolate cupcakes, loaves of wheat bread, packages of raisin pitas, bags of garlic rolls, full sized frosted cakes, a red velvet cake, a six pound carrot cake and packaged chocolate chip cookies, then he unloaded his cargo into plastic bins and placed the green and blue bins on the floor in front of his counter. He'd done this thousands of times. Paul Down's at his mission in a pawn shop.

On some mornings the old women were first and on other mornings the bent over, stoop shouldered men pushed at the door ahead of everyone else, saw the pastry and snacks, then stuck their mangled, gnarled hands and wrists into the bins and scooped up a few items then left the store satisfied.

Paul worked quickly.

The Narrow Gate had brought comfort to thousands of people through its decades of service, a single dilapidated door opening to the main thoroughfare of Dubuque that fed anyone in need or want.

The numbers could hardly be compared to what the city of Dubuque had done, numbers having a meaning all to themselves and truth having another meaning, one the science and the other the Christianity of the heartland; statistics less easily understood than the word of mouth and the touch of a friend, the alliance of friendship and the first step on the way home. Paul's Narrow Gate Mission was so far ahead it might be said that the straight lines, the grant writing books, the boxes, the engineer's plans, all of the system's plumb roof lines and square angles, its self promotions and rehabilitations with HUD money, its removal of old buildings for a creek project, for a gambling casino, its speeches and parades, had not meant one little thing.

When a hollow faced old woman reaches out for help she finds Paul Downs. The same woman calls the city manager's office and is referred to another phone line.

She called me and asked that I mention her story. When a poor man hurts so bad he has to pawn his grampa's watch Paul asks him if he needs a box of food. A pawn shop in the redemption business.

The 17th Street Pawn stands like a sentinel, wary, vigilant but willing to listen, always that welcome, how-can-we-help stance, feet at shoulder width, in case someone pushes. The corner landmark faces Central Avenue. Central is the street of history, the main street; of change but sameness, of winners and losers and stories that begin with the birth of the heartland, Dubuque being the first city of Iowa, where the first canoes landed and the settlers dug in, calling themselves 'badgers', gutting out winters to dig out of the lead veins and supply the shot and window frames, bullets and hinges for the nation.

Each step of the unloading and unpacking of his van involved Central. It was where Paul dodged the big trucks, watched for the turning cars at 17th and tried to remember to return to pay the meter.

The ritual conversation at the mission and pawn concerns two items: justice and deception, what's fair and what's real.

Now the impoverished walk on two legs, have brains, get nose colds, fall and get up, breathe and cry, have children and are buried.

In the research literature the impoverished are not different from the wealthy. It has been an illusion of class, the same illusion struck at race, that genes were somehow different. The genes are all there on the street.

Dubuque calls itself the Key City, a port that lays like a thumb print inside a curve of the pouring mud and talking water of the Mississippi River.

Central is filled with ghosts.

Life along the main, curling street of Central is a river pool filled with catfish, snapping turtles, diving beetles, dragonfly nymphs and algae. Predation celebrated by the bars, used car lots, delis, pool halls and pawns.

Hope springs from the pawn.

The American Dream for Paul is in living frugally and giving abundantly. He unpacks his load and lays it on the floor.

This is a gate of love. For Paul and many others, the poor men and women and their children are the regal heirs of the heartland.

The poor are not inferior. The impoverished are not shorter or taller, not thinner or fatter or more self absorbed. They don't have more of an entitlement attitude than the very rich.

Paradoxically, research in 2011 suggests that the lower classes may have a higher moral character. Witness the Benz, the BMW, the Jag, the Bentley disregarding the stop light and highway speed in statistically significant numbers, larger by far than the forgotten class.

That nothing can be done, that the problems of the poor cannot be fixed, that's unacceptable at the corner of 17th Street.

Paul Downs and his cohorts, acquaintances and friends, they do not believe nothing can be done. Today, Al carried in a few dozen boxes for Paul, broken down, corrugated boxes, that he delivered into the basement.

On Monday and Thursday they move quickly from the street to the basement.

The basement is the Neanderthal darkness. It drops behind a make shift wall. It was dug out by men and mules. Its walls are crusting limestone.

Al comes from the older, depression generation who believed that everyone was in it together and hell or high water, each of us is accountable. No questions asked. Al's a cancer survivor and stands up for anyone who cannot stand on their own.

Paul told a story about Al.

For years Al has parked his van in front of Paul's store on Central Avenue, has pushed against the great winds that are storms from the diesel trucks as they flare past the intersection of 17th Street. Like a postal carrier, Al has confronted all weather to get food from the van to the hungry.

Paul began.

"Was a sale of fish last week. HyVee grocery on Locust was practically giving it away. After a purchase you could redeem a coupon inside the box to buy the next box at a quarter.

There's a sale now on butter. A pound for one eighty eight."

Paul spends an admirable amount of time looking for food bargains.

"I told Al about the sale, he goes over there. He starts small but graduates to armfuls of fish, great and ominous boxes of fish and he lays them at the check-out counter. You know Al…"

Al's depression era mind dances between savings, frugality and worry about the future. He marches with the eternal moral of helping the least among us, visiting the poor and the prisoner. His ready smile has been a beacon and his white shock of hair a reminder to pass it forward.

"So the fish sale is going very well and Al piles his fish on the counter. Then he opens the fish, box after box, and he finds each coupon, points to the next box in the line so he can have it for a quarter. But… some of the boxes do not have a coupon."

Paul chuckles at the thought of an earnest man demanding his due, the rain now falling with justice. Al has become a special ops soldier, rejecting anything but complete victory. Al's a stand up guy true to his ethics and loyal to all his friends.

"Well, Al makes a fuss, I think he went to the service desk or the store manager, but finally, he got what he'd gone there for. All is well that ends well. Can't you see that? Standing at a HyVee checkout, moral outrage dripping at your sides, wanting that fish …where's the coupon…"

The story, of course, is a never ending one, a battle between those who fight in trenches for those who cannot fight. Al has cancer and regular check - ups. He's passed eighty years old and his efforts are not without pain.

That's how it happens, the genuine love is given without reward, people moving in and out, carrying the loads of others, doing what needs to be done.

The crock pot stew began at 9:15 that morning with eleven little cans of chicken that Paul dropped into the white basin. He found a can of red beans and he dropped that, mixing it into a pasty, clay like pastiche of red and white. Then he added the larger cans, one six pounder filled with tomato paste and another seven pound can of pork and beans. He ladled some more beans and found more tomato, then stirred. After he adjusted the heat he let the batch of goo simmer and watched his store till a conversation began about Jasmine, the hoarding lady.

Jasmine has nothing but junk. You have to be real with her. Martin Buber would approve. Dialogue trumps possessions. Life is about I and thou. If I and it, something's gone awry.

Jasmine has hundreds of boxes of stuff.

She has been an aged poster child of eccentricity for years. Her appearance is often accompanied by a panic in the store. When she stumbles in the door employees dash for hiding places. Poor folk who know her take stock of quick exists. She stands four foot six and as wide as that, as feisty as a bumble bee and persevering as a mule, and she complements everyone by confirming to them their normalcy.

Despite Paul's singular efforts to help clean it up with his sometime employee and friend, big Jim, her home was condemned.

Jasmine's home is surrounded by boxes, furniture, lamps, broken table legs, books, magazines and wet newspapers.

"You know she's nuts. She's lovable, but nuts. I can't help her. No one can help her.

She won't let anyone help her. You know last summer Jim tried to help and he did and when he told her what to do about her home she blamed him for the mess and accused him of theft and larceny. Said she was missing things." Paul worried.

The home begins at the curb and it spills from the side entry to the driveway and onto the retaining walls, flows to the front yard and around the side to the back then gorges itself at the garage. Parts of a life pour out like rain on a field, dribble spots and gullies then erode, twisted in tourniquets and boxes.

Jasmine built a lean – to, plastic garage in front of her brick home to shelter thousands of knick knack items. Barely a path had been made to lurch through the home. Despite sleeping in the car she held onto physical health.

The home's retaining walls appear like a dreamscape. The dozen cans of paint setting along the edge wait for the house painter who never arrives. Nor does the moving van to assess the dozens of boxes of old papers and wet magazines. Furniture sets in the yard, an end table waits by a reading lamp, weights seem ready for a high school footballer, a fish tank, emptied except for rainwater, hides under weeds.

When Jasmine tours the lot she heads for the brick garage where her daughter's ferrets have left a smell unlike anything the earth could have produced naturally, a skunk death smell that wraps around the debris and furniture as if Stephen King had paid a visit.

Paul loves her because she is eccentric but he says he wants the current trouble to end, recognizing how he enables her.

"Jasmine's got my truck and a man from church who's out of work is helping her."

"Hope it works out…" I said.

"Well, I know it won't but we've got to try. Besides the city is coming next week. She's living in a motel, her daughter's in a motel, yeah. They have the home but there's no room to move. Since they condemned it she has to make the inspection or that's it. So I'm going out there and see what we can do. I don't know…"

Jim stands by Paul and he's willing to help but he can't. Jasmine threatened to sue him or have him jailed. He stands in an Army jacket that's rags at the elbows, at the chest, at the neck and around the zipper.

"Yeah, if she'd listened to me she wouldn't have the problem. I wanted to help and thought it was going good. It's why I bought my van. I thought I was employed but she changed that. She can't live like that. She needs help."

Love doesn't pay the bills.

"Yeah," Paul says, " We've been losing money for years now." He acts as if the connection to God is through the poor.

Some hoard. Some need. Some hide. Some give. Some take. Some give and take.

What's wrong with giving everything away?

"What fasting in the time when boyhood dies had put the distant seeing in his eyes, the power in his silence? What had taught that getting is a game that profits naught and giving is a high heroic deed?"

('The Twilight of the Sioux' by John G. Neihardt)

XIX. DANCE LIKE AN INVISIBLE MAN

The two middle aged men sauntered along the crumbling sidewalk at the beginning of Garfield Street where the alley bends to the cement entry into Eagle Grocery Store. Each a victim of the age when men's hair grew to the shoulders, the age now passed, but their hair filled with white and gray and they moved slowly.

I knew each man and saw in their wobbly gaits the ends of their hopes, dreams they'd given up years ago.

The shorter man had fallen to the plague a few months before, drifting in a daze when he stooped by the deep curb side in front of the grocer. It was Jimmy Mitchell. It was the day the police surrounded him and the stretcher carried him, the day the last spiral had begun. I stopped that day to ask my friend Jimmy if he was okay and the police asked me to step away. He looked like a rabid dog and was disoriented and tired.

The taller man was also a friend I met at the pawn shop and he played with a pony tail, whipped it over a shoulder as if his youth was not a remnant on a worn patch of a raggedy coat of arms, as if his hair still stood him up with the Sampson's of the earlier time. Scott was haggard. His gaunt eyes filled with slivers of lost youth.

No work. No insurance. No home.

Both men wore rags in their eyes, dark, lonely shards of the mouthfuls of asphalt they'd claimed in countless falling downs and risings, morsels left over from falling down in fits of drug and alcohol fueled rant and laughing at nothing but the wind as it descended upon their old shoulders.

No one tells their stories but the wind and the few who survive them. The younger men playing along the first base line of this descent can still laugh as these two old and dying men do, but the truth stands here and it doesn't retreat. These are invisible men.

In the summers they have hiding places and stairwells, basement dungeons they wake in when the working people tramp across their thresholds. They are friends to crows and to mongrel dogs. Once, a woman from Dubuque commented on one of my published stories and said, "The author is making this up. There aren't any people like this in Dubuque, Iowa."

It's hard to see them even when they stand in front of your car as you wait for the light to change.

Once, when confronted with the seamier side of Dubuque, last summer, a Human Rights Commission member said, "Where are these people?"

"Go down to the flats and knock on some doors."

"Why we're here because we have had problems ourselves."

"Then you should be sensitive to these stories."

A year later no one sees them. A thousand years earlier, a thousand years from today, have you seen the sad old men or the sad old women?

The ancient moral of the story is that we make a deal with the devil. If we can have a better life, will we allow one person, maybe a small number of people, to live in hell. The devil says,

"Sure, I'll let you have a little prosperity, but those people over there, the ones walking in the alley, those who talk to crows, they'll have to pay."

Invisible.

One day this week Roy came home from Virginia to say howdy. He went to 17th Street where he found the two white haired, hole in the shoe, hands in the pockets and eyes to the ground…old friends.

"Good to see you!" He said to each.

A hug offered and given back.

"I had no idea about the heart attack," he later said about the shorter man. "So, open heart surgery, heh?"

The Virginian, Roy, had been away just a year. The spiral moved quickly.

The white haired, bobbed haired, short friend, good ol' Jimmy, told some of the story about the daze at the grocery, the cops and the stretcher. The trips to Iowa City and his refusal to quit, those parts went unsaid. The scar from neck down through the sternum, the vacant look and the shuffle, "Well," the Virginian said, "He looked pretty rough."

One other friend responded that standing curb side now, asking for money, a last slide before the final epiphany, was the road not chosen now taken.

"You know how it goes."

Scott with the pony tail, he's been seen at NA meetings. He's still working on a moral code, a sober style, a packet of truths in hand and eyes set for the breath beyond the bottle and the pipe.

"I wouldn't give him any money. You know that doesn't help. He just spends it on stuff." The Virginian said.

One year the pony tail lived under a stairwell. One year Jimmy lived under a bush. Now they watch each other's back.

Someone told a joke the other day. Asked the scarred old Jimmy about wishes.

"Would you rather be able to fly or be invisible?"

"I'd rather be able to dance."

Jimmy lost weight the year before the church ostracized him. They conferred, asked each other and finally, made enough of Jim's drinking that he left. It was too bad because he loved to play his guitar in church.

Jimmy always leaned to the right side of the stage in church, sat on a stool, studied his guitar, stared at it, loved it and picked it. He made it sing a soulful, sonorous song, a sound of wind, a spiritual sound to touch God. The stage and the guitar became Jim. He lit up, looked like an ember in a fire of spirits, a ghost in a dance, a soul found, sure, ready and glad.

No one ever paid attention to him. Maybe that's what it was. He worked at the mission, sweated on hot days and swept the sidewalk when the snow fell. I can see him there, leaning with a broom, his shovel stuck deep in a drift, pulling on a cigarette. The simple things mattered to Jimmy.

It took a few years but mysteriously, slowly and inexorably Jimmy found he'd lost his foothold on that church stage. These things take time. Jimmy missed a service then he went on a short bender. He loved the 17th Street Pawn shop and he gave everything he could to the Narrow Gate mission.

No one could have worried about a couple of missing days. It was Jimmy, after all. The minister said it was a shame. How he found out we never knew.

Then the slide, Jimmy trying to hide by drinking rubbing alcohol or vodka with gum, mints and Powerade. That was the stuff that clogged his heart. At least that's what Scotty said. That, and the smoking. Jimmy was no kid, either.

One day he went to stay with Otto. Otto lived up the hill from the mission. Otto liked to drink. Jimmy liked that. When we tried to coax him down he said it wasn't any use. He couldn't quit the drink, he couldn't quit a friend and no one cared but him and Otto. We quit trying to coax him but we kept praying.

When he found out that the minister and the wife of an important member of the congregation judged his drinking with severe old testament brimstone, Jimmy had enough. He was hurt the church woman had been so severe. He had watched her babies from birth but now she didn't have time. He started to drink alone and didn't care anymore. I saw him stoned so bad he didn't know up or down. It's a miserable sight, watching a friend go to hell.

Jimmy knew how it affected us. He said he hated to do it to us but he couldn't help it. Sometimes, he picked up that tough love and got mad when we lent him money. He'd say, you should know better, giving a bum like me a dollar. Don't you know better?

After a year of carousing he asked us to give him a reference so he could get admitted. The care facility wasn't where he belonged but he didn't belong to himself anymore.

We visited often but he became expensive, craving cigarettes. That's all he did for two years, smoked and of course, played cards. He loved cards.

It was a sad day when they let him out. I saw him on Main Street, and he saw me and ran to the car when I stopped at a stop sign downtown. He said he was sorry, he hated to be a bum, but could he borrow a few bucks. Said he hated to beg and all. I should have known he was at bottom but then it was Jim and he never seemed so bad.

He did the public intoxication thing for a long time. He'd be sloppy and the cops would pick him up. He'd do a little time then get out and redo the same stuff. Cops seemed to like helping him. He liked it that someone cared. He just kept getting drunk, getting arrested and going to jail At last, they put him in the county psych unit again but he skipped. They didn't expect that he'd clear out but he did. Good ol' Jimmy.

Near the end he picked up with Otto again. He also followed Scotty around but Scotty didn't want to be responsible for him so he ditched him.

There is no law, human or divine, that alcohol respects.

Jimmy had been to the hospital some twenty times for alcoholism. He'd been out of the Julien Care Facility for the year, released after spending two years there after he tried to drink rubbing alcohol, a drink that could have cost him his life.

It was a bad day when I saw my friend as I drove by the Eagle Grocery Store on Elm Street. He was surrounded by four policemen. I pulled over to the parking lot at Eagle. It was afternoon. My friend was slumped on the curb, fifty yards away. His face was pale and he held his head in his hands. Two of the police were bending over him.

I left my car and walked toward my friend. I didn't know what was going on but I knew he didn't have a family and that he had a history.

As I approached one of the policemen walked toward me.

"That's my friend," I said, "Is he okay?"

"Yeah."

"Hey," I waved to get his attention because he seemed far away, hurting over some hidden pain, doubled up and slumped on the parking lot curb at Eagle. The ghost of a future he didn't see.

"Hey," he said and nodded. He looked weak. I turned to the cop.

In the foreground a siren roared. The EMT truck pulled up. Another friend, an EMT, said hello. We frowned to each other and the medical team surrounded my friend at the curb.

One man strapped the stethoscope to an arm. After a check, the man shook his head.

"It's not good."

My friend tried to stand and wobbled. The cop next to him held his arm.

The medical unit raised their gurney and strapped him down then wheeled my pal to the truck and I raised my thumb and called his name, prayed he'd see that he wasn't alone. After a while, after he was stabilized, the truck drove away.

The next day, after being taken to Iowa City, after the tests returned, the doctors tried an angioplasty. They thought they could open up his arteries, maybe apply a stent to help the blood flow. They stopped short because my friend had a closed artery. Then, the decision to open him up for heart surgery arrived like the sunrise, sudden and slow, all at once.

As the winter ended some of us worried out loud about Jimmy. After he had the open heart surgery, an operation they were compelled to do because he had a heart attack in the parking lot of the Iowa City hospital, we started to consider his mortality. He didn't take much notice of it, being more concerned with hand outs that could get cigarettes or alcohol. In the end, most of us think he'll die from the alcohol.

"Have you heard about Jimmy?"

"Not a thing."

"Hope he's alright."

"He could be dead."

"Yep."

I saw him on the way to school one day in late February. He was walking along Washington Street in Dubuque, ambling as if he didn't have a care in the world. His hair, now gray and dirty, was too long for him, unlike the barbered cut he'd always held. He looked too thin and he walked with his face to the sidewalk. I couldn't stand driving past him so I turned in the Walgreen's parking lot and zipped the couple of blocks back to pull over to the curb.

"Hey, Jim! Where you going? Need a ride?"

"Well, hey, Tim! Yeah, sure. I'm just going down the street to see a friend. He owes me money."

"Get in man."

The clouds of that late winter day still set inside me as I retrace Jimmy's last few months. Once in the car, he answered my questions about his whereabouts through the cold and desolate, Iowa winter.

"Oh, I've been staying with a friend. No, not Otto....yeah, I'm okay. Say, he's right here. Pull over...oh, wait a minute, his car's gone. Can you just give me a ride downtown?"

"Well, listen, Roy is in town, you know that, right? He'd love to see you. He's only heard about the heart surgery and is probably aching to get a look at you. He's staying with his girlfriend, just across from Paul's. You know the place, a few blocks from here."

I may have been too convincing, too truthful, too lacking in a con to suit Jim. He smelled and he coughed and his jacket was torn.

"So here," I said as I pulled toward the deep, ancient, limestone curb, "He's there." I pointed to the red brick apartment building and Jimmy nodded.

"Say, listen," Jimmy said and I should have known, "Can you give any money? Whatever you have. Twenty. Can you give me twenty? I have to get some groceries."

"Sure, let me see."

Jimmy smelled like whiskey and tobacco smoke, a twisted urine scent of body odor and metropolitan damage. He seemed to be sneering now.

After I let Jimmy go with a ten spot that February he snarled in a subtle way, looking to me as if he was angry that I fell for his con. He seemed to judge my enabling, like I was no longer a friend - "Why would you give me one thin dollar when all I'm doing is killing myself?"

A few weeks later, a friend of a friend saw Jimmy on television. He was playing gospel, had a guitar and sang of his love for Jesus. We gathered round a computer after we heard and watched him tell the audience that he'd lost all his friends and family, too. A young University of Iowa student gushed over his guitar and another hovered around him like he wore a halo.

I don't know if it was his attitude, the show of sobriety that he'd said he'd had for many months, or that he'd gotten better at his chosen craft.

"I know he hasn't been sober that long." One of us said.

"I don't like the way he's referring to us as if we gave up on him." Another said

He's better at con now. Maybe that's the thing.

Jim's drunk wood alcohol, rubbing alcohol and most any liquid containing alcohol. The spirits own him as he owns them, in lock step to the end of the sidewalk.

"Yeah, the public intox. I've been down that road." That road has been dozens of hospital and jail stays.

His hands are roughened now by the weathering influence of alcohol. The scars are not subtle. Little nicks beyond sight are within, those slights of society he's felt when walking along a sidewalk he's built and having someone's gaze rivet him from a position of status.

"Oh, I'm fine," he'll say as if to draw attention to the paradox of being fine after falling down, time after time.

Age spots have grown like little tomato seeds. His skin is thinner and his hair greyer but his voice holds. When he's feeling right he can sing and banter like a choir boy though he says he's more like a bantam rooster. Dylan's rooster or The Stone's rooster or Chuck Berry's.

When a friend questioned the wisdom of leaving the care of counselors, social workers, meals, warmth, a roof over his head, Jimmy said simply, "I don't care."

Friends have heard the 'I don't care' line a thousand times. Why they haven't tired of asking why he doesn't care is bewildering. Maybe it's because they love him and in that refusal to accept that he will die, probably soon, from the various ailments of his behavior, they know he's going out his way...

He worked at the Narrow Gate for years. He kept to a routine. If and when he drank, it didn't get in the way to prevent work. You can ask anyone who knows him and the first thing they want you to know, "He's a great guy. I love Jimmy."

Soon after the heart surgery, Jim was drinking a twelve pack daily. Then he was leaving ..."Going AWOL..." as friends referred it. He left and returned to his friend's home till the friend gave an ultimatum. Jimmy tried to abide but couldn't.

"He's trying to kill himself," friends said. "It's suicide," friends said. "I love Jim," friends said.

Jimmy lived on the streets. He was picked up for public intoxication. He panhandled, sometimes showing the wicked, crazy line of scar tissue that began at his neck and dropped down his chest.

For a short time he was wanted, with a warrant issued. He escaped from his confines during the summer and found an old drinking friend.

He eats, sleeps, walks, plays cards and watches himself grow old.

Whenever the subject arises, he says matter of factly, "I'm responsible. I did this to myself. I made this."

He built the sidewalk to his destination, pour by pour. He formed it. This is where the sidewalk ends. Some day, his friends say sooner not later, he'll be dropped in a hole, covered with dirt and a few prayers will be said. Everyone will say, "I loved Jimmy."

XX. STAN'S AMERICAN PAWN

Stanley stood at his counter by the watches and games, sprinkled gems of gold and silver, and he diligently cleaned a computer screen. He held a spray bottle while his eye drew to the cash register. A young, orchid faced woman asked about a price for a cell phone. She wore a do rag and her razor thin face screwed tightly to a frown.

Stanley placed the plastic bottle on the counter. He said the phone was twenty dollars then he returned to his cleaning. The woman shook her head and whispered, but loud enough to be heard.

"Food…"

"Did you say…you have to eat?" Stan asked, incredulous about the statement. She stared at him with a hard, dry, cold look.

Stan had learned the pawn shop business at 17th Street and had spent twelve years at the Narrow Gate, working the pawns and helping at the mission counter.

The woman nodded. She placed the red cell phone on the counter. She stood as firm as a soldier, stark to her task of firing again, watching the trench in front of her.

"I can do fifteen," she said.

The recession appeared like a shadow then, whirling above them, a long cloud of rain and a grizzled rumbling in the pits of their stomachs. The woman had a hungry look in her lean face. She said she needed to eat.

Stan named his store the American Pawn shop. He was born in India. He was often as likely to help a street urchin as make a profit though he was known as the king of the stakemen.

Both the pawn shop owner and the customer knew the precious value of each penny and every second, of things lost and found. Somewhere Caesar's picture, the issuance from Jesus, in the form of founding fathers in this age, was passed above the welfare of the poor.

Somewhere a proverb was being twisted, somewhere in time the raggedy tired had been left behind. Both Stanley and the woman knew the score. Stan okayed the cell at fifteen.

A five dollar savings to make a difference in the day's daily bread.

Time is made into fractions, precious moments laid into a grid, deposited like ant's eggs in a tax and moral code.

When the transaction was done the woman thanked Stan and ambled out the door.

Now, a young man who had waited for his turn, showing his insolvency with a sad faced stare at the floor, with brown, greasy hair that fell over his collar, seethed in his own darkness. Stan had moved to the register now and looked at the man.

The young man seemed to have become something indiscernible from the economy and the pain, reaching out to the world with colors and tattoos that said many things and nothing at the same time. His attire appeared to be a trumpet call from Gideon or from an angel during the beginnings, when some say heaven and hell were made by decisions that now affect everyone. He might have been a prodigal son.

Red and green winged dragons flew down from his shoulders, his black leather coat an old symbol of defiance. Upon each knuckle a tattoo of one of the suits of the playing cards rose to the eye. Blue clubs and red diamonds sought relief from poverty, from luck gone sour. Index finger a heart, middle finger a club.

On the wall by the corner files and the phone a yellowed, tin wall sign with numbered tickets hung from a hook. The sign, titled "Complaint Department." Next to the numbers a greeting, "Take a number." A hand grenade stands in the shadow.

On the city streets, poverty stricken citizens are holding on with cat gut and guitar strings. The devil has his eye on city streets. In the great recession, the real unemployment rate is 15%. The last figure about the unemployment pain heralded a drop but this was for Wall Street's benefit.

In 2013 it was said that 25% of new college graduates were unemployed.

One early winter day, a solitary figure ambled down a poor stretch of a Dubuque street. He was headed to Stan's.

The shadow man wore a guitar on his back with the strap hung low to his waist and he strolled down Central Avenue from 17th Street like a man with an agenda. He stared straight ahead with a cold eye on the cement and occasionally he glanced at the rooftops of the ancient buildings that dot the boulevard. Brickwork looks down through the dream. Tradesmen from Europe laid it with cornice and style. They placed cornerstones to last.

The cloudless sky shimmered blue and the morning temperatures were in the twenties but the man with the guitar wore only a gray, hooded sweatshirt. The Silvertone guitar rustled upon his shoulders. It was precious to the young man.

After he crossed the embedded threshold tiles at the entry to the American Pawn shop, once a hardware store where wooden barrels filled with nails were scooped and sold to the growing city, he passed the Dale Earhardt Jr. photos at the front door. He then sauntered toward the counter. The shop owner was eating chicken from a Tupperware bowl.

The man with the tattooed knuckles stood in shadow at the counter. He passed his Fender across his chest as the shop owner now drew cash from the register.

"You pay it within a week and I cut the interest. It's an incentive."

The black case held a beloved black guitar. A temporary fix people of the street understand. These are inexplicable times. Hard times.

The hawk faced youth with the tattoos talked about luck. The shop keeper said, "You devil you…"

"Some people have said I have Satan's eyes," the young man said.

The somber self assessment did not elicit a blink from the other five people in the store. No one questioned being the devil. It's the story that comes around, again and again.

"I have sinned," then look into the eyes of poor allies and nod.

"Hey man I'll be right with you." Stan said to the young man with the Silvertone as he finished chewing the leftovers from the bowl. Smells of chicken and noodles drafted the countertop.

When the transaction was done the young man from the sidewalk held his Silvertone up for inspection.

"What do you want?" The shop owner asked.

"I got to get forty, fifty," the young man said as he tugged at his hood.

"No! What else you got?"

The young man said he had a Gibson circa 1939 and the clerk's eyes widened.

"You bring that down. I'm interested," he said.

The young man took his guitar back. He turned and walked out the door. The sounds of a familiar silence greeted him as he retraced his steps.

Stan's store is diverse. On another day while sitting on a familiar bar stool in front of Stan's counter I saw a young woman at the counter.

Her toe nails were pink but the enamel was chipped and worn. Her feet looked tired. Her tan sandals were torn and her blue dress was loose as if she borrowed it or found it in a bin at a second hand store but her face was young and her hair shone. She was a black haired young woman about twenty years old who stood between glass topped counters. She seemed to be a cherub at a communion rail, waiting on a wafer, hoping for a sign, eyes intent and lifted up, for hope is a tantalizing aspect of life, sometimes a shadow on a distant trail and sometimes a flame.

She carried a gold necklace and a cell phone. In a tiny box were other jewels and jewelry. Her poor pockets of silver and gold were frayed but her voice practiced a more confidant sheen despite the wise man's psalm of robbery and despair that connects to silver and to gold. She was pushing a camel through the eye of a needle. A bid for freedom had been foreshadowed in her approach and the pawn broker quieted as he strode to gaze upon another sad story in a litany of sad fables in the age of trampled dreams.

The moon was a sliver of light in a pale sky that morning it broke across the threshold of the Dubuque, Iowa, pawn shop. If the moon is amore the poor are more bereft of affection than ever.

Poverty is a killing field. It consumes children in dark forebodings and removes life's energy from their play. In the neighborhoods of the poor are broken bottles, broken sidewalks, broken windows and broken dreams. Health care is depressed, education has less quality, alcohol and drugs are more prevalent and violence is more frequent and more entrenched. Generations pass. The poor pass along mangled and broken hopes to their children.

The poor watch the liberal cry foul and listen to the conservative cry independence. They watched when Nero fiddled and when Hannibal crossed the Alps and when Napoleon put his hand in his pocket. They know the world builds itself up on their backs. They know poverty does not go away. The war on poverty failed. The Bible tells the story of a short, brown man who was hung on a cross, whose sole mission was to walk among these, the less fortunate, the poor. The poor have beatitudes but little else.

"I can't give you much for your stuff," Stanley Samuel said and he smiled and behind the smile was his sadness, too. "Let me look at this necklace," he said and turned, looking through his jeweler's orb, adding a drop of chemical to determine the exactness of the gold.

"It's just twenty four penny weight, not much," he said and seemed stuck, with her, on a trail of tears.

"I need four hundred," she said and the man drew a breath and said, no, he couldn't do that.

"I need it for my rent," she said and he smiled again and the weight of the world tucked itself onto them then.

"I can give you $150 for everything here."

Her rent was due in a few days. Every penny counted and she accepted. She tightened her sack dress at the belt that hung on her hip and thanked the clerk as she walked out into the slim light of the moon dappled, tear addled sidewalk. She didn't cry now but kept her head up and she walked in the same silence that the poor hold, on her way to a cross, somewhere, on a hill, somewhere, alone.

Stanley's parents live in Dubai. He visits them every few years. He's an honest, hardworking man who came here for the Bible college but stayed because he fell in love with an Iowa, farm girl. He learned the pawn business working with Paul and he said that without Paul's advice about heart, he would not have done well.

He introduced me to many stories but the one about Stacey was special because it concerned how our lives become harder, through no fault of our own.

Stacey's story drops a hammer fifty feet from the American Pawn… at 16th street.

"I was in a really good mood that day," she says. She smiles then the smile dissolves. Stan introduces us.

You read the news. Three men arrested across the river in Wisconsin, charged with a first degree robbery at Cash Central in Dubuque. Central Avenue. In the middle of pawn shop row. The news copy ran three paragraphs, second page. Maybe you don't remember. Stacey Oswald does.

"It was a good day," she says about the morning.

Then two men walked into Cash Central. It happened fast.

Stacey says it seemed like forever.

"I was texting on my phone. Two guys walked in. I set my phone on the desk. They just stood there." She says the men wore masks.

She's a young woman with a pleasant smile. A pretty face but not a person you'd put into your memory bank for outstanding radiance, not Hollywood not celebrity. She's more like a beatitude. Careful, thoughtful, concerned committed.

She says it was a cold day. She remembers the clear sky. She says she began to feel

overwhelmed with the two men, hands in pockets, staring, scanning the room.

Cash Central was on the corner of 16th and Central in Dubuque. In 2012 Jerry opened a pawn shop in the space.

Large picture windows face the street. The views are clear. On the walls of the store are peg board displays filled with cell phones and the wood floor of the business is divided by glass display cases of green, yellow, pink and blue phones. A sign says Cash Central, Payday Loans, Cash Advance.

"One of the men walked around Jim and put a gun to his temple, his arm around Jim's neck."

Stacey says, referring to Jim Quayle, the owner of the store.

In deposition she says, referring to the thinner man, that he simply told her, "Get down." She says she looked down: "At the floor. I didn't want him to see me look at him, give him reason to hurt me."

"I froze," said Stacey, "I'm trying not to make contact. I'm just terrified. He has a gun pointed at me."

She's thinking now about her life, about her children, about those precious moments of life as the gun roils across the space in front of her face. Guns feel like no other thing in this life.

A cold, dead power, an aesthetic, some say.

It may be that someone you know drove by that day. Maybe you did.

Stacey was on the floor, on her knees, nine millimeter handgun at her eyes, tall, 200 pound man standing over her.

"I stared at the floor and he started pushing buttons on the register. 'How do you get it open,' he said."

The second man, whom she says was Anthony McCollum, rifled through the register. When he was done with the cash drawer the gunman dropped it. The crash, a boom, a scraping clash of noise resounded like a shock wave through Stacey Oswald.

"Please no! Please no! Please no!" she thought.

"…ing move! …ing move!" Stacey says he told her. According to deposition,

Brother Mario was now with the store owner, in the back, trying to get money from a safe.

Today, among her memories are the black boots that her assailant wore, black leather

that fused across her eyes, dug into her and stayed, holding her like a bird in a cage.

"Those men robbed me… they totally affected… my life."

"He just held his gun over me," the pretty mother says, "Then the other man said, 'Just shoot! Just shoot! Just shoot!'"

A van waited outside. Antione Grant is reported to have been the getaway driver. According to testimony, the McCulloms ran to the vehicle. No shots were fired.

Traffic rushed past the 10 a.m. robbery.

Later, a detective said the gun pointed at Stacey had been loaded. He said the bullet was not yet into the chamber.

In the deposition the ordeal revisited itself through attorney questions. For five pages an attorney for the defendants asked about the gun held in her face.

One hundred twelve questions pummeled Stacey Oswald about clothing the robbers wore, colors, textures, stitching.

"There's many, many coats out there," Scott Nelson, Esq., said in deposition.

"You've asked that enough." Stacey's attorney responded.

"I still see him," Stacey said of Mr. Nelson.

Of the three men, Mario McCullom received 25 years, Anthony 15 years and the driver, Mr. Grant, 10 years.

The story does not end there though.

On November 30 of last year a check, 'Case Number…Code MV

The State v. Antoine Grant, Joint and Several Restitution' appeared in her mail.

The amount, fourteen dollars and eleven cents.

Stacey sees a therapist on Mondays.

American Medicine Dreams

The man walked into Stan's store with a blue box marked Clancy clutched to his chest. It was the Aldi's brand. His arms wrapped around it like it was his child. A tortilla chip stamp was stenciled on the side but a brass colored gas torch and its tube were packed inside the half shell box. The green and red of the hose seemed like a Christmas color but the tubing that fell over the sides seemed like a snake.

He resembled Everret Koop, the 1980's U.S. Surgeon General. His white, chin strap beard coiffed and his cheekbones high, he smiled then slammed the box onto the counter.

"One hundred twenty five!" He screeched like an owl. He scratched at the box and smiled a confident air that beamed across the counter.

"Now you know I have to look at it!" Stanley smiled back, calling the man by name.

When the clerk sauntered behind his register the man said, "One fifty! I need one fifty!"

"Now…." the small businessman drawled as he stared at an invoice, "What did I do for you the last time?"

"This is now. I have to have one fifty. You know I'm good for it."

Standing nearby the man, a woman whispered incoherently but the mumbling did its job of distraction.

"I'm good for it," he repeated, now an upper hand in the psychology of the deal, "I'll pay you right away. You know it."

It was ten days before Christmas. The torch was how he made a living.

"I can go one twenty five."

It was here, in this moment underneath the compound bows and behind the metal detector that the white bearded man drew all the sincerity out of himself, a pleading countenance of prayer and hope. His eyes seemed to water as he said, again, "I have to get the one fifty. I'm good. I'm good for this. You know I'll pay you."

Stanley seemed to melt, to follow Paul's advice about having a heart. He smiled and looked above the rims of his eyes and said, "Yes, okay."

"You still junkin?" He asked as he prepared the paperwork to consummate the deal.

"Yeah," the man said, his tan workman's coat slung to his knee and his greasy, blue cap tilted upon his head.

"I get some city business, you know. They do those rehab jobs and I get a little tin and what not."

While the man waited for his receipt, he spied a friend across the counter.

"Hey man. What are you doin? You workin?"

"Yeah," said the taller man with the brown leather coat and butch haircut, "Had some concrete work this summer."

Soon it's Christmas. Tradesmen aren't building nest eggs. There's no stock certificates hung in their stockings. They trade in tools for temporary gifts.

Two women followed the Clancy's box pawn and one of them pawned a ring. The other said she was worried about medication. She said the availability was low. Stan said Merry Christmas.

As they walked to the door, the pawn owner asked, "What's the medication?"

The sad faced woman with the shaggy, brown hair said it was for her cancer.

Snow was forecast for Christmas.

Tiffani

The Bible study was held in the store front church on Locust where the Easter colored, purple curtains prevent walkers from invading church privacy. Each week the serious faithful open the book and review its meaning. Each Sunday the pastor exhorts his small following to live and breathe the sacred text. The Tabernacle of Faith studies the good book as redemption and regards it as God's word.

Tiffani Allen is one of the faithful from the little church set in the retail store front in Dubuque. She and a friend had just finished that week's Bible lesson. Tiffani said she'd give her friend a ride home that Tuesday. When she arrived at the home near Nineteenth and Washington she parked and she and her friend began to talk. She says she pulled the keys from the ignition. Within minutes she saw a police squad slide in behind her. The bulbs came on and lit up the night. The two Bible stewards shared looks. Just done with instruction about the powers of their faith and the corrupting influences of this world, they wondered about a police car pulling up behind them. More cars soon surrounded them.

"It's about midnight and it's 19th and Washington and your van has tinted windows and we see you sitting here," Tiffani says the police officer said as he stood by her window. "You are parked about a foot away from the curb."

Tiffani says she wondered what could be wrong with how she was parked. She and her friend were confused. Maybe this was a case of mistaken identity.

"I'm coming from Bible study and have driven my friend home," Tiffani said.

"How much have you had to drink," she says the young officer asked. She worried about race as an issue. The patrolman was black.

"I'm under the influence of the Holy Spirit," Tiffani remembers saying.

She remembers he said, "It's not racism and I hate it when you people say that…" She says then that the world of man became fury.

"I had a cell phone and it dropped. It was dialing. They drew their weapons. I yelled into the phone, 'I'm being arrested!' All I could hear was click, click." A gun was drawn and cocked.

"I'm nervous and I see weapons. I asked if somebody had robbed a bank."

Among the conflicts that night a half hour after Bible study was the request for proof of insurance. Tiffani says she had proof.

"I did have but I was so freaked out I couldn't find it."

Her heart began to race and her blood pressure rose. Her throat dried and her muscles tensed. The police lights slapped the trees and sidewalk and houses. The officer stood in shadow. The other squads waited nearby. Sounds of police radio squawks filled the street. Two black Bible students sitting in chaos who were planning to review their study then say goodbye.

"They searched my car." She says. She says she was not informed about rights. She was handcuffed and placed in the first police car. Then she was taken to jail where she was bodily searched and put in a cell with two other women who had beaten someone so badly that Tiffani says, "His face was swollen beyond belief…"

Tiffani Allen was charged with Driving with a Suspended License, Failure to Surrender Her License and Having No Insurance.

The young mother and Bible student asked the police to help her after she arrived at the jail. She told them she had seizures and asked for her medications. She says the police refused her.

She told them stress brings on the seizures. She says she was ignored.

"It's a big Tuesday night…" one of the officers laughed. Tiffani tensed. In jail for driving violations after she had been sitting in her car talking with a friend.

While in the cell, the two other women threatened her.

"Hey, church lady!" One screamed. "We could beat you up if you're not nice!"

"Church lady, don't cry," the other one yelled.

."I started giving them scripture. I didn't sleep. I was a mess."

In the end she endured. She's been forced to pay fines. She's making payments.

She says God keeps her strong.

The Mail Order Bride

She moved like pudding. She squeezed into the two foot space in the corner by the glass display counter and her bulk shimmied as she hovered over the short man with the coal black hair. Her clothes were garage sale attire, musty accoutrements that wrinkled while she bounced from foot to foot.

Stan stood at the counter.

The man stood still, pressed to the counter, a counterweight to the big woman, and he talked to Stanley. Everyone at American Pawn focused on the tiny space of the counter where Stanley stood by his cash register. The customers were bearing anger, money and confusion. The dialogue was shadowed by posters of Scarface and the Godfather. Pacino and Brando glared at everyone.

An argument had begun. The brown faced Stan understood.

"I'm telling you, man, you're crazy! You've spent how much, now? Nine hundred dollars? What is that? You'll never get a dollar of that back!" Stan was adamant and direct.

The pawn broker screamed, laughed, jiggled in a delightful howl. He danced and pushed at the shock of the scene, leaned into the story from the middle aged man who had sent a thousand dollars to West Africa for a woman he now believed was boarding a plane to come to Dubuque, Iowa.

"You've never seen this woman, you don't know her, you're sending money so she will come here! You've done this before and I told you, it's a scam! You're getting ripped off!"

The short man, fingers digging into his licorice black hair, frowned. His cell phone rang. He pulled it from a shirt pocket.

"Yeah…" he waved at the pawnbroker, stepped back several feet from the counter and turned his head to face the door.

"This is too crazy! Someone should write a story about this!"

The heavy woman stared forward impassively, unblemished by the conversation, a bystander or an involved party, no one seemed to know, and she presented an unfazed aspect, watching the hysteria, unfettered by the histrionics. She stayed close to the dark haired man.

"He can't send more money there. There's easier ways to get a woman."

"He's married, what about that?" One customer eagerly chimed.

"His wife cares about him." The obese woman said.

The black haired man then ambled back into the fray. He shook his head.

"She's at the airport."

"She's not at the airport, fool. You've got to quit this! I'll give you a hundred dollars if she ever comes here. It's not going to happen!" Stan yelled.

"He has a wife who really cares about him but…" The heavy woman spoke. She seemed to care.

Now, the woman's obesity was frightful but the tar haired man held his space, ignoring her size and the way she penned him to the corner. She was connected but disconnected, as if she didn't hear the conversation, believing and not believing it, knowing the truth and not knowing. Her bulging waist and fleshy, sagging arms, wide, sack like neck and her pasty complexion made her a ghost. The big woman overwhelmed the man like a huge shadow.

The energy between them was unclean, too, like an unwashed sink. The sad, fat woman hung over the conversation, a bird flapping away in silence, giving breath but taking in more, taking in the scent, the flavor, the taste and the memory and taking it in deeply.

"Are you married?" Another customer directed himself to the poor woman. She nodded.

"I'm his wife!"

Her eyes filled quickly, her cold tears poured down her cheeks and she rushed to the front door, cheeks lined by the streaming pain. The black haired man kept talking about the exotic beauty he'd purchased, a mail order West African doll, the pageant winner he'd meet in Dubuque after she stopped over in New York then Chicago.

When three young, raggedy clothed men entered the store with a box of electronics, the man walked hurriedly out to the sidewalk to see his wife. Customers looked dumfounded, scratching and blinking. One man looked at the wall photo of Marlon Brando.

The three men changed the conversation

"You sell that?" One of the fresh faced customers asked as he pointed to the Marlon Brando photo with the caption, 'I'm gonna make him an offer he can't refuse.'

"No, man, I've had that a long time. Some things are not for sale."

Standing on the pitted sidewalk of Central Avenue, the married pair growled, then they walked down the sidewalk into the dark afternoon.

XXI. THE HEARTLAND CAMPAIGN

*{Field of Dreams director Phil Robinson liked
that title – The Heartland Campaign}*

The temperature at the city's clock tower is sixteen below zero today. The cold, wide gutter iron that sets curbside to pick up the runoff down Central Avenue is smoking with clouds of frozen air from underground that billow upward toward the deep blue skies. Inside the pawn shop Roy pops open the cans of beans, macaroni and sauces that become the grist of survival for the street, for the hungry of Dubuque, Iowa.

The oldest pawn shop in the city shows a smiling face. Inside, Roy talks about people.

"A fella came by for two months. He had come from elsewhere and was waiting on disability checks. He ate here every day. The man said, 'I'll tell you a secret but you've got to keep it to yourself. I live under the bridge.' I wouldn't tell anyone. It's no one's business. Anyway, after about two months, his check came in. He got himself a little room and last I heard he's okay."

The shop holds a litany of life within its bowels. In the basement bread and staples line the shelves. At the front door the wood shelves hold dozens of loaves in bags from area food stores.

Plastic deli servers contain sweet rolls and buns.

At the far end of the store guitars hang from hooks near cases of videos and miscellaneous wares. On mid aisle shelves televisions and computers set waiting for owners.

Outside, the cracking sidewalks show white haze from the car's splatter of salt and grime. When Roy finishes filling the black Rival cooker with can after can of pork, beans, vegetables and sundry foods, with the hill of can goods depleted, he pours sauces and pepper, flakes of garlic and whatever is on hand. He does this six days a week.

"You ever see the guy who walks the streets in the Columbo jacket? I hope he's got a roof today…"

"A man used to come in here some time ago," Roy says, "He found an old refrigerator and hauled it up to the bluffs somewhere. He filled it with papers and he lived there that winter. Don't know what happened to him."

After several minutes of stirring and waiting Roy opens the cooker and the steam rises out from the huge pot and the smells of tomato, garlic, pepper and beans mingle in the steam and pour toward the gray front door. A short man with a blue coat and blue stocking cap enters. The two men greet each other and Jimmy, the other employee, walks from the end of the counter where he's been cleaning.

"Yeah," the man in blue says, "I've got a truck full."

Jimmy smiles and opens the door to the freezing wind and Roy says to the man with the Samaritan delivery, "It's cold out there. I can feel the cold rolling off you." Roy laughs and the man smiles. The man says," Say, I've got some candy for the children, too." He walks out to his van and brings in orange, Halloween M&M's.

Jimmy returns with boxes of rolls and bread, sweet rolls and candy. He comes and goes several times, filling the wood shelves inside the door with the food staples.

No one has asked these men to give the staple of life each day but they do. The cold from Siberia can harm a man in minutes today and a man without food could die on the street. These men seem to know that. They talk nonchalance as if this is a part of every human beings lot, to give without reward.

The store pays out cash each day for the people of Dubuque who pawn precious goods,   music boxes and parts of themselves.

"We have a couple that comes here. Both of them work part time. But they don't have enough to make the rent so they bring in what they have to cover till payday. We hold things and send them out again. The loans aren't much. This couple works but they can't make it."

A thin man with a white flecked beard strolls in from the corner at seventeenth and rounds the entry like he's been there before. Roy and Jimmy say, "Hey…" The wizened looking man stares with sunken eyes at the shelf of food.

Jimmy says, "Help yourself."

The man's eyes dart from person to person then he reaches out for bags of bread and rolls.

Jimmy asks, "You want some buns?"

"No. I have some. Thanks."

Jimmy helps him fill a bag of food and drops a Halloween roll of M&M's into the sack.

"Thanks…."

The man bundles up quickly, pulls his arms into his body and walks out the door. His breath highlights follow him as he ambles down Central Avenue.

Roy and Jimmy go about their business.

The building once housed a furniture store. Once, a rescue mission. Today, the 17th Street Pawn Shop keeps bellies full and offers warmth from the cold. No one asked them. The cold never goes away.

It's been more than a year since Roy said that business had picked up. We all reflected on the meaning of that, more than a year ago. We stood at the counter of the 17th Street Pawn shop, by the food of the Narrow Gate, a handful of grown men discussing the subtleties of existence, looking for answers.

That was back when Paul was still allowed to give away hot food, a meal to stick to a man's belly and add to his hope. Something simple like chili, a pot of beans and rice, some deer meat and beans and cans of vegetables ladled in over the top. Roy said more people than ever were coming for food. More invisible people who knew the trouble, who could have told everyone

about being hungry, homeless, alone, unemployed.

Back then, a daily group of hungry people waited their turns, sometimes coming in groups for the box of food handed out upon demand.

Back then Paul was still allowed to cook for the hungry too, filling the bellies of those without enough. They came in every day with a sad hello, a turned down optimism, sometimes a hearty smile, but always that sense of weariness that you see in someone who's had a run of hard luck and hasn't pulled out, maybe never will pull out.

Last summer the city of Dubuque told Paul, "No more!" No more giving away hot meals, no more handing out free, cooked food to those in need. They gave him a form and told him to stop.

Oh yeah, they suggested that Paul could read the fine print, he could invest some small fortune in remodeling to meet their standards, but for now, they said, "No more. De nada. Finito."

Maybe this shouldn't bother anyone, and to tell the truth several people said I should write it down back then and get the facts out for Dubuquers to digest. That was back then, about the hurts of the invisible people. I don't know why, I let it go. I wrote about them but ignored economy and mercy. Someone once said that the understanding of consequence guides behavior. Maybe I thought nothing would come of it, who would care...

The pawn shop sidles up to some poor sections of Dubuque and as the poor got poorer, many downtown asked the same thing, "Is the prosperity ending, finally? We know it can't go on forever."

Today the decline is so swift, the losses so far away from what our leaders understand, and, leadership and finance is not beget by gazing at the sun the way the Sioux did to gather a vision about economy for the tribe, about the right direction for the family. Our leaders have gone to ten thousand dollar a night resorts to discuss it over Pina Colada. For us at the pawn the tendency to doubt the sacrifice and self discipline of the wealthy is commonplace and wise. We know not to ask, "Where have all the flowers gone?"

The falling down the slide has come and if you think you're secure, ask an old man or old woman from another time, a time of loss and sacrifice and slim hopes; can bad times happen overnight, what if the whole "sucker goes down"...as President Bush delicately put it? Ask a resident of the flats of Dubuque. Ask a regular at the second hand stores, Goodwill, St Vincent's and others.

Psychologists used to say depression fits among the depressed because they are understanding reality - the depressed may be lacking defenses most of us use - to understand reality is to be depressed.

Today, it seems, we all face the thought of hunger aligned against security and the wolf at the door.

Today, at the pawn shop, we don't review the needs of the poor much anymore. And when we reflect about leadership, we remember. The big step is doing something. But first, people have to care. About everyone. About ethics. About invisible people who aren't saying, "I told you so."

And they could have, even as their food was transferred to other door steps with other forms.

Downtown Brown

A member of the .01 percent, Edward Conrad helped to build Bain Capital. In May, 2012 this builder said the great, growing income inequality is a sign the economy is working. He knows privilege. His economy sails in a blue, driftless sky.

Standing at the mission counter where nearby a family heirloom is pawned to pay the rent, an old, wrinkled woman wipes at a tear. The unforgiveable powerlessness in the economy is pain that only those who have suffered understand.

The economy is teaching millions of children about helplessness. At the mission and the pawn, Jesus Christ is taught. Who can say if this is hope. The suffering is greater than the black time of the 1930's.

Downtown Brown wore the same grey baseball cap for months and his long, brown hair fell in locks around his ears. He lived above the pawn shop. Every day he walked down the stairs on the rickety staircase that was tied to the exterior, whitewashed wall , holding the rail to keep his balance, watching the steps for the grit patches to hold him. Sometimes he opened the store and mission. He greeted people on the street like a brother would and he knew their pain. Sometimes a child would greet him and he would invite the child indoors for a hard candy or a cookie.

Ron Brown walked with a stoop shouldered gait. He tugged at his scruffy, salt and pepper beard. His clothes were second hand and they were dirty and torn like flags upon a field of defeat. But his toothless smile did not waver in times of hardship.

He worked at the meat packing plant for 12 years. He was the electronics wizard of the 17th Street Pawn shop.

He smiled and it was a signal of friendship and it survived in times of homelessness and times of hunger. His spontaneity and quirky humor engaged him and it cost nothing, as he said, "To smile and be positive."

And Downtown Brown loved children. These qualities made him a builder of lives.

"Now there, what do you say," he'd say to a six year old child standing at the counter of the pawn shop, parent wrestling with a bowl of chili from the mission. And the child would stare in wide eyed wonder then slowly push his hand away, knowing the candy was his and quietly respond, "Thank you."

Downtown Brown has friends that come from the street, from every stone and stony place, through the mud and through the rain. Some come from referrals. He fixes things. He lifts and clears the fields of pain.

He will wire a house, add a radio to a car, fix a computer and a television and sometimes, if he feels the squeeze in a man's face, will finish the work and walk away. No charge.

"Well, there, Mr. Tim," he said, " The reason I have lots of friends is because I don't get into anyone's business."

Downtown Brown greets everyone as mister. It's a calling card.

In the early morning when the delivery man from the downtown mission leaves his leftover pizzas from the nearby Pizza Ranch on the pawn shop counter for the mission people, Ronnie Brown rants. He likes to kid and he likes company at the counter.

"He was the toughest guy, that there, right there…"

The delivery man smiles at Downtown. He has worked at the packing house with Ronnie and knows the killing, the cutting, the packing, the weight on shoulders, tired backs, cold floors and smells of dying, people so tough they worked with a tourniquet after losing a finger.

Ronnie spoke like you knew the unsaid things of his mind and then he smiled. He said when he worked at the packing plant the pizza delivery man was a tough steward, a supervisor who didn't mince words if he felt the job hadn't been done.

The delivery man from the Main Street mission said he wanted a remote starter for his car.

"What kind of car you got?" Ronnie asked.

"Hyundai."

"Well, that's about a buck forty."

"Sounds good. When can you do it?"

"How about Saturday," Ron said and the two men agreed.

Downtown Brown will do the work on the man's car at the curb of 17th Street, a foot tall curb built for horses a hundred years ago. He'll put his hands in the gutter to lift dropped screws and he'll smile. When he's done he'll thank the man for the work.

Standing in the muddy economy with cash that pays for a meal.

People that are accustomed to the rain.

The term 'beloved' is used to describe Downtown Brown, as if an apostle is in our midst.

If the twelve were alive today they would be smelling of fish, work and the dusty roads of hunger. Take down the flags of hurting.

Babies are crying.

"Okay, miiistttter Tim," he'll say, respecting, even as he mocks, laughing at the insanity life brings.

We're all going away. Into a nightmare. Going like the money, like the jobs, like the security of a dream. Gone like the candle light.

In the economy of poverty, families are made in circumstance, by years, experience, adventure, tragedy, empathy and loyalty. Love grows here and that's a true foundation for equality. Trust matters in democracy. As Matthew Modine tries to explain, Jesus was communist -

Help me mister, brother, sister.

Family is a tribe, a culture, brothers and sisters, parents, those coming and going.

Help the children.

In 2005 Ronnie set himself up in the dilapidated apartment on the second floor at the corner of 17th Street and Central and he's been there ever since, for the pawn and Narrow Gate mission, whenever anyone calls.

The freight train rolls a few blocks away and the rush of the poor fill his dreams but in his world, without two pennies to rub together, a wealth and wonder fill the hollow sky.

The dogs bark in the alley.

In the pawn shop by the crock pot, where a stool waits for his weary feet, tacked to the bottom lip of Downtown's counter, a sign reads, 'Candy Shop.' The old men say hard candy was the treat they remember when the 1930's rumbled on top of their parents and ran their families into the ground.

You have to see in the distance.

XIII. THE POORHOUSE

The problem with poverty is that it seems so normal. It's that big bulge in the bell shaped curve, that swollen center that the numbers can't hide. For the poor it's fear of another move south, away from hope, another mile from the dentist and just across the street from a shorter life span, no car, no job worth holding, no prospects.

"The problem is the interest in the poor. No one cares." The speaker today in the pawn shop is a funny faced man named Telly. He's picking at a bowl of food from the mission. His triangular head has been sharpened from a rounded skull cap to a pointed chin. The oversized ears create a cab door effect as if he's headed somewhere else. Howdy Doody of the 1950's.

"You know what they do in Libya? If you steal, they shoot you."

Telly's on a roll and he knows it. When he commands the floor everyone looks away, hiding their faces like ostriches their heads. The children of poverty, in this peek-a-boo dialogue, know

Telly knows, too. Once he starts, he's wound up like an eight day clock.

Everyone at 17th Street heads in the other direction when they see him coming. It's said that when he was a child he fell on his head. He never recovered. He's unable to understand nonverbal cues and he's also slow with directions. He likes attention and on a slow day he's accommodated but when business is good, his constant pulling is distracting. He likes the pawn shop and he likes the library. He can begin at opening and stay till closing, asking questions, roaming aisles, addressing anyone who's breathing. It doesn't matter if there's no eye contact. Telly likes to talk. He rambles. Despite his manners, the regulars at the mission care about him. Grudgingly, sometimes.

Telly scoops the chunks of gray meat and the potatoes into his white bowl. The shop, like so much of impoverished geography, has been way ahead of the economists for years, keeping the mission in a corner where the hungry have come for food for twenty, long years. When the rich were adding to their largesse the poor were looking around, still asking questions about where all that money came from, what was the source of those mansions being built everywhere.

A fearful anxiety creeps into the conversations.

An old man with blown up, bushy eyebrows confronts a new dilemma.

"Did they get Gaddafi?"

The television news is spreading out the conversation but Telly's still eyeing the crowd.

"Way too many wars," Telly's now back in the fray. He picks up a loaf of bread and shuffles toward the electronics shelves. A store employee anticipates the move and slips into an aisle, away from the jaunty, jabbering Tell.

"You know what bothers me?" A coup now shadows Telly, an insight the others are hoping to avoid. In some ways this denial, this gullibility, this inability to control a dialogue, is what brought them to the places of their lives. It takes a colder man than these to break bread in the stock market. Perhaps the evolutionists among the wealthy are right; these men don't have what it takes.

"Let us eat, please…." the unspoken breath of the yellow toothed hungry. Alas, Telly knows his route today includes the library. He comes full circle with illumination. He's a movie opening klieg light.

"Jimmy Carter, a genius, and they made him look like a fool. He averted nuclear disaster, what could he do?

Oh, if I knew the answer, I'd be a millionaire."

The subject of malaise is too familiar, of hopes crushed from the falling bluffs at the river in this Iowa port, barely missing the Mississippi's angry torrent this spring.

An old woman with a red shawl walks inside, her back bent, a crow's nose and gnarled hands her signatures, as if she grew from a tree. She spies the boxes of bread on the floor under the shelf of televisions.

"Bread today?" She asks and the pawn shop owner nods. Near his big, outstretched hands is a pamphlet about the Bible. Paul's a Christian who understands Maslow's food in the belly first then the good word, if any are still applicable.

"Okay if I take some?" The old woman asks and the crinkles at her downcast eyes are too difficult to remember, pained eyes that have become trauma, shame and sorrow.

"Help yourself." The man says and works up a smile.

Telly rants on and on but no one pays attention this morning. He asks about aliens and no response. He refers to a secret, government airplane and no takers.

Telly's now seen the desperation of his continued control of the conversations this morning. He scrapes at the bottom of his Styrofoam bowl. He pushes at a last word.

"I need to get a computer…I think that Facebook has real people on it."

The Picker

The brown Jeep holds onto the curb on Central Avenue like a tugboat tied to a wharf. It's an older model truck and the bed is filled with last year's brown leaves and empty, plastic pop bottles. The truck shakes with rusty patches and quilts of rolling dents and divots. The driver talks to himself. He's seated in the stalled truck, arm akimbo, hung over the window. He speaks toward the grimy sidewalk but is miles away, eyelids darting to and fro. His voice digs into a deep bass drum.

"So I don't know," he speaks to no one there. When people speak to themselves in front of the Narrow Gate mission it implies faith has had a rough time.

Is he preparing for the pawn broker whose shop he's parked in front of. Perhaps a contest of wills comes. Maybe he's lost in thought.

"Yeah, and so…" His face shakes like he's in a dream, like he's thinking in that rapid eye movement stage.   His movements clash, jittery, swift hand signals, turns of the neck and jagged facial tics swarm the air as if he's tied to a hitching post next to the tugboat.

This is where the poor come who lack credit. This is where the poor find refuge in selling their possessions to pay for a meal. For millions, the economy looks like this.

"Hey!"

In the store, the electric customer starts the dialogue. He wears a red baseball cap. He wears the cap backwards and the bill is lettered with the word Zoom.

"Yeah, so I don't have my glasses," he begins. He moves without rhythm, randomly cranes his neck then lifts one shoulder to his neck as if he's been a fighter. Wrenched with an old pain he tells the story of lost glasses.

"I had them on a store counter. I looked away and they fell off. The clerk didn't seem to know what happened. I picked them up and…"

Here he sounds low and he lays his voice to a stuttering whisper. The effect engages everyone. As he twists from the counter it's clear that he's disabled by something.

He limps now and asks Paul for a guitar.

"Let me see if I can play that. I used to play. Was pretty good, too."

The tanned acoustic trades hands and the deep voiced man finds a cloth chair by the counter, places the guitar on his lap and begins to search through a red coin purse.

"I used to have it here."

"What are you looking for?" Paul asks.

"A Fender pick. I always have my Fender pick with me. Makes me feel like I'm any good, know what I mean?"

Now he turns the cap. Zoom sets above his brow. He removes the cap then shifts it to a lower space over his forehead. His eyes are hidden. He strums but nothing like a song returns from his touch. When he stands he talks, again as if no one in particular were his listener.

"So what is it…"

He bathes in a shadow that cries in pain. Maybe he's a soldier. Maybe he was struck by a bullet, hit by a truck or walked on a mine. Maybe he's just poor and he had a stroke.

"No damn good!" He says into a cupped hand. Others in the shop ignore him. He turns away when another customer ambles in the door.

"Hey man!" The deep gravel of a voice in a drum, Zoom tilted upon the forehead.

"Hey man. I know you. How are you?" The new customer wears a white cap, a gold chain dangles around his neck, a whitish stubbed goatee is like sand across his chin.

The two men eye each other and they separate. Zoom walks the guitar back to the counter. White cap addresses a new topic.

"That your Jeep out front?"

"Yeah."

"You could restore that, it's a nice style."

"Yeah man, no cash. Know what I mean?"

Just then an isolated customer expands.

"Is it true that nice guys always finish last? I don't know."

It's a sentimental doubt that tastes like a soothing wine. Maybe we win some. Could there be happy endings? The taste is now sour and the endings unhappy. Paul swats at the silence now and lightens the bitter taste.

"Nice guys may not be at the end of the line but they can shake hands with the guy who is…"

The laughter spurts and shimmies.

After a pause, the deep voiced man with the limp and the jittery hands that paw the wrenched guitar neck, walks outside. He talks to himself as he goes:

"I need some tunes for my Jeep."

The black man with the gold at his neck switches into another gear -

"Have you heard this one?"

"Once, there was a Zebra. He died. When he got to heaven he met Paul. Now Paul asked him what he was but the Zebra was stunned. Paul said, ' Are you black with white stripes or white with black stripes?'

'What do you mean, what am I?' Now Paul said, 'I have to know what you are before I let you in heaven. Go now to God to ask him.' So the Zebra went to God. When he asked God, God said, 'You are what you are!'

The Zebra went back to Paul and Paul asked, 'What did God say?' The Zebra said, "You is what you is."

It was then that Paul, weighted down by the heaving conversation, understood. He said, "You're black with white stripes."

Old Jim

In every direction from 17th Street and Central to city hall, the street hangs a worn face. Five pawn shops, a few taverns and a gun shop litter the crumbling facade. Here runs the giant John Deere tractors that have been sold to every corner of earth. Change and status quo meet and confront each day.

The corner at 17th Street is a holding tank for castaways and characters, of routes to other places, and it stands outside of time, entrails of birth and death converging, newborns rocked in cradles and murder committed in nearby alleys.

Privilege and lessons meet each other on the worn paths of tragedy and goodness, places where wisdom intersects a story and becomes a living soul.

If someone says faith is above reason you can be sure. Hard times here. They gave up thinking about it.

The coffee pot with the burned scale on its handle sizzled the last drops of black coffee and the dregs rescaled the pot. Paul pulled the chain on the open sign in his window. He'd been open for an hour.

Paul began to laugh. He dug into the stew in the bowl placed in front of him. The deer meat and gravy, mixed with corn and beans, hugged the bowl and steamed upward into his face.

"I just don't understand some people." He said. It seemed the others were thinking the same and

the hard life let go with a group catharsis. Who understands people?

The men at the mission laughed and suddenly the old man who had become a regular raised his hand and his eyes came to life.

"Hey, follow me!" The white faced, old man with the green pants had need of attention. The others saw that. They understood his pattern of leaving the group to isolate someone. He couldn't seem to get enough attention.

I followed.

The old man's teeth were crooked and his smile was a crooked gate. His girlfriend had been using cocaine and he said he felt responsible. He wanted to get her help. The old man had been living in a garage shed throughout the winter. Everyone said he was tough. His eyes said he was crazy.

"Come here. I want to show you something." I'm given to amiability, but have suffered with my own kindness and now I felt like I endorsed the insanity but followed the old man down the rickety stairs into the basement. The low ceiling forced our heads down. The deep shelves that were affixed against the walls were sagging under the weight of thousands of record albums and a pallet of apple sauce, still covered in shrink wrap, hugged a shadowy corner.

"Now look here at my record collection. I've got Mantovanni, Oak Ridge Boys, Chet Atkins…"

"Man, I'd say you have it all." I answered.

Kindness can sometimes appear offensive, contrary, even cynical, but the wild eyed old man's manner said he understood ambiguity.

"Why, sure. Say, let me show you the bikes I've been working on…here! I sand 'em down and when I'm done I'm going to paint them blue and silver. What do you think about that?"

"Really neat, I'd say."

I kept my distance from his presentation now, suggesting by affect that any juror might be inclined to acknowledge that the old man showed something alien in his eye.

"A fella would have to go a long way to find better work than this, for sure."

Upstairs another white bearded old man was slicing sausage on a paper plate.

"I hope we don't have to go downstairs. I've seen the bikes, I've listened to the records and I've seen the sanded chairs. What's up with him?" One of the boys had said.

No one knew how long the old man had been without work and no one knew his age. The confluence of facts about the white bearded, grizzled old gnome made it difficult to offer compassion. A brief theme had arisen about the old man being a con man but the men at the mission couldn't abide the idea. A consensus was forming that he was nuts but most of the men at the mission let it be.

"I do the chrome color first then the blue."

"Well, sure. That makes sense."

"You get any breakfast?" The crazy eyed man now stepped close to the stairs, leaning by the shelves of bagged, black beans. The basement lights flickered and the old man seemed to be falling asleep. I walked to the staircase and nodded.

"Let's see how that deer meat tastes!"

Now the old man's eyes became filled with kindness and sadness, turned down at the corners, and when he flicked off the lights the pitter patter of mice dashing across the cold, cement basement echoed up the stairs.

Have you ever seen old men, tears in their eyes, looking for something lost that they never find? The world passes them and covers them in new languages of the internet. They look at you when you watch them and they shrug their shoulders. The old men's parents built prosperity and now they stand, each alone, searching the horizon for hope. They're desperate not to let you into the secret pain they believe they can hide.

What becomes of dreams?

The counter of the pawn shop is as unchanging as the sea, a drifting desert that dries up the dreams of the invisible people who come to trade their heirlooms. Each pawn holds doubt. The doubt is cast far into the future, deep into the psyche - a customer's return to pay is filled like clouds are filled, ready to dissolve, ready to rain. The broker knows it. The poor man knows it.

"I'll try to get back by Friday." The poor man says but Friday never comes. After a month the broker pulls the item from the shelf and adds a tag then places it on another shelf, for sale.

The old men were once young, cloudy eyes clear, unsteady gait strong.

Old Jim is like that. He was once a working man and he takes pride in talking about work but he does little and he knows that.

The old men of poverty cannot understand the world. Looking back they say it was so fast they couldn't tell you about tastes except they were good or smells except they were joy. Now they have the future but it's only the past, confused by the clouds, and the future grows dimmer.

These old men have been stoned in the market at Jericho.

"Hey, did I tell you the story?" The fluffy bearded Jim asks and does not wait for a response, "A guy had a garage delivered downtown. Next day he comes to inspect it before the carpenters build it. It's gone."

Jim talks a lot and he pesters people that come into the Narrow Gate. The movies shot in Dubuque have enjoyed these neighborhoods because they are decrepit like old men. Field of Dreams and F.I.S.T. and Take This Job and Shove It. Old white faced Jim lives a role of age, see through skin and tired eyes.

Here at his crossroad conversation the white faced man laughs heartily.

"Somebody came while he was away and piled it onto another truck and carted it away."

Now the straggly beard becomes a rope the old man pulls as he laughs then finally he points to his audience and instructs them with the pointer. Life is hard and devious.

The old man is a grim witness to an economy of vampire casinos and amped stock brokers, and, no one else but dreamers.

When he sneaks downstairs into the basement, another old, toothless man with a gold t-shirt, Iowa Hawkeye Pride stenciled across the chest, comes in the front door. His white hair grows down his back from an unkempt, balding pate. He talks like the old actor Walter Brennan, gums his words and licks his lips but smiles too. He's looking for allies.

"Jim here?"

"He went downstairs."

"Thanks," the toothless man says. He shakes his head as if it were a bobber and he shuffles away.

A young couple bring jewelry to the counter. She has a cast on her right hand. Someone asks if she'd like candy and the candy bowl that's hidden behind the counter appears like a rabbit from a hat. The petite young woman smiles.

"Milky Way!" She laughs and says she needs some chocolate. When the clerk asks her how she broke her hand she says, matter-of-factly, "I hit a guy on top of the head." She laughs again.

Soon the two old crows arrive at the counter. The hungrier of the two asks if he can borrow some money.

"You have any money?" The toothless smile shows a gap of dark roots.

"No, can't say I do," the pony tailed Downtown Ron Brown responds.

A weight of silence pours upon the people by the counter, a truth about present, past and future weighs upon the shoulders. An empty plate is set before them and the toothless man becomes a motherless child.

"I need the money to buy wax. I've got two cars and if I can get some Turtle Wax I can clean them today. Can make fifty."

Making fifty would be a good ending but it's another part in the endless links within hunger and loneliness.

The old man with the shaggy neck implores with a sad sounding truth, wistful and melancholic, like a crucifix of despair hanging around his neck.

"You know I'm good for it. I don't get money till the fourth but I can make some today. Just need Turtle Wax."

"Okay, let me see. How much do you need?"

"Six bucks is all I need. The Turtle Wax can't be more than six bucks. I have to give up smoking, I don't have money for that."

The toothless, sad faced man, white complexion and turned down wrinkles set upon his smile, explains a larger story like the poor want to do, pleading for a prayer to be sent to heaven, for someone to listen.

"Yeah, I've got six bucks," Downtown Brown says as he digs into a wallet, "Don't go to the True Value, though, it's more expensive than Ace…"

Here the old men shake as if a palsy has overtaken them. They stare into each other's eyes but they don't see what the young people do and as they leave the youth turn away, as if to cry. The old men are schooled in this pain and find victory for another day. As they leave they smile as if the past cannot catch up.

Old Jim wore his olive green pants for days at a time. They were holstered by a belt but the trousers were without loops and the belt rode high upon his hips. Jim was an old man. A white beard, scruffy and reaching like weeds upon a fence, was stained with his last meal. He smiled with his jaw drooping but a spark of joy lit his face.

"Hey Tim," he said and reached out his boney index finger, "Now they've got me listed as a thief in the landlord association. How can I find a place when they dirty my name like that?"

"Old man," I thought, "God's in his heaven and you have lived in a shed all winter…" But I couldn't bear to say these things and I saw him smile and I saw his hope flicker. I wanted to ask for mercy for a man who has harmed no one.

"I don't know what I'll do. You know it's not the truth and I need a place."

It was a long, cold winter. On frigid days, below zero, he'd fall inside the store with ragged clothes and his smell, pungent and sour. He had one leg with which to stand but he spoke loudly.

Maybe we should hear more than words.

"Hey, I fixed that place in Wisconsin, had a deck and all. You should have seen it." He spoke as if he owned something.

After a customer told his story about building and remodeling the old man touched my sleeve. He'd been ousted from the garage he slept in but refused to talk about it.

"Come on downstairs. I want to show you something."

Have you ever seen the face that expects a yes, an okay, an approval that without which a slow dying begins? It's sadness come to being, animated on the hangman's loft.

No - no, cannot be spoken to the requests of the dying children of life. A song sung in pain cannot be ignored.

"I have been working on it for a while."

The thin, rickety stairs of the pawn shop angle, steep like a jacket hung on a hook, left for a cold morning. The frosted air that dried the century old walls smelled of damp earth.

"What do you think?" He smiled, rubbed the hair at his chin. Bright shop lights fired the low ceiling. Record albums lined decrepit wood shelves, a pallet of canned potatoes and hundreds of boxes of cereal, beans and cherry pop tarts stood up as if sentries to the old man's work space.

"Look here, this chair!"

Standing in the dust, a tan chair waited inspection.

It was wood, a replica of an old design, a flat seat, spindles, a curved back. It had been antiqued with green and gold tissue streaks across its minute cracks, but the old man's work showed outside the morning, outside the lit corner of the dark basement. The old man had sanded it with his weathered hands and the smooth surface felt like an infant's cheeks. The smell of sanded wood rushed in the air that blew from the cracks in the walls.

"What do you think?"

The dusty work of long hours smelled of initiative.

The spindles were loose and the legs wobbled but the old man imbued it with faith. The dark corner seemed like the manger, wreaths and magi stood by him.

"I worked hard on that one. What do you think?" He waved his arms to show off his dungeon room. "I have everything I need here. Got the radio, the light, a sandwich. Pretty neat deal."

He stood here, in the middle of the mission warehouse, a dank basement where daily food stuff waits to be boxed for the poor. He picked up a picture frame.

"I did this, too."

On a stack of other frames that he'd sanded was a picture of Jesus kneeling, praying at the garden. The old man smiled. In the corner shadows he seemed like the crucified carpenter.

"Thanks," the old man said, then turned back to the basement, the damp, ancient cave where he worked, now the only secure place in the world.

XXIII. STANDARDS

Money is like an image in a dream set aside to be remembered or forgotten.

At the Narrow Gate the lunch is served at the counter. The traffic from the street roars past. At the American Pawn cash moves quickly. At the Dubuque Pawn, across the street from the Road Ranger convenience store, Mike and his guys liked to smoke. Before he was sent to prison for being the ring leader of a crime spree, according to the police, he would have said that under no circumstances can you share this story. Since residing in Fort Madison, Iowa, in prison, his pink Nintendo story fits his myth and the ironies and paradoxes of poverty and pawnshops, gates and those blamed and those blessed.

Mike dragged on his smoke like it was a pipe. His fist was tight then he smashed it in the tray to his left by the bird cage. His Cockatoo screamed and Mike glared. The bird quieted. Mike's six four and two forty. He's been in many street fights and likes to talk about them. When the bird irritates him he moves his hand and the bird understands. A few of his friends were standing with him and eating.

While the men shared KFC's fried chicken a big girl strolled up to the counter, fresh from the street and carrying the smells of smoke and dust with her as if sadness could be brought to life. Her denim overalls snuggled up at her breasts and held her bottom like a flour sack. She placed her fat hands on the counter and raised her brow and eye in anticipation of delivering a fast pitch, readying her tale, composing as she watched the big man to see about his disposition, his willingness to allow for what she had to offer.

"Can you tell anyone who comes in that you bought my pink Nintendo? It was really stolen and I can't get it back. But if you would tell the police or my mom, that would help."

The big man could be a kind man, an understanding man, but he had a limit. He'd gladly pull his wallet and contents, fill a grocery sack, tell the cops he planned to hire a man in trouble at the

bench of a judge. He wouldn't entertain fools.

"So, let me get this straight. You want me to lie to the cops, fib to your mom, and this is about stolen property that I could go to jail for?"

"Yes. Oh, please! You help me, then?"

"You want me to go to jail in case you get into trouble?"

"You're such a kind man."

"I should go to jail so you don't have to?"

"I hoped you'd understand."

"Better me than you, is that it?"

The husky girl primped her hair, tossed her hands away from the counter. She turned her thick neck and the folds of her fleshy face creased like a dollar bill creases when pushed at a soda vendor slot. She lifted a leg then fumbled at her strapped chest pocket, dancing and fidgeting. The big man looked at the black man by the counter then looked to the counter man Big John who sat nearby on a stool.

"Good chicken." The black man said, a fact he wouldn't have noted except for the tension the fat girl created.

"Are you crazy?"

The big man now felt the fury of the request, the down right paradox and irony of the unmitigated, straight eyed, harried boldness; the undaunted and dimmed uniqueness that transpired and coveted, clung to and slipped over his transom like a sharp clawed little bug that hung from a lintel and waited for an opening to dash upon the fresh fruit of the season.

"It's a pink Nintendo. Just a little toy. I loved that pink Nintendo."

"Girly, why would I want to go to jail for you? I mean, are you nuts, or what?"

"Sir, I'll get in trouble. They think I stole the Nintendo but I lost it and I can't help that it's stolen."

"You want me to go to jail. I'm supposed to take your place in a tiny little cell and wait for some gorilla to come breathing down my neck and wanting to drop …get out of here. Now!

Get!"

But the roly-poly girl would not quit.

"All you have to do is tell the police you saw my Nintendo. You had it here for a little while."

"Sweet heart. I don't think you understand this. I'm sorry you're in trouble. Now get out of here before I call the cops."

When she turned and walked to the door the big man began to tap his fingers on the counter. He looked to the black and he looked to the giant counter man. He ran his fingers through his hair and tugged at his shirt. The heavy girl moved slowly. Her back side wobbled like a wheel on a wire, a to and fro like a possum walking to the woods.

"Don't come back here."

Gold Standard

"What's the crown worth," the old woman said. She held a gold crown tucked inside a sandwich baggie. The man at the coin shop stared at the bag. The shop windows gleamed with an unrelenting heat.

"I'll be right with you."

Paul was despairing. He had to turn in coins for cash. Business was bad. We waited for the clerk.

The white haired woman waits. Waiting is what poverty does.

Wait when the abscessed tooth shreds away the nerves, wait when the dark spot changes shape

but the doctors cannot help without insurance, wait when the baby screams and the ears drain but the money, the money isn't there - forego the medicine.

The human skeleton on the Central Avenue corner could have walked a production line but his dinosaur bones rattle. Nature did not interfere in his decline. His bones will be tossed into the tar. The work line was closed by an entrepreneur.

Nature does not create employment, causing a child to scream from a swollen belly. If nature had a thing to say, if …the starving parents could hunt or farm.

David Beckmann, president of Bread for the World, one of a group of coalition partners concerned about this world, this stark, biting hurt, notes, "I don't think they want to make kids hungrier, but if you have deep, unspecified cuts in spending, you will make kids hungrier."

What would Jesus do? The July 26 Washington Post wants to know.

Ten thousand children starve until they die, each day, each day they choke, before the angels come. The free market, so what. The industrialized nations accept unemployment. Poverty tags along. The economist says, "What do you want me to do?"

That's the way it is.

"Went on a diet, that's right. Nature took her course, lost weight. Don't eat diets do it every time."

The year long unemployment is ragging the factory worker, he says, through the gaps in his smile, "I don't eat so my kids can."

Institutions build income, make markets, trade to other nations, make corporate decisions, the struggle of the fittest. It's all on paper. No one's to blame.

The corporation gets more rights but the old woman with her crown torn out, she's ready to sell for rent.

Ever sell teeth for income?

Nature did not create this poverty. An unrelenting hunger, homelessness and psychic wreckage dances on the street.

"Gold's going up…"

And, "The Dow…"

The scarecrows don't care.

At the coin shop the elderly, white haired woman stands at the door. Scoliosis bends her back. Three men have passed through in ten minutes. One waits. She leans on a glass counter by the stacks of pennies.

"Gold's up…" The man makes small talk.

Two hundred and fifty $25 boxes of pennies have been lugged to a stand by the door. Pennies from jars, pennies for rent, for a meal, for burying gramma. The six foot tall, red safe stands behind the counter where the young man reviews a stack of quarters.

During the lunch hour the wealthy broker asks, "What do you want me to do about it?"

At the counter, George Washingtons before 1964 are worth twenty six times face value.

The man at the counter screens the old woman's gold molar.

The word Liberty is stenciled on the safe.

Neighbor Wes

The hurly burly figure stood near the railroad tracks looking up at the tall building with the aged, wood dock off Jackson Street in Dubuque. Stallone's movie 'Fist' was filmed near here. 'Take This Job and Shove It' was filmed nearby. The husky man stood a few blocks from the pawn shops, equidistant to city hall. Nearby, the gray highway rumbled and his cries were droned off by the noises of the city. A rain fell. He walked to the rails. His energy had disappeared like the sunshine. His pockets were empty. He'd been evicted after being fired. His breath came in shadows.

" I was crying my eyes out. I went up under a rail car, trying to stay dry. Then up on the rail. I saw a train coming towards me. I said, 'I can't go out like this.'"

Wes Howes had worked in Peosta, supported himself in a room at the end of Main Street. He was 45 years old. One day, two years ago, while bicycling for groceries, he fell from the bike after a seizure.

"I never told them about the seizures. I never told anyone. I'm ashamed of them."

In the pouring out of his pain his pupils swell and lids fill but he only slows in his telling, for breath, and he works through this place he's in as he speaks. And while he speaks you think of the place where he's walking, down the cobblestone street of Jackson, by the abandoned old buildings.

"I started having seizures in the early 80's. The first one, I was talking to a fella, in a chair. The next thing I know, I was in the hospital."

The big man begins to pick at his hands as he talks, as if he needs to recover his feelings, as if his hands remind him about being alive. He says he fell from a tree when he was a boy.

"When I was young I remember my father telling me I was in a tree and I fell and hit the ground head first."

The glasses he's wearing are tinted. His dark beard is flecked in white streaks, his round face like an infants, evoking helplessness, innocence, trust. Thin creases show around his eyes and a line runs along his scalp where receding hair gives up to a crest down the center of his head. Faint, gray scar lines appear around head and face.

"I went to the police station," he says, the next stop after the rail and rain, "I was sitting there about an hour. No one came out. Then I pushed the button. I told them I was about to end my life. I went to Two West (Mercy Hospital's Psychiatric unit). Dave came up to interview me and we talked for an hour, an hour and a half. I was just crying my eyes out."

Dave Smith is the administrator at Julien Care who brought Wes to the facility after the stop at Mercy.

"I still cry a lot."

This hurting man has the Bible belt, heartland work ethic ingrained inside him, repeating, insistently, about work and independence.

"I don't like askin' nobody for nothin'."

As he sits, he adds his hands to his hips, pushing away from the chair and table. The story about falling from a roof spills out as Wes tries to bravely offer a smile.

"A few years ago. I shouldn't have been working there but I had to work. I never told people about the seizures, never put it down when I applied for a job. I was on a roof. I took a step back from an edge and fell. A guy on the second floor said he saw me reach out my hand as I went past. I hit concrete head first. I split open my head, shattered my wrist. My eyebrow was hanging over my eye. Arm was broken. Over 200 stitches and staples."

Feelings sometimes roll over the dam in such a spilling that the words don't catch up.

"I had a seizure at a church. I fell while I was coming out with my girlfriend. It's the last I ever saw her. She told me, 'If you hadn't lied to me.' I didn't tell her about the seizures.

I'm ashamed of the seizures. I'm embarrassed by them."

As he sits in the cafeteria with the sunshine streaming in and the smells of turkey and gravy drafting through the big room, he frowns and he thanks you for listening. He says it made a difference that you listened. You hope he finds another path, honest work and some of God's mercy.

XXIV. PAWNBROKERS

The world of the pawn is serious as a claw, a sharp point populated by those who understand life's peculiar deals and the strains that unprompted tragedy play upon on us all. It is a world of barter and trade, poker face to poker face, sometimes loss, sometimes covetousness; a dry glass plate under a microscope, and for each trade the fair value of a thing and the equity of it and the thought of a man's spirit is conceived on a scale understood and confusing all at once; accepted and denied and ignored, all at once.

The pawn plays a role in local economies, easily moving many millions of dollars annually; money that is loaned and exchanged and that changes in transactions, a coin for a dollar, the dollar for a tape, tape returned and added to a box of CD's and jewelry that becomes a wide screen TV; a man takes a loan on a gold watch, later pays interest, buys an old record, decides to sell his reciprocating saw and finally, weeks later, pays for the watch that began the cycle.

Those unable to receive bank loans are given credit, credit they may not get elsewhere. This credit economy is a large, ambulatory financial system that underscores the economy and affects every strata of society.

"What can I get for a fifty inch TV?"

The man in the pin striped suit needs extra cash, has an appliance, unloads it here on Central Avenue. When the barter is done he exits to his convertible Lexus and drives away.

Justice and its accompanying soul visit each dollar that passes over the pawn counter. The breadth of interaction and the meanings of possession and humanity conspire across the counters in the making of esteem and loathing.

Some return to the same shops, some shop for better buys, better arrangements, improved attitudes. The pawn brokers know their customers and the customers, some will refuse certain of the pawns.

Paul is legend for helping the poor and the transient who cannot buy a lucky charm. One is niche for guns, one for jewelry, another has computers as focus, one simply hustles and another, newer on the street, makes improvements by inches, learning and selling.

"Hey, Jay!" A broker said.

"Hey, Ken!" Another broker in another store to another familiar face. Daily the crowds of regulars make rounds and the owners and their employees make the usual acknowledgements, the world of Iowa and its politics and the rumor and the fact, the wisdom and the ignorance

blending in the meltdown of conversation and creed and custom.

"I found a place and I'm going to be alright," an old woman said in the dead of winter. She'd lived under an old heat vent near Spawn and Rose Lumber company. She said she'd found a place nearby.

"Good for you, darling. I'll keep praying," Roy, the one time social worker said.

Have you ever seen a frowning spirit placing an heirloom given through grandparents, held in a drawer, esteemed and loved, weighted by years and sentiment and set on the counter of a pawn shop, watched while the broker weighed it and dropped his chemicals upon it and eyed it through a little jeweler's orb, pitched its worth, as if dollars could measure the family and the gift of generations then, waiting for a response, you saw a heart drop an inch and a tear pushed away from the corner of an eye?

"I just need a few dollars till my paycheck," the man said and you hear it in his voice and so does the pawn broker and you see the humanity as the broker doles out the money and smiles into the sadness and says:

"I trust you. See you at payday. Have a good week!"

Meanings of the measure of what is owned and what a man has come to be worth is placed upon eternal scales and inspected and the dollar transcribed like judgment is at hand.

The riddles of the book of Judges, following Sampson's remarks about the honey and the strength, these abound in a pawn shop, in a city, everywhere a man has lost the job, the will, the luck; where the wheel has turned and he's behind the eight ball and the hand shows eights and aces.

Legend has it that pawns have been birthed wherever gambling takes root. The dice, the wheel, the cards, the horses, the dogs; each venue will swing an old door that opens a profit from a page, a seal, a title to a car, a home; that without title and only in hand, a stereo, a TV, a computer, a watch, a ring.

A sad man, brown skinned, having trouble speaking English, walked into the 17th Street shop. He steered toward the DVD's and then, composed, walked to the counter where the pawn broker waited.

"Heh mech you gave?"

"I'm sorry, what did you say?"

The man shrugged and tried again.

"I'm really sorry, I can't understand you. Say again…"

Finally, after fumbling with a white plastic bag from a big box, after stationing his DVD movies in a row, the man was understood.

"Sir, we only give a dollar and two of these are scratched. You want to pawn them?"

The slouched shouldered man nodded and the pawn owner said:

"Sir, it's okay and I understand but you must know that I can only give you three dollars and the interest will be five. We have a minimum interest…and…"

"Okay…" the brown faced man said, "Okay," he said again.

Okay, as the first step in a thousand mile journey. The mountains at the horizon are wide.

Once, after a story I wrote about the 17th Street Pawn appeared in Dubuque's paper several people commented that they had no idea about pawn shops except that they were where the poor went, where the disenfranchised malingered. One reader said he never understood but after reading, he saw it differently.

When the pawns are struggling, the poor are a rung below the bottom on a ladder someone built, but no one can repair.

Inside the pawn shop the Irish green that covers the door bullies the eye.

The hand lettered 'Thank you' above the door flutters like a red wing, becoming an autonomous advertisement.

In Iowa, it is as if the pawn shop and its accomplices are wishing for your return, sorry for the loss, but thanks for the juice.

There is very little to be thankful for if you've you just pawned a family heirloom, if you lost your job and need each dollar to feed your children, if a hospital bill overwhelmed your budget, if the rent is due, if you dropped a tooth in the bathroom sink, if your shoes have holes on the bottoms and if, just like millions of other worn out, dragged down souls in the economy no one understands, a never ending unemployment debacle, an induced recession the bankers will never account for, never have to admit as theirs, never find consequence knocking on their doors like the gloved late night knocks of the millions who have lost their homes - if, you're one of the worn out cast asides who buoyed the wealthy, expert bankers, you see black everywhere, dark ditches cloud your every step.

Enter the pawn shop.

A clean shaven man, brown hair unkempt like he slept on his left side, wearing a leather jacket, quietly whispered to the pawn clerk, " Wedding rings."

"Yours and hers?" Paul the clerk, asked, knowing the circumstance.

"Yep." The man dropped his shoulders now, tucked his neck close to his torso, hiding as he stood at the counter. Ten feet away the steam of hamburger and potatoes, gravy and onions and corn, mixed into a goo, drafted the breathing air.

"And her necklace?" The clerk asked.

The man nodded behind his wall of losses. Paul shuffled into the warehouse in the back room, behind the gray, steel door to find the items. He returned quickly. He was acquainted with the defeated man's property, a tribute and a cheer without saying so.

"Alright, a man's wedding ring," the pawnbroker said as he picked inside the little white envelope that contained a precious symbol, pawned in return for the right to stay alive on a raft in a sea of trouble.

"Five diamonds," Paul added. Now, he was up and out to the back, again.

"So, what's up with you, guy?" Paul's son inquired of the leather jacketed man.

"Chain with cross?" Paul asked as he hurried from the back, clipping his sentence, speedily completing the transaction.

The theme of pawn shops is simplicity come to life, a genie smoking a hookah pipe, squatting upon a stool. You sell your item, accepting their offer or you trade, this a more unusual exchange or you pawn the thing for whatever the pawn owner and you agree upon, this becomes yours, when you buy it back with an interest rate tacked onto the back of the receipt. Everyone involved either knows or senses the smoking light is always on.

"Chain with cross?"

"Yep."

In Paul's store, the ethic of the downtrodden is served. Mashed potatoes and pork, deer meat and gravy, all this goes along with the transactions. A box with oatmeal, crackers, canned peas, cereal and a bar of soap and a loaf of bread accompany each customer, their choice.

Now, the man at the counter, fidgeting and shifting his weight from worn out shoe to worn out shoe, picks up the black, hand sized calculator for the clerk.

"Here."

"Thank you."

A pause of silence, a moment of heads down, prayer like mediation. What will it cost, finally, to retrieve the wedding rings and the necklace?

"Two hundred eighty eight."

Here, the man holds a wad of cash, folded, and like a crying handkerchief, creased and stained. He sniffles. Paul counts."Two eighty, two eighty five…"

The cash register punches everyone in the midsection, bursts at the drum of the ear, pounds relentless chords of hurt into the room. Ching Dahoor, Dahoor, dahoor, ching, ching.

Paul passes the change and the receipt. The man accepts his portion of the inferno, Dante stands aside. The green door looms. The message harkens. The gravy whets the mind and sours the appetite.

"Thank you."

"Thank you."

"Coffee?" Paul asks.

"If I had the time," the sad man says.

"Okay, thank you."

The man walks into the twilight.

A few minutes pass, just enough time to stave the breath of Houdini were he under water in the nearby Mississippi River. No applause follows the return of wedding rings and necklace.

"Okay, I'm going now." Paul says to his son, seated to his left.

"I'm going to deposit three hundred in cash into the bank to cover the checks I wrote yesterday." In hard times the pawn shop should be doing well.

Around the corner a poor man pushes a baby carriage with his wife. He's wearing second hand, black sweat pants and a torn, purple Vikings jacket. He's waiting in the line of ghosts that fills up outside. Together, he and his wife stroll down the walk. It's midday and he's not working.

What's Left

The last time he stopped in the pawn shop he dropped his head when he smiled. It was another day. Same passed over dollar. He'd exchanged wedding rings. Now, he stood again with his wife and teenage daughter. They were selling old DVD's. When they dropped the movies from the white, plastic WalMart sack at the counter, they were willing to call the three hundred dollars they had invested in entertainment a wash. Poverty cannot afford entertainment nor long term possession nor large dollar credit nor heirloom or sentiment.

"Seventeen dollars," the man had said. They pocketed the cash.

The day his wife unloosed the wedding ring when he walked away from the counter to the store shelves to distract himself the family accepted a hundred dollars for their band of hope. The visit before that he had come alone to retrieve their two rings. He paid two hundred for the pair. He spoke some biblical verse and prayed.

The couple does not wear their symbols long. Poverty feels empty, nauseous.

Today, he wore a sleeveless, black t-shirt drooped over his blue jeans. His gold necklace still hung at his neck but his half hearted smile reappeared when he said hello to the clerk at the scuffed countertop. He didn't speak as he pulled at the wedding ring, twisted it, turned it and grimaced, trying to create the nonchalance a prosperous man might present, but the sobriety of exchanging the old dream still tightened his throat.

"A hundred," the clerk said.

"Yeah," the sad faced man said, now a lighter feeling sweeping across him.

On the counter, two cellophane wrapped boxes of peanut butter waited to be loaded into a donation box for the mission.

"Man, I remember one winter. All we had was cheese and peanut butter. We spooned the peanut butter on the brick cheese and ate. It was good but we didn't crap all that season."

The man laughed and the few others in the store chuckled but the serious business of living stilled the mood.

Stew boiled a few feet from the counter with smells of mushrooms and onions percolating into the trade of his wedding ring. The ring would be recovered when the hundred and the juice was presented.

"Hey, this lock box…" The sad man said as he looked to something for conversation, the silence a hurtful ghost standing by his side.

"We tossed that…" another pawn shop clerk said. Now the man held the gray box he picked from the top of the garbage. He turned it like a tackle box meant for fishing lures.

"You have a nail file?" I can open it with a nail file." The man in the black tee said.

"No. Just leave it."

"I know how to open these."

"How's that?"

"My wife had one for drugs. I needed medication so I got her nail file and opened it."

"Why?"

"It's for pain. She worried I'd take too much. I only take two pills now."

When the deal was complete the clerk handed the man one hundred dollars. He put the ring in an envelope and sealed it.

"I really liked Johnny Cash," the man said, "He had a hard time, they say."

"He did."

"Okay, thanks."

The man turned to face the door and hesitated. He looked out to an empty future. He held his left side then while he held the door to look back and as he walked out the door, he rubbed a space under his heart.

A Ring Of Hope

At first, the middle aged woman with the turned down corners at a mouth that she bit, offered a silver totem from her left hand, but it wasn't worth the five dollars she needed to cover her rent. She smiled.

"Okay, what about this one?"

She only needed a little money. Five dollars to fill in the rent.

The clerk behind the pawn counter did not offer mercy but returned her smile. She tugged at another ring on another finger. The clerk placed it under his jeweler's orb and scanned. He looked like a pirate with a patch but the middle aged woman held a steady gaze.

"Sure, I'll give you five."

"I didn't know what I'd do and I can pay you back today."

Gold was rising and the band of hope shrouded the face and the clerk stared. Faces rise in dreams and nightmares, in darkness and the dark cloud follows us all.

The poor are losing. Rings are being traded for rent.

At the exchange of hope, a short line waited. For the middle aged woman with the flour white face, the glimmer of prayer is gone. In the short line behind her a second tragedy stood- a man doing day work, biding time.

This is not Currier and Ives. It is not a holiday.

Behind the grey man a half dozen green, plastic bins flowed above their rims with bread, spice rolls, large chocolate cupcakes, oatmeal, M&M and chocolate cookies. One last box of lemon rolls perched above the small hill of one bin until a white bearded, sharp shouldered man bent to lift it from the hands of God. Some days the bread is fresh and the mission customers walk away with a taste of God's mercy.

"Thank you mister," the sad faced woman said when the gold was dealt and she picked up the small change given for her band of promise. Under the eyes of these forlorn are rings and each ring has been darkened. The power of a long war has been against them.

The politics of the poor has been that mercy would see the day. The hungry children of God have trusted their faith but their faith has not stopped an inexorable change in prosperity.

For years the pastors and priests have extolled them to live the life of faith, a camel will fit through the eye of a needle sooner than a rich man will enter heaven, they have been told. So they abided, the poor and their children, they abided. The Narrow Gate promised.

A series of clouds that mires the world now rolls outside the doors of the pawn and the mission. Those who failed to demand more are left behind. The humble inherit handouts.

The man in the blue cap stepped up to the counter. His best poker face became a candle. He shone everything he could remember from better days, knowing an upbeat face gathers. He dumped a white, plastic sandwich baggie filled with electric wire onto the counter.

"What do you want?" The clerk asked.

"What do you give?"

The clerk thumbed these wires from computers, the alien black strings of a dozen cords, the little square boxed ends and the tiny silver teeth like ends. He hung them from a hand like a rosary, stared into the wide eyed wonder of the poor man with Labor Ready stenciled to his head.

"Five bucks."

Five dollars for attachments and connections whose value might have been in the hundreds. The poor man didn't know. He needed the money.

"Sure."

Later, the stereo sound of a young couple with a DVD player commanded the clerk's attention. Walk a mile in these shoes and judge not - throwing stones at angels left in alleys…, the devil haunts the hungry.

A short conversation grows about mutual friends, one sent from a Mt. Pleasant prison cell to a Fort Madison cell. "…it was because of a snitch…" a young woman confides. Now she confronts the desperate money.

"I bought it for three hundred." The graceless woman says. She goes high. Her eyes are the eyes of a fire.

"Fifteen," the clerk says.

A deep breath, that release after holding on for too long, added her fire to the cold room and she picked up then lugged the DVD player under her arm and left. Her boyfriend took a box of chocolate cookies from a bin and trailed behind. These are the next generation of abiding spirits, the younger people are angry, they catch the closed doors of the world falling into its own pits and its own losses. The closed fist of poverty is growing into an army.

----

*"Suppose a white man should come to me and say, Joseph
I like your horses, I want to buy them."*

I say to him, "No, my horses suit me; I will not sell them."

*Then he goes to my neighbor and he says to him, "Joseph
has some good horses. I want to buy them but he
refuses to sell."*

*My neighbor answers, "Pay me the money and I
will sell you Joseph's horses."*

*The white man returns to me and says, "Joseph I have
bought your horses and you must let me have them."*

*If we sold our lands to the government this is
the way they bought them.*

(Chief Joseph, Nez Perce)

XXV. SHADOWS DISTORT

The black minister opened the door to the pawn and he stood firmly by the door, looking at the white faced crock pot and smiling. He used his eyes to communicate and they told stories of poor little children and single moms. He sermonized very little as he stood and he and his friend the deacon, a heavy chested man who held his head high, were just saying hello. They have a place and the place is a church where the sing song camaraderie of sermons about tough times presents hope.

The church is an old store front. The street number is clear on the door but the face lacks a cross or a sign. The plate glass window is covered by an old purple curtain. The church is an address, a state of mind, a place in the book of life. Thirty black and white adults and children come. Others follow.

"We're just a little country church," the minister says and he smiles and he leaves that mystery to float into the room and fill it.

The room is 40' x 25'. The evidence that this was once alleyway shows with a doorway and window that are boarded. The black marked wood covers for the window and door set behind the pastor's lectern. The floor is a dull gray and the tin chairs creak when the congregation sits.

"And you remember the old rhyme when you were a child," he begins like a wave, like a concert, like a rendition of Mozart in which the wave slowly rolls then the crescendo comes in power and grace. He speaks of grace and the people he preaches to understand something special is happening here. He's midway into a two hour opera and he's sweating and roaming the room.

"That hen asked who would help plant seed. No one came."

Someone in the seats yells about his teaching and bringing it on and he's sweating and his voice comes into the room as harsh as if he's breathed coal dust. He moves with the strength of an athlete and the people pay attention. No one's kidding here.

He speaks about being down and about not caring and asking for help. He moves to his hands and knees and crawls then ends up on a distant chair.

"Jesus, Jesus," he says and they feel his story come to life. They live it and have lived it and he in turn dignifies and rebukes and holds each in the way only the very best of ministering does, tells all to account and to heed. He's part Al Green and part Martin Luther King. He's serious as life and death.

"Then the duck comes and the hen asks if he would help reap. And he won't. And comes another and that old hen keeps asking. Mr. Pig, will you help me grind the seed. But the pig doesn't have time. The hen asks who can help bake the bread and no one, not a single one, comes to help."

"Tell it bishop," a woman yells at various points of his sermon and others chime in like the wind above the crescendo and he gathers them and they frown and he pours down with the words of his sermon. But the words are words and the emotion is spirit.

"And everyone's there to help that hen eat that bread…" He partakes of every syllable with evocative grips and each member attends.

The people in the little room nod and some bend closer to the preacher and he says several times, "It's quiet here."

But they respond at intervals and the messages roll away from passages of Deuteronomy and the Psalms.

"God is with us," the young man says and he leaves not a shred for anyone to doubt as he adds and adds in a voice that rises and sweeps. He turns and cajoles and walks from one end to the other. The children near the front window, the small window that opens to the street, sit politely. When it's time to sing they sing as a choir.

"Know who your friends are," he says and rebukes and gives without any thought for ending what life brings. "God is with us. Don't blow it."

A lesson from the book and from the rhyme and it's a take home meal that is being devoured.

"He's anointed," a deacon says and if there were a bible to swear upon as an oath you would vow it's so.

"God's gonna break you down and build you up," he says and the woman in front begins to sway. "Yes, sir, and you know you can't afford Ramen noodles and you can't believe you can go down farther but you go. Two days later you've got some money and you're arrogant. You forget. He is with us. It wasn't you."

Then he raises his great voice, practiced and spontaneous, at the same instant somehow, "Do not blow it!"

"And you know when the stress is so great you can't talk to answer how you feel but you answer. Who has not been able to pray?" He considers these elements like Francis Bacon considered nature. "You have a part time job or you have a day job. You don't know security.

You worry there will be work tomorrow. He is with us. Oh, Israel, children, do not blow it."

When he talks about a shadow he says that shadows distort. Somewhere between the delivery and the sound, the rhythm and the words he does not leave a humble station.

"Shadows distort things."

He speaks about a mountain and it becomes a stone and a woman in the abyss responds.

"Teach it, preach it."

On a Saturday night, driven to build the new church, set inside a new building now, a sacred journey's night and day from the purple draped store front, six black men stood at the roster and stared back into the church at the congregation. Three wore gray suits and three wore brown suits. High vaulted ceilings curved over their heads. The dark brown wood that covered the corners and filled the walls reverberated the song and the repetition of the speakers, important to the effect, each adding and subtracting, one yelling for Jesus and praise, one louder, the leader and the next leading; the surface of leadership from Jesus and follow and follow and they spoke, each of whom began slowly like a train leaving a station but inched ever quicker till a great roar descended upon the church, each tearing at the calm, each growling and howling.

"Let me hear you! I said, give it up for Jesus. Praise the lord. Huh uh."

Some stood at intervals, some jumped and some rocked back and forth. Singing became spontaneous, boisterous, loud. A young man in the front put his fingers to his ears as the loud speakers did for them what decibels do to glass as it shatters, stopping at the atomic vibrato against the silence.

"And it's your flesh, uh huh, the flesh tells you to do this, do that uh huh and you know that's not the way, uh huh, and you follow his way, uh huh, he said, 'I am the way, the truth and the life', uh huh"

Fifteen minutes of short jabs as quick as Ali ever dappled, jabs with power, a force that moved the crowd. The minister sped along the ceiling now and dropped his right then a left, bam, bam, bam.

"If it's not the lord then who you going to? If you died where would your soul be five minutes later?"

The clapping and dancing raucous as a carnival, one preacher jumping thirty inches off the floor, slamming his dunk and spinning three hundred and sixty degrees, wiping his brow with a gray handkerchief. Like James Brown unable to stop after the frenzy, he walked to a calm pew on stage then returned, spontaneous, uninhibited, one long jump to the audience then jumping up and down, turning, spinning, raising arms, a flailing, reaching wonder.

When he was done only smiles hung on their faces.

Women had begun to sob and the tears rained upon the pew while their hands flailed. One began to issue incoherence, vocables rapidly passing as speech then shaking hands skyward and sobbing.

The quiet in the congregation were captive as song birds, peace had disappeared, reason was foregone and tension the hallmark of purity.

"Clap for the preacher," the voice yelled and the clapping hammered at the smith of the word.

The young girls sang, the women screamed, hands clapped. One here began to make noises, another the noises of an unknown language. Tongues flapped and fell, jaws berserk, hysterical and uncontrolled, people swayed and the choir roared in heavenly harmonies. Then the preacher jumped, pounced like a jaguar onto the floor and threw his arms back and howled and jumped like James Brown never did, working crowd and spirit, clarity and confusion colliding and blending.

"Let me hear you!"

"Praise the lord!"

In the beginning, song poured out from the stage. A brief, quieter tone started the ramshackle business, a teen read the first lines of the Bible:

"In the beginning God created the heaven and the earth and the earth was without form and void, and darkness was on the face of the deep and the spirit of god moved upon the face of the waters."

Once words were given to the void the church began to erupt. Pews shook, the bedrock of the Mississippi River might have been crumbling in a nearby slough.

The middle aged, elder group of pastors and bishops on the stage sat impassive, overseers, immobile and yet pleased. The people were raising the roof. The wind might have drawn a lesson, the sea would part, rapture would fall like feathers from the sky.

"Huh uh and praise your god Jesus! Let me hear you huh uh! Praise him and his way huh uh!"

The level of sound stopped conversation, quit silence everywhere, walled heart beats, opened eyes. The red drum set pounded like a deep heart, the electric red guitar squealed as if a stuck bird, a goose, falling and crying in rhythm with the drum and then came the saxophone, whirling and swirling, breezy and long then easy and short, swift blooms of grace chiming across the wood pews and sailing into the back room.

The first preacher began, swilled on about praise of and expansion of Corinthians. Corinthians ten and turning pages.

"Your flesh won't lift you. And it's the flesh that trips you, the mind that won't get you but the lord, praise god, mighty Jesus uh huh."

Preacher first called on flesh interests and overcome by its intensity, tense the obstacle and the higher tension the victory.

"My voice, you can see, isn't strong, but I've got the preacher behind me. Praise god, uh huh."

After each line of a dramatic and intensifying nature. The spirit rose to a cliff and dove headlong, repeating the huh and uh until the journey, now sanctified, shortened with swift, small lights of words. The rhythm drew the crowd and the clapping grew as if waves slapping a rock shore.

When, after two hours of screams, catcalls, barks, horns, strings, songs, dances, and the word, breathless, a white haired preacher from the rostrum, seconds earlier calm, now storming with squall and line of pressure, stepped up to the plate.

"Twenty dollars now for the host church. Who's giving twenty?" Then he squealed and rubbed his head.

When the money came in and the screech was done, another preacher, a larger man, spoke about baptism.

"I know someone needs baptism." Then a few minutes, "I know there's one more person needs to be clean." Then a few more minutes, "NOW I know, sure, someone on the right side here, I can feel it, needs to come up." Then, a few minutes beyond and after the parties to whom he'd compelled had arisen, "I just know, one more person needs the holy ghost. Not need baptism but you need the holy ghost. I'm waiting for one more person." And more minutes hung in the stilled, guilt loaded air and he said, "Now god almighty, one person, I know, one more before I go yet, who needs to feel the joy." And minutes turning into hours, heart beats as loud as thunder, again, now after another person the gall rose in his eyes and the words repeated.

"So come on now, I know it, I can feel it, one more and I'll sit down. One more person to get the joy. You know to come up here, get the joy of Jesus, you need the joy of Jesus. You know who you are." And another came. The clapping kept with his pace and the small eared youth who had played the guitar now sat behind the drums and flailed. Bah boom boom boom.

Hard Time Refugee

Jonathan asked me to help with his move to Cedar Rapids. He needed me to drive to the landfill and to load his belongings into his U Haul.

He's been a customer at the pawn shops. He's well liked. He's had a tough time.

I knocked on his door at ten a.m. on a boiling August first, in the summer of scorching heat that melted plastic in the street , visiting like a scourge of the Bible. One of his sons met me. The big man was rousing from a late night of saying goodbye to Dubuque. It was a long goodbye. It needed to be.

Living a few blocks from the University of Dubuque, he had said, yeah, this is a good neighborhood, my kids are safe and we're happy here. He noted that the lawns were cut, the houses were tidy and the trees shaded the clean sidewalks that the joggers roamed. The family could walk to the Dairy Queen or opt for Beecher's real ice cream in the friendly parlor by the gas station fifty yards from his front door.

Jonathan is a black bear, not a Black Panther, the black men of the 1960's that rose in Oakland, California, and roamed to many cities in America and elsewhere, asserting their rights, only to be swept away. Jonathan is warm. He's cuddly. He's sincere and kind. His rules are ten commandments and a golden rule he learned very young.

The black bear knew of Eldridge Cleaver, Bobby Seale and Huey Newton, and the others of the Black Panther Party. Too, he saw the pictures of the 1968 Olympic podium where Tommie Smith and John Carlos, America's medal winners in the 200 meter dash, dropped their heads and raised gloved fists to salute human rights. The third medal winner, Australian Peter Norman, had worn a human rights badge to signify solidarity with these black athletes. The photo went everywhere.

In the photograph, Smith wore a black scarf to represent black pride, Carlos kept his suit unzipped to show his allegiance to blue collar workers. They stood shoeless but wearing black socks to represent black poverty.

During that age, the FBI chief J. Edgar Hoover called the Black Panthers the "greatest threat to the internal security of the country." It is recorded that Hoover oversaw a program of surveillance, infiltration, perjury and police harassment.

Forty years later my friend was patrolling Dubuque, Iowa, streets, knuckle bumping black acquaintance and friend and stranger, looking to help the poorer quarters. He wore buttons. He wore rasta braids. He told me many times, all he wanted was peace. By the time he left he was watching out his window, fearful of the police. More than ten years in Dubuque, he became paranoid.

He became a member to the all white community task force that discussed black housing, crime, employment and safety. He asked tough questions. He told them he wondered about racism in Dubuque. He admonished them for their failure to address racism. He spoke with the chief of Iowa's human rights commission, Preston Daniels, sharing horror stories of police profiling and alleged oppressive agendas in Dubuque. He spoke about jobs.

The bear met with local NAACP leaders. He was asked to contribute. I was with him that day when the local NAACP head told him to be careful. The white police and the white cloud agenda were volatile. Dubuque had been a national travesty after the cross burnings, he was told.

Two years ago Jonathan was angry about the shooting in the back at the local pawn shop. Preston Daniels said he didn't have the funds to pursue the case. We shook our heads when he said that. Jonathan pressed on.

After meeting with the NAACP chief and Mr. Daniels, my friend and I stood by his car. I told him to be careful. A farm knife set on the floorboard of his car. It might be called a weapon if a three hundred fifty pound black bear possessed it. Jonathan didn't think about that.

Jonathan wanted freedom. He wanted everyone in Dubuque to see the failed justice for the poor.

Two years ago he went to court in Des Moines with a local bar owner. The bar had been surrounded every weekend, for years, by police. The alcohol license had been rejected.

In the end, the Des Moines judge rejected the city of Dubuque's liquor license ban to the bar called Players. Surrounded at four corners with extra police at the front door, the only black social gathering place in Dubuque, Iowa, the only one that the police surrounded, surrounded like it was a rail car headed to Auschwitz or Dachau, Players would stay open.

Jonathan now said he was being followed.

The bear had been shot twice, standing alone on street corners in dangerous neighborhoods of Chicago. He suffered from PTSD.

Jonathan had come to Dubuque with hope that the hard times were over.

Hard times.

The hard time is that space between good times. It lasts only as long as you can hold on. It's a desperate space that takes every ounce of energy to beat back, being filled with coincidence, tempted to the wrong places. These are times that you stand outside the time and observe, thinking to yourself, "It isn't happening to me, thank God."

The hard time is the one that you think over and then decide, this is the last one.

That hard time.

Jonathan is a black man. It shouldn't matter. It does. In Iowa it matters. In Dubuque maybe more than any other geography in America, it matters. The mayor will say it doesn't. The city council will say it's not that bad. The city manager will be offended. White bread folk from secure neighborhoods will look away from the comment. A commissioned survey about violence and safety will say that everything's about perception. As the ad agent says, perception drives reality. Dubuque is very good at driving.

That hard time.

After KKK style cross burnings in the 1980's race became a national hot button for the city founded by priests. The lens focused in Dubuque's neighborhoods where white supremacy made its loud, thunder clap.

Imagine a black man's surprise when he learned that race mattered but learned the city line had been, "It won't happen to you and you can thank God."

The hard time that whispers it's unreal. The time that tells you to doubt your lyin' eyes.

In the city Barbara Walters and Stone Phillips observed had some peculiar notions about black and white.

That hard time.

My friend is the father of six beautiful children. He has tattoos of their names on arms and neck. He's three hundred fifty pounds and he's a magnet.

He's a graduate of the local community college, a member of the NAACP, a member of the city's Safe Community Task Force, a member of the Democratic party, an acquaintance of the biggest politicians in America, photos with Mr. Biden and Mr. Obama and an activist. It's the activist space that seems to push the hard time. He's been in the wrong place more than once.

Choice. Of course it's choice. Then think again about how choice becomes that opposite and equal reaction, that Newtonian puzzle of oddity and mood when you're innocent and the truck runs you over.

In May, 2010, Jonathan sat in his car with the ignition off, staring out at the scenery in a park where the Vietnam memorial graces the river. He and his wife were looking for a placid, quiet space to share.

He said the cop searched him and his car, charging him with violating the demands of his temporary driver's license, though the car was parked. Then the charge of possessing a weapon, that farm knife that still laid at the floorboard of his car. He went to jail. He was stripped and left in a cell naked.

Friends told him to duck, to get out of the limelight, get out of their way.

In October, still working through the courts from his arrest at the Vietnm memorial, a cop named Paolo, the cop the black community will allege is racist and dangerous, the one who trained the policeman that had earlier arrested my friend , pulled him over. He said he knew Jonathan was driving illegally, which Jonathan denied. He said he'd give him a chance. He asked his fellow officer to call Jonathan's place of employment to verify part of the story. Then he arrested my friend.

In June, 2011, a video shows a man breaking a bottle over my friend's head at the notorious Player's tavern. Jonathan showed the court the video but the judge decided he was guilty of Disorderly Conduct and Public Intoxication.

This spring my friend agreed to give an acquaintance a ride from the bus station. His license still valid, he took a meandering route from his home by the university to the station and said en route the cop named Paolo followed him, drafting each of many turns, slowing and speeding as Jonathan did. At the bus depot the cop pulled up to my friend. He charged him with being an illegal cab service and driving while his license was barred.

Across the country now, courts are using the plea bargain to provide justice. In effect, the cop arrests and makes the last judgment. A poor man cannot afford an attorney. Despite innocence he may plead. The consequences are lighter when he does.

The Dubuque judge offered a deal. A fifty dollar fine and court costs if Jonathan pled guilty to operating a cab service and the other charge would be tossed out. The city of Dubuque clerk told him he most certainly did not need a cabbie's license but no matter.

Jonathan has spent eleven thousand dollars in fines and costs to defend himself in recent years. He showed me the receipts.

Since he offered to help the tavern owner with the case against the city of Dubuque, since that court hearing in Des Moines when he sat with the tavern owner defending the right to run a small business that caters to a black only clientele, Jonathan was arrested four times. In each arrest the same cop was involved in the case work.

I watched his baby girl in her extra large tee shirt, the one that daddy had given her. She hopped on his burned out lawn and called to him. We were loading the U Haul. His beautiful wife strolled out to greet us. His other children lifted bikes, toys and shoes to the van. They all worked hard. No one complained. He wanted to buy them ice cream after they were done.

I spoke with him several times after he moved to Cedar Rapids. He said he's happy. No one's following him.

XXVI. THE CAMP TOWN RACE

She's wearing old clothes today. She believes in front porch conversations, real people and a neighborhood. She wants to bring back Dubuque.

Thursday, Angela reviewed the colors that the volunteers would use on the store fronts of Central Avenue. She agonized about the right shade, the correct hue, the appropriate combination, the possible alternatives that would cover four stores.

"Yeah, an earth tone, that deep red. Finale, that's a good one." She spoke about a final review of color to cover a purple store.

From many long years of obscurity and demise, jobs headed elsewhere, flattery left for others, the phrase of twenty years now gone but still suppressed, "Last one to leave, turn off the lights."

Some obsess with the line, 'What Dubuque makes, makes Dubuque.'

This was a factory town.

This stretch of main street meanders inside Angela's domain. She runs it like a tribal warlord, first strategy, then redemption.

Odds favor the Washington Street Neighborhood group that is rehabilitating the space called the 'flats' because Angela will not let failure enter the tree lined streets. She's caring, energetic, tough as necessary and sweet as home made sundaes.

"We're gonna do this thing. I love this community and we're going to change it. It's getting better all the time."

When money is an issue she goes to volunteers, she sells local businesses and she crafts an argument about family and front porch Iowa that no one resists.

"Thank you for your help," she talks to everyone this weekend who has lent a hand to the Community Days of Caring Project.

She's there at inception, handing out paint buckets and brushes, tarp, gloves and good cheer. She'll be the last to leave, carrying buckets, tarp and weary but happy, she'll hang tough till the end of the second day of clean up.

Central is the main path, the street that horse drawn buggies once traveled, the avenue that city hall still hovers over, watched by a gold domed courthouse and newly risen parking ramp. Angela watches over her long swath of street as if she's curator of city spirit. She studies it like a surgeon, thinks about it like a mother, considers the song it becomes and the muse that it is, a place of variety. The place of origins. It is here that city fathers considered future events, placed their hands over their hearts and promised to keep this port on the Mississippi River a vibrant place.

Fifteen people met Friday morning on Washington Street to pick up supplies and gather last instructions. Once assignments were reviewed a volunteer named Joe blessed the day's work.

"We've given you all spray bottles. Spray before you scrape. We have dusk masks here. If you want to wear them, we have these cover all's. Put tarps down before you work…"

Angela watched her teams converge to boxes filled with gallons of paint, scrapers, rags, bottles, blue gloves, plastic gloves, yellow rollers, brushes, pans and tarp. The True Value contributed.

"He asked how much, I said ten thousand, we agreed five thousand." She doesn't say the money was promised. Angela wants financing. The True Value on Central wants to help.

Angela smiles an impish grin.

The crews panned outward in the neighborhood, some taking porches, some doing sides; one active clan roving along Central.

Thursday night, after picking the colors the owner of the purple store changed, wanting purple again. Friday morning would be another obstacle.

"Maybe we can talk to him. His wife now wants purple but let's play it by ear."

An hour into the scraping one team leader meandered away from the purple store to discuss color.

"We finished scraping and began to apply that red. Is that right?"

"Yeah, I think so," the other team leader said.

"I think we better call Angela, someone said the owner changed his mind…"

If ever the raven comes calling, the neighbors can be sure Angela will be there.

"I talked to Dan, the store owner. He said he'd be down at noon." The team captain said. Angela responded:

"Alright, wait till noon. We'll pull that crew and move them to another site. Let's wait for Dan."

Noon came and went. No Dan. Angela paced.

"Give it to one, then we have to get it done."

One came, not a whisper.

"Give it another fifteen minutes, then we're out of luck..." Angela's last word.

When he drove up alongside the partly painted store front, Dan appeared stern, frowning.

"I like the red." He said, "My wife does too."

Angela grinned from ear to ear.

"That street flows, now." Angela said.

She sat with five other women on the aging, hard cement surface, feet from the speeding John Deere tractors set high on semis, rumbling to deliveries, crunching the street like predators.

They sat in front of the 17th Street Pawn shop. The city manager was expected to stop.

As she sat, Angela listened. She savored a bag lunch and conversation. Ladders behind them, buckets around them, tarp and street traffic washing away the silence. An old black man stopped to tell a story. Perhaps he sensed the women were tired.

"Once, there were three bored brothers. Doo, Dah and DooDah." The women laughed. The man continued:

"They had a boat and were at this great lake. But as luck would have it, DooDah drowned. Now, the problem for the two brothers concerned which one would tell DooDah's wife.

'You're telling her.'

Doo said to Dah, but Dah was defiant: 'No, I'm not going to tell her!'"

Now, the man began to sing the rest of his story, much as Stephen Foster might have in a rendition of his famous, 1850 Camp Town Races.

"Finally, Doo acknowledged the horrible message... had to be delivered..."

Pause…

"At DooDah's house, that afternoon, he knocked on the door… DooDah's wife answered, 'Yes?'…

'Guess who fell in the lake and drowned?'…

" Camp town race track five miles long, doo dah…doo dah…"

XXVII. DILEMNA FOR THE DISABLED

The two of them and a dog named Sassy live together in a poor house in a sometimes noisy neighborhood of Dubuque. A picture of Jesus looking up to heaven hangs on the living room wall. A glass curio cabinet in the den shelves an angel, blue plates and glassware. On an end table to the left of an easy chair, medicine bottles, a spoon, a hairbrush, 32 ounce cups, salt and pepper shakers, a black ashtray and a little wood box set in the yellow light that falls through their window shade.

Curt stares at Linda and she smiles with a toothless smile from her broken wheelchair.

"We fall down all the time. It's the MS," Curt says. He says he comes home after errands to find his wife on the floor, waiting for help to get up.

"He ordered me to marry him," Linda says.

She says he nags.

"I said three times, 'Marry me, marry me, marry me.'" The bearded man says as he strokes the neck of their Jack Russell terrier.

They were married eleven years ago in a little ceremony in East Dubuque. Both Curt and Linda have Multiple Sclerosis, a chronic and degenerative disease marked by neural and muscular impairment. Both use a wheelchair.

Curt had been a regular at the pawn shop, sometimes trading and always enjoying a hot meal at the crock pot. Often, he'd share with Linda by carrying food home, tied by a bungee cord to his wheelchair.

Sometimes without transportation, without enough food, without soap, without bare necessities they hold fast to the hope that is born from love. They guide each other: to the sofa, to the door, to the cupboard; up from the floor after a fall; up the stairs, up the little incline at their back door, up from a wheelchair. Curt smiles and then she smiles.

"I let him do most of the talking. He likes to talk." Linda looks up from the incline of her chair.

Curt unfolds the recent trial like a towel hung upon the backyard line. He rubs his hands as he begins.

"It was August first, I remember. I sweated a lot that day. In the morning I went to Dutrac and took out cash like I usually do. Then I went to Eagle and got cigarettes and chocolate milk. Later

I went back to the bank. It was 3:38, I know because I had to get a copy of the receipt that I showed the police officer."

Curt's routine had been to drive his wheelchair from the area of five points to Dutrac to get money for bills and necessities. It's four blocks. Like many recipients of social security he and Linda depend upon the monthly stipend.

The wood box on the end table is where the monthly cash is laid.

"It was about four o'clock, after I went by the Family Dollar. They came up to me and talked. He was a black man and bald, in his twenties, I think. She was white and heavy. I remember exactly what he said. He said, 'Give me that money!' I gave him the envelope. It was more than five hundred dollars. He hit me then they ran. I chased them in my chair to 32nd Street. I don't know what I thought I'd do."

Curt says he should have stood up, that he should have fought for their money.

"I cried," Linda says about his return home that night.

"My hair was soaked with sweat and I cried," Curt says.

The money would have paid bills. Linda points to the kitchen when asked about food.

"We've got a whole bag of food," she says.

"As long as she's alive and my dog's alive, I'm happy," Curt says as he stares at his wife.

"You talk a lot," she says. "I worry about him." She cranes her neck from the wheelchair and looks away.

"I'll go out of my way if I think there's something different, now. I'm afraid," Curt says about the ordeal, " I won't go to the dollar store anymore. Ever again." He looks at their gruff little terrier. Linda sips a stale Pepsi from a straw.

"Sassy didn't leave my side." Curt says and stares at the ceiling as if he's holding his tears to the heavens. "It's weird but I look at everybody now. It's different."

Two people with a disability trying to make it, trying to find a little comfort, a little of God's mercy, a little of the human touch in working class Dubuque, Iowa.

"We're doing okay," Curt says, "We got Linda's check in and we can pay the utilities."

Later, Curt says the same to a member of the Dubuque Community church. He smiles. He thanks the church friends for their concern and he rolls toward the church pantry where he and

Sassy wait for a friendly face. Linda waits for them in a seat nearby. She can't move around so readily but waits and watches the musicians before the service.

Their home isn't much but a white clapboard built with saws, hammers and nails, sweat and promise of a dream. It leans on a thin lot, close to its neighbor like working class homes of Dubuque do: remnants of the European style of closeness. The old back door stoop falls in the alley.

The sky was blue that afternoon. Curt saw the man easily but doesn't talk about the details. He reported it to the police.

"I've never been afraid like this." Curt says. He frowns like something more was taken from him.

"I stayed home for two weeks. Didn't go out of the house."

Sassy barks and wags the tiny tail and saunters toward Curt. He brushes the short hair backwards and Linda offers a glance of wonder. She shakes her head.

"You don't think someone is watching, do you?" Curt asks.

The philosopher William James gave thought to this mean street of society. To James it amounted to more than turning away from these forms of poverty and violence. He said that if millions of people could be "kept permanently happy on the condition that a certain lost soul on the far-off edge of things should lead a life of lonely torment our moral sense " would make us immediately feel" that it would be " hideous" to accept such a bargain.

Linda and Curt do not complain. They understand the bargain. They look over their shoulders as they help each other out the door.

XXVIII. THE DREAM DENIED

Denise Hall left her home in Chicago sometime in the early afternoon of November third, 2007. She crossed Illinois with her children in tow and all her worldly possessions neatly stacked in a rental truck. She headed for Dubuque, Iowa, a home on the Fifth Street hill and a dream of starting over.

The city on the great river impressed her. She spoke about Northeast Iowa Community College and the short walk to classes. The widow had gazed at the city lights that fired up the river horizon and been converted.

She was encouraged by the closeness of the post office. When the wind was right she could smell bread from the nearby bakery.

She noted coffee shops and craft stores; at the corner light red geraniums had set in a bowl. The nearby cathedral loomed as a symbol of God's presence. The Key City had been built by people with dreams like hers.

"After my husband died I wanted to try something new…"

She says she was exhausted the night she moved, her two children were weary. That night her dream drifted into twilight.

"…Imagine getting a knock on your door," she wrote, "It's the local police department. They were not here to see if everything was okay or even to ask if I needed some help, which by the way, I did. No, that wasn't it at all…they got a call that some blacks were breaking into a house on the block."

The widow notes that she was unnerved. Boxes stood in tight rows in the truck.

"I need everyone to stop what you are doing and tell me who is the one holding the lease to this place," the policeman said.

"My kids were there and they did not understand any of it," the widow said.

After handing the officer her identification, she asked the movers to be patient and attended to her children. According to the widow the officer returned the identification but then demeaned her:

"Well, here is your identification back, but you only have one hour to move your stuff into your place and if I come back in one hour and see someone moving into this unit I'm going to lock someone up."

Looking back, the widow may have overlooked the news of September, about the gathering of 200 in a nearby park; about the summer stabbing that the Dubuque Telegraph Herald called a "...racially charged Dubuque homicide...," about the public defender's concerns for a fair trial; about the Dubuque NAACP's 19th annual dinner to address the racialization of justice – their note about Iowa: 13.6 times as many blacks are imprisoned as whites; about the quote by Dubuque Police Chief Terry Tobin that the recent killing involved "racial slurs"; or about the photo of a lynched black man that appeared on the Dubuque Telegraph Herald Web site. No one apprised her about the climate at the port.

In class she tried to hold back tears. She rubbed her face, she dropped her eyes. She remembered a local restaurant where she saw an Aunt Jemima figure on the wall. She said she felt eyes following her in the white spaces.

She said she's not afraid. She said, "It's not my fault."

At the Phi Theta Kappa ceremony in the Spring of 2009 at Northeast Iowa Community College Denise smiled as she stood. Her children watched her when she walked to center stage where she accepted a flower and applause. She had studied her way to honors.

In June the young widow moved to Country Club Hills, Illinois.

"I can't take it anymore," she said after a neighbor urinated on her mail box.

According to Dubuque police Public Information Officer Scott Baxter, "No report was taken" on the night Denise moved to Dubuque. "Nothing was officially filed." A call titled 'Suspicious Circumstances' is listed for an incident police responded to at 580 ½ Fifth, her dream home, on November 4 at 1:51 a.m. No complaint addresses the defiling of her mailbox.

The widow's story stands inside a community recognized as one of the "100 Best Communities for Young People"; one of the "Best Small Places for Business and Careers" and during that year she moved to Dubuque, the coveted award of All-America City, one of ten cities nationally to do so.

The snow drifted from the heights, flaking down in plates of white, then spinning sideways. In the first week of February, the weathermen reported the cold spell rivaled the winter of 1996.

Inside the gray battleship door of the Narrow Gate mission, two men stood behind the linoleum counter drinking coffee. They watched a box shaped television set in a row of twenty TV's. The movie, The Ox bow Incident, played in black and white.

"It's a fearsome thing what a mob will do," the bigger man said.

"No conscience in a mob," the other said.

A hanging took place in the movie.

The food mission hummed alongside the pawn business. The two businesses survived as meager hopes on a poor street. A man might buy a wrench then help himself to a bowl of stew. The pawn's Spartan profit paid for the meal.

The two men stared ahead at passing scenes of the hanging tree.

"Anthony Quinn was a helluva actor." Roy said.

"He's innocent, wait and see," Jimmy said.

"When they toss the ropes over that branch they'll find their consciences and be shamed," Roy said.

"I finished the door jamb with an extra lock," Jimmy Mitchell said and he swept the long bangs of aging, brittle hair from his forehead. The stocky Roy smiled at Jim then pulled at the Styrofoam cup.

"You put in some extra time to add the lock."

"Yeah, but the neighborhood."

" You're always going the extra mile, Jimmy, and I appreciate it."

Overhead, a dozen, dusty pool table lights hung from the smoke stained ceiling. Ads for Miller, Schlitz and Bud in neon colors of blue, red and green slung across the rectangular tiles, suspended by bronze colored chains. On shelves behind the computers and TV's a thousand videos fought for space, squeezed and crammed into the wooden shelves.

By the front door, wood boxes held dozens of loaves of bread, rolls, buns and pull aparts.

A shaggy bearded man stood by the door. He clapped at Henry Fonda when the mob began to initiate its foul thought. Roy stood up from his chair near the black edged coffee pot.

"Weather don't know what to do next. Pile up more snow or freeze our feet or both," Roy said. "How you doing?" He asked the bearded man and they both smiled. The freezing wind was seeking to sting and the bearded man tugged his beard as if to say, "This winter's too much."

The big man watched the opening door. He offered the store as a home to everyone who entered. In the corner, a mash of beans, deer meat, potatoes, corn and gravy steamed its wicked scents into the room.

"Want some stew?" Roy asked the shivering man. "You need a mean bowl of this goo, extra pepper and even a few radishes set in to keep it lively."

The man reached out for the ladle at the crock pot where steam rose. The aroma of the deer and onions seduced each shaking customer. Roy pulled the top from the cooker, "Dig in. That's what it's there for."

"That's kind of you, big Roy. Glad to have something to warm me up."

"Take as much as you like."

Roy turned his head from the man at the cooker to his friend Jim, and said, "I'm listening to you, Jimmy."

Steam rose from the cooker in a white cloud. The man filled a paper bowl with the beans and tomatoes, then laid down onion to surround the deer meat. He dipped a big spoon and tasted it.

"This here's delicious. Thank you."

"Want some donuts, or rolls?" Jimmy asked the man.

"I'd take a roll with this. Yes, sir."

Now the man folded his cap and put it in his pocket.

"I've been walking up and down the street, trying to make a dollar or two, shoveling the walks. Seems half of the stores I stop at tell me a guy named Robert's already been there, or Robert's got the business. You fellas have any work?"

"Tell you what to do," Roy said, "You finish all you want, eat up the stew. When you're done, walk out there and just shovel. That's all, just shovel. After each job you walk inside the store and ask if they'd be willing to pay a little something. You tell them you know times are hard. You did the job for free, but if they wanted to help a fella out…"

"Say, mister. That's a good one. I'll try it!"

Later that morning, Roy lifted an old door that had been refit with locks and jambs and placed it in a truck. He could see fifty feet in the heavy, falling snow. Small drifts rose in the alley and at the curbs.

"Too cold this good day of the lord," the barrel chested Roy said. He rubbed his hands and slapped his sides.

In the foggy air, he spied a vision in a slanting snow. A bearded man filed into the nearby barber shop with a shovel in his hand. The man lifted a thumb up and pulled a bill from his pocket. He waved the bill.

Roy smiled in the flurry of snow and torrents of chilling wind. He stood with his friend Jimmy. The two men balanced the door in the jamb for the coming freeze.

XXIX. THE COMMUNITY CHURCH

In working at the pawn and mission I became a part of the whole. I began to attend the church where the Narrow Gate's regulars went. In Dubuque it had the reputation as being the place where the down and outers were served. It's where Paul and his family went. The first time I went the pastor spoke of joy. It was a refreshing tome, a light, a change. So I sat curb side and I sat in church and I learned.

When I was invited to go to the church, I was honored to be accepted. I took notes. The emotion and the church doctrine was new to me but the fact of this great faith that Paul showed every day stirred me and inspired me.

I recall my mother saying that the beautiful fact about faith is that it only takes your belief to move mountains.

"The minister said this morning that everyone was a vegetarian before Noah," Paul's dad said as he stared at me and winked.

"Oh, yeah," he said, "We were all vegetarians before the flood."

"Where he got that, I don't know," Paul said and frowned.

"So you're right about the diet," Paul's dad added, referring to the meatless diet question, adding the unspoken message that my family were all meat packers in Dubuque.

I was compelled.

You know, Paul's dad Bill is an imp. He's fun to be with and down to earth. Better qualities you cannot find. He tells those stories about chasing Ruth around the house at age eighty, then looks the other way as if it's true. I felt at home with the Down's. People who didn't take life too seriously.

"Help yourself to a muffin," Paul said in the Dubuque Community Church kitchen. He waved his fat fingers toward the rail between the kitchen and church where plates of red dotted, cranberry muffins and cakes, rolls and pastries with white glaze and cinnamon rolls, set by a steaming pot of coffee. It was like Narrow Gate west. The smells of the coffee and the muffins tempted all who passed. When Paul brought his infant son in his arms and smiled I understood he could be signaling that it was my turn to carry the child. I moved quickly to the kitchen cabinets where I retrieved a cup then to the coffee to fill my hands.

Church was starting.

The coffee was warm and went down with a fresh, clear taste. It left a pleasant aftertaste. The lights went out. Service began and we walked into church. I sat in the last row, a purple row where two other lapsed believers hid themselves.

The first song included the lyric, "Let it rise." I understood the sentiment and looked through the cross shaped glass windows above the front of the church where the guitars and the drums and the lead singers stood. The tall, gray barked trees that visited me from the windows told of my morning run, filled with birds, colors of skies and grass knolls of melting frost.

The next song reverberated more of church dogma about lord and lord and our lord, awesome and a man. I worried about being seen as an infidel, one with his own beliefs but again reckoned each to his own. Their beliefs were a mystery but something Paul was doing with his life, and tending to poverty with such diligence, had come from this place.

Keeping faith.

With my feet planted as I did when I was a child, I kept my eyes to the floor. I sang only when the lyrics were of my own understanding.

Fifteen minutes of singing. In the first aisle, in a front row, long haired Renee, Paul's beautiful wife, flailed herself with waving hands. She struck the sky again and again with thrusts of her hands then waved. She swayed and she rolled and she sounded out louder than any person in that church. Her long, dark hair, tied by a cord, swung upon her back and her nine children, all swayed and waved.

The singing lifted the angels from their sleep. The song, "Old Wooden Cross" came in with a twang and a drum roll, a voice picking away at the church lights, drowning the choruses of saints somewhere, each church member fighting, climbing on each other's shoulders in song and rapture. I saw the pastor grab himself around the shoulders and sing in violent rhapsodic joy; he yelled, "Oh Jesus. Oh, Jesus."

I remembered childhood and seeing the man on the cross and hoping I would understand.

The throng fought back tears and swayed. The church rumbled and the song lifted and the pastor cried.

"Oh, Jesus. "

In their finality, the songs tired the group and they sat. The pastor moved to the center and checked his microphone. He looked around the room from his spot under the lights, careful, deliberate, sincere, devout, touched. He accorded each face he turned to with a beatific smile. He began:

"Wow! My friends, what can I say? That today we'll talk about resurrection."

To the minister's left, a few rows out of his reach, a healed disciple called.

"Who is that?" The preacher inquired, "Who calls? What did you say?"

And the voice tuned up, raised his solemn voice toward the sky with an increased volume.

"It's me pastor, Chris."

"Oh," the pastor stared with eyes widening, "It's Chris! What is it Chris?"

"Well I'm just blown away. Your sermon is exactly what we all discussed earlier at Bible study. And, the youth group studied the same. It's unbelievable!"

I knew Chris to be a good man. Within this space I learn to let it be, learn that a mystery of faith has profound consequence, that people who are homeless, whose behavior cannot be measured, will climb a staircase to save a child in a burning building.

The preacher looked around, again, scanning, looking for eyes and talking ever more solemnly.

"Of course. It's the spirit. No coincidence my friends! Amazing. Ours is an awesome God!"

Behind the minister a deacon reverberated, "Awesome. Hallelujah. Our God truly is an awesome god!"

I whispered, "What others, among gods, are there. You fellas have competition…?" I wanted to find sunshine. It felt like confrontation but it was about love.

The seriousness of the church can bring clouds. It becomes laughter, too, as if humor may relieve despair in the hard times.

Then the pastor began.

"I was thinking. And you all know how I think…"

He waved his arms. He pulled at his ear where the black strap of the microphone tightened against the lobe. Pulling at his dark red sweater, a shirt of medicine, like a shaman, he brought his forefinger and thumb to his lips, drying the moisture that congealed around the corners of his mouth. He licked his lip.

"We're all like a tube of toothpaste. You know what a tube of toothpaste is filled with. And then you squeeze and what comes is toothpaste. Of course…"

It was beginning to seem like a pawn shop scene when an ex-felon waltzes in and finds the booklet about Jesus and feels compelled to share his 'walk with Christ'. I hoped people were genuine here.

Miracles are tough to understand. Once, working on a crisis line, a woman told me that the first clue to the truth is how far the believers will go to 'share' their story.

The congregation stilled. The preacher touched his nose, rubbed the edges of the shine upon his nose and tugged his nostrils, inflamed now like he was refreshed. He squinted like a man peering into the souls of the faithful and then he riled and revved and hunkered down to the message of The Resurrection. It may be the most powerful message of the church and it applies everywhere.

"I was thinking," he said and began to cry, his voice trembling and lips quivering, "I was thinking about the lord. About how he died for us. And you know he was tortured. The greatest torture mankind has ever devised," he said and a fever appeared to descend upon him. A red swelling might have moved up the temples of his face. He swung out into the audience.

Was he talking about the torture of the poor?

Pastor continued.

"They tore at his flesh. They used a cat of nine tails with glass and steel and I don't know.

They skewered his back till ribbons of blood and flesh drew away to show bone and gristle and he wore a crown of thorns."

Pastor had seen Mel Gibson's "The Passion." I remembered a thousand poor men had walked to the Narrow Gate and been revived, hope given, a fresh word instilled.

I drew my head down and placed my hands together at my waist, prayerfully attending the floor.

"Now Jesus had pressure. Great, eternal pressure. He bowed to the father. Finally, like a tube of toothpaste," he said, "Nomini sabu sabu tattoo…" Or, words the minister accessed from literature, meaning, "Why have you forsaken me?"

The pastor has shared his 'tongues' with the congregation while I have been there. I have no judgment or assessment to offer but that the faith is tangible, real, living.

These serious moments choked off everything but breath. Occasionally, a word from the rows to either side of the preacher proclaiming majesty: "Hallelujah Jesus. Jesus is lord."

Everyone was ready to drop every dollar from their wallets. A pin onto the carpet might have sounded like acorns plopping outside on the parking lot: pop, pop, pop.

"And," the minister began to spill the tears,

"He was a man. He was god. He could feel our feelings. He was one of us. And… Jesus, in that moment, that one instant, as he said to God , who he was and wasn't," …now a rising crescendo, "At that moment, we know, we know: he took on all the sins of the world."

Here the pastor decried the unfaithful, saying, this was all the sins ever to be and that ever were.

"It was then, my friends, that Jesus and God split. God left him. And they were two."

It was accepted by everyone in that church.

Of the mentally ill who have stood on that raggedy carpet of the pawn shop, their missing piece of rational thought floating away, these symptoms – those unforgettable lapses when someone loses grip of their mind - the pastor's sermon fluttered around madness. None in church doubted.

The love that is given in church is not mystery. Nor the hope that inspires people to help the downtrodden. Neither is faith that overcomes the riddles and obstacles of the economy.

Is inequality damning the country?

"I was with my wife Carol." Pastor pointed to his wife. She had the countenance of death, white faced, gray at the temple, she slouched over her chair. "Carol, the saint," he said.

"I came home from work and I said to my wife, 'You cannot believe the day I had at work. The pressure. People are fired. The economy, what can I say. I can't take this crazy pressure.' And, Carol, like a saint, walked away."

Here the congregation began to laugh. The laughter seemed like a cauldron of pressure leaving; a boiling sea steaming off a great swell of waves, as if a typhoon had churned through and some of the power had to be cast off.

"Ha. Ha, ha," they cried.

"And what," he said, "What happens to a tube of toothpaste when you squeeze it? And I was filled with pressure. And what came out of me was bitter, was mean and filled with anger. Now," he continued, as if we could take more.

"Now, you think you've had a bad day? What about Jesus? He's hanging by the nails. And those nails, nails, by the way pounded into his wrists, not his hands, for this too, we know. You think you've had a bad day. Jesus had a bad day.!"

The psychologist Albert Ellis tells us we are born to be rational and irrational. We choose.

Faith does not have to be rational. It is said to move mountains. The minister pounded his hand with his other hand, slammed his right fist into his left. He scowled and breathed as if a fit had overcome him.

"You don't know what a bad day is. And, so, I went into the dining room."

Now he was sobbing. In church. He's trembling with emotion. I cannot watch. Others shade their eyes and stare at the floor. White haired women begin to stop breathing. An old woman with gold rimmed glasses, hair as pure as white clouds, as arctic frost, looks away from the minister and places her eyes as if drawn by locks, to the floor, where safety and sanity seemed to lay.

Screaming as loud as any man I have ever heard, in any speech or court or assembly, yelling and screaming, he calls the spirit and sends us into his living room:

"I have marriages that are falling apart. I have people who are losing their homes. There's people with illness and trouble is everywhere."

He's angry now and all of us know it.

"I have pressure," he screams to the ceiling in his dining room and I can see the wallpaper there, "Why me?" He asks god.

Then he calms as mysteriously as a wind at the river. The waves slow and the people, some of whom have begun to cry, are enthralled.

"Then, the holy spirit came into the room."

The people are hanging on to his every word, as if to say, "More, more, more"

"I said to the holy spirit. ' I can't do this, I have marriages and illness and troubles, my job is a mess and the economy is in trouble and...' ; the holy spirit spoke –

'Man what is wrong? Fill up with me.' And he spoke, ' I love you.'"

With this the man recovered himself and the spirit left. In the Dubuque Community Church, the mystery of faith stilled every man, woman and child.

XXX. BEGINNING OF THE END

In the cold morning during the first week in February Paul opened his store an hour late. He said he'd been there at eight but had no money. His friend Jim said that seemed odd and Big Jim might know these things but Paul stared him down and Jim quieted. Then Pat, who was working through an employment agency after he lost his job at the window manufacturer said that Jim should shut it.

"I have to do my laundry. I don't have any clothes. Look at me." Jim said, using the Red Herring defense, redirecting like an attorney in a fine, pin striped suit.

The ruse would only go so far. Each day Jim walked the sidewalks of the poorest sections in Dubuque and each day his clothes were tattered or grimy, dirty or stained. The laundry was not a new excuse and Pat called him on it. Jim admitted to a lazy side but this morning had chosen to recuse himself.

"Yeah, that orange t-shirt reminds Jim of the jail jumpsuit, that's it."

"Sure, I spent a little time in jail, but not much," Jim said as he stuffed his mouth with the morning pizza that the rescue mission had brought. Jim shrugged off Pat's comment and wiped his mouth with his sleeve and his dark haired belly showed.

Recent conversations about that one last party were dissolved. The glory of sending one last song to the streets seemed a distant horizon. The fellas knew they were the last stand. The dance was ending. The decades had caught up. Time could not be fooled. Christ was not coming in time. The poker game they'd had with him had fallen short of the mark.

Other pawn shops were open by now and Paul's business would have to lag behind and it did. The store did not compete but endured and the priority for Paul was not profit but helping the poor.

Some days the majority of customers came to get free food. The falling down, white washed building was a crumpled chalice. Paul was committed and everyone on the street knew. He offered hot meals but his shelf goods had been substandard for a long time. Sales were nonexistent. Across the street at the American Pawn Stan had five customers who wanted to sell or trade and he was hopping. Paul rested his weary arms on the counter and looked into the television above his head.

On May 17, 2012, after more than twenty years Paul and his wife had begun to talk about closing. Paul had resisted but Renee wanted to quit. She said she'd like to do missionary work and the plan she had was to go to India in the Fall. In private, Paul said he couldn't, his love has been for the poor of Dubuque and the mission.

For three days now Paul has moaned about his losses. He has forsaken the business he built here, now letting his son Daniel manage. The cost has been losses in sales and a new crowd of people who walk in for free food, talk shop and leave. They're a younger crowd now, an unemployed group of mongrels, whiskey on their breath and drugs slowing their speech. People at Paul's church have begun to talk about the end coming.

Big Jim asked another customer what his impression had been, the customers of the pawn shop being away for a year and the man responded that the people seemed different. Jim said , "Yeah, they are and they're no good."

The street was alive Friday, June 1, and the fables from the grim lives were moving as they do, jumping and sorting themselves, finding the crazy patterns that Rorschach said had meaning and portent and might be used to effect change. There is no change on the streets but motion and it's queer and tough and funny.

The coffee pot with the burned scale on its handle sizzled the last drops of black coffee and the dregs rescaled the pot. Paul pulled the chain on the open sign in his window. He'd been open for an hour.

"What about the time, at the auction, when he bought a head and a wig?" Paul began to laugh. Jim had gone and they needed a story. A big Jim story would always lighten the load.

Paul dug into the stew in the bowl placed in front of him. The deer meat and gravy, mixed with corn and beans, hugged the bowl and steamed upward into his face.

Paul spoke about Jim's spontaneous, disruptive behavior. Jim's temper could be trouble and everyone understood that he felt he was always right. He'd get mad at simple things but that's what was lovable about the middle aged man who always did his best and who never forsook a friend.

"Later, after he had been looking at the stuff he bought, he felt he'd been had, taken advantage of - he got mad and beat up the head and threw out the wig."

This scene of big Jim holding a mannequin head and hitting it, this tale of life and displacement, punching a reflection, hitting a dummy, frustrated, without a way of escape from the hard street, its truth tapped us all.

The men at the mission began to laugh. The old black man in front of the counter elbowed the old woman and they all laughed. Their eyes lit up and for a moment, life became easy and peaceful.

The End

Responses to the Frontier Dubuque Survey,
100 respondents gave the following:

1) 79% said yes, a power elite exists in Dubuque.

2) 76% said racial discrimination exists in Dubuque.

3) 82% agreed or strongly agreed there is discrimination in Dubuque.

4) 74% disagreed or strongly disagreed that justice is fair for all people in Dubuque.

5) 60% said racial diversity is being resisted.

6) 64% agreed with the statement that media shows bias in Dubuque.

Regarding safety, 100 respondents surveyed:

1) 41% said some areas are dangerous.

2) 30% said it is less safe today than a few years ago.

3) 88% acknowledged a less safe Dubuque.

59% said there is hiring discrimination in Dubuque.

43% said there is not fair opportunity for employment.

67% felt the newspaper is controlled by an elite group.

PHOTOS

Pat, also known as Double P

Al

Stanley

Jimmy

Some of the fellas.

A busy place

Paul Downs, owner of the 17th street pawn and Narrow Gate

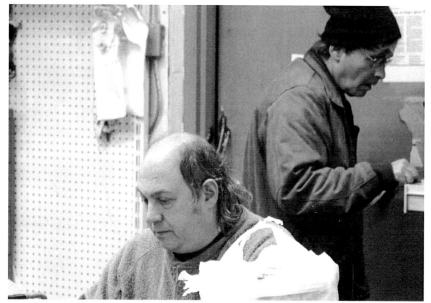

Paul and Jimmy

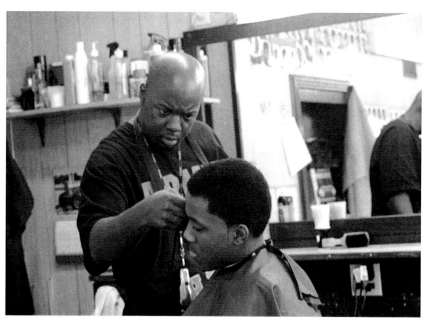

Makiah trimming a customer

Neighborhood friends

He shared stew and traded at the pawn shop.

Good ol' Jim

A friend to the store

Stan and customers

The long shot where Kevin Costner and Burt Lancaster walked on Central Avenue. The corner has seen meth deals and murder.

Easter Sunday

Billy, Stan's manager

The famous gold dome

Ron and Al

Pensive Adam and the prayer magnet

Harmony and Renee Downs

Note Frankenstein on the balcony of the American Pawn

"There are no crime problems here,
there is no race problem here...
um uh, strike that,... race problem, well, yeah"

– as if he heard what he had said, finally...
as if he knew he couldn't stretch that truth any longer.

(Housing Director of Dubuque in meeting attended by Iowa Public Radio,
July 23, 2013 following the HUD essay in the Cedar Rapids Gazette)

230 - T.W. Trenkle

Photographs and drawings are done by the author.

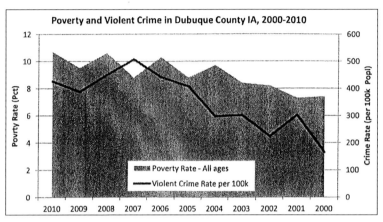

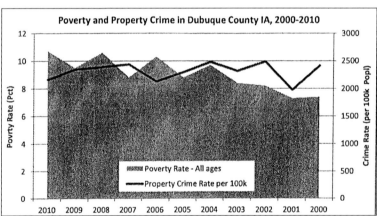

VARIABLE	2010	2009	2008	2007	2006	2005	2004	2003	2002	2001	2000
Poverty Rate - All ages	10.7	9.5	10.6	8.8	10.3	8.8	9.7	8.4	8.2	7.3	7.4
Child Poverty Rate - Under 18	13.6	13.3	12.5	11.2	12.1	11.5	11.2	10.4	9.3	8.0	8.8
Violent Crime Rate per 100k	425.9	386.8	450.3	507.1	440.9	408.0	297.8	301.8	224.2	302.1	164.6
Property Crime Rate per 100k	2161.1	2345.5	2386.9	2436.9	2127.8	2296.4	2481.6	2318.0	2487.1	1974.3	2411.4

AREA: Dubuque Co IA

NOTES: Crime rate includes crimes known to law enforcement. Includes all jurisdiction within the area.

SOURCE: Poverty rates from SAIPE, US Census. Crime rates from UCR, FBI.

Mother, mother
There's too many of you crying
Brother, brother, brother
There's far too many of you dying
You know we've got to find a way
To bring some lovin here today.

What's Goin On, by (Marvin Gaye)

NEWS REPORTS

PUBLICATION	HEADLINE
New York Times	It's Hard To Summon Sympathy For Big Banks
Telegraph Herald	Dickenson: What, Me Worry?
Telegraph Herald	Job Numbers Take A Hit
Des Moines Register	Racial Divide in Hiring in Iowa
New York Times	Can The Working Class Be Saved
New York Times	Jobless Report Is Worse Than Expected;
New York Times	Banking On The Brink
Miami Herald	When In Trouble, Nations Look For Scapegoats
New York Times	Ever Closer To 1982
New York Times	Mission Not Accomplished
New York Times	651,000 Jobs Reported Lost In February
Newsweek	The Great Jobs Question
New York Times	Steep Market Drops Highlight Despair Over Rescue Efforts
New York Times	Things Are Not OK
ABC News	Top 1%'s Income Grew 275% From 1979 To 2007
Washington Post	The Growing Tension Between Capitalism and Democracy
LosAngeles Times	Corporate Power Grows Stronger As Government Wanes
New York Times	2 Parties Place Political Focus On Inequality
New York Times	Progress In The War On Poverty
New York Times	A War On Poverty At 50
Telegraph Herald	HUD Accuses Dubuque Of Racial Discrimination
Telegraph Herald	Downtown Group Talks Tensions
Telegraph Herald	Study: Section 8's Impact Murky
New York Times	The Unemployed Held Hostage Again
New York Times	Good Poor, Bad Poor
New York Times	Why Inequality Matters
New York Times	The poor, The Near Poor And You
New York Times	Winning The Class War
New York Times	At Grave Risk
KCRG TV	Dispute Over Girl Led To Dubuque Shooting
New York Times	The Mutilated Economy

SUBJECT	DATE
	12/12/2013
...says the loss of 1,000 jobs In July par for the course in the summer	8/25/2008
	1/5/2009
Biggest in U.S.	11/12/2006
	2/11/2012
Rate Rises to 9.8%	10/3/2009
	2/22/2009
	2/20/2009
Steepest job loss in 50 years	3/6/2009
Few jobs/Rise in child poverty	10/2/2009
	3/6/2009
What if they don't come back	9/4/2009
	3/1/2009
Economy remains deeply depressed	2/5/2012
	10/26/2011
	11/24/2011
	11/19/2011
	1/8/2014
	1/8/2014
	1/6/2014
Police: Shootings Not Part of Gang Activity	6/21/2013
	6/26/2013
	1/20/2011
	11/27/2010
	12/19/2013
Americans remain a lot poorer Than before crisis	12/15/2013
1 in 3 Americans (1Million) either Poor or perilously close to it	11/23/2011
More poverty but American companies most profitable quarter ever	11/26/2010
Millions going down for the count	2/21/2011
	1/13/2010
	11/7/2013

PUBLICATION	HEADLINE
Washington Post	Study: Rich, Poor Americans Increasingly Likely To Live In Separate Neighborhoods
New York Times	Billionaires Row And Welfare Lines
New York Times	Welfare Benefits For Big Business
Washington Post	End of The Magic Show
New York Times	Of Janitors and Kings
New York Times	Letting The Banks Off The Hook
New York Times	Who Will Stand Up To The Super Rich
ABC	Police Say Employee Pulled Trigger In Dubuque Pawn Shop Shooting
Telegraph Herald	City Officials Calling For Calm
Telegraph Herald	Speakers Call For Unity
Telegraph Herald	3 Arrested After Armed Robbery (Briefs)
Telegraph Herald	Racial Disparity In Drug Arrests
Telegraph Herald	Dialogue On Police, Race Finds Conflicts
Telegraph Herald	Robberies, Burglary Keep Police Busy
Telegraph Herald	Man Charged With Homicide
Telegraph Herald	Should City Fund Social Services
Wall Street Journal	Billionaires On The Warpath?
New York Times	Number Of Families In Shelters Rises
New York Times	A Recoveries Long Odds
New York Times	Getting Older, Growing Poorer
New York Times	When Class Trumps Identity
New York Times	Rich People Just Care Less
Los Angeles Times	Global Economic Crisis Spurred 5,000 Additional Suicides Study says
Telegraph Herald	Stabbing Coincides With Rally For Peace
Chicago Tribune	85 Richest People Own As Much As Bottom Half Of Population
New York Times	What Happens When The Poor Receive Stipend
New York Times	Caught In a Revolving Door Of Unemployment
Telegraph Herald	Struggling To Survive
New York Times	Children In Peril
New York Times	The Inequality Problem
Wall Street Journal	Are Companies Responsible For Creating Jobs?

SUBJECT	DATE
	8/1/2013
	10/25/2013
	12/25/2013
Missing trust	2/24/2009
	9/3/2010
	4/18/2011
	11/13/2010
	1/19/2010
Fatal stabbing	8/31/2007
Aftermath of murder and racial tension	9/30/2007
	1/4/2008
Worse county in the worse state	6/5/2013
	12/16/2010
3 Incidents During 10 Day Span In November	12/9/2010
	8/26/2007
Bishop Bomber Suspect Denied Pretrial Release	11/2/2011
	12/14/2010
	9/11/2010
	9/13/2010
15% of population poorer	10/6/2013
389,100 millionaires N.Y. City	10/29/2013
Research shows people with more social Power tend to dismiss those with little	10/5/2013
	9/18/2013
	3/27/2012
	1/20/2014
	1/18/2014
	11/16/2013
	11/20/2011
Poverty and family homelessness are a rising emergence of what amounts to a 'recession generation'	4/21/2009
	1/16/2014
	10/28/2011

PUBLICATION	HEADLINE
New York Times	Wars, Endless Wars
New York Times	Job Creation Basics
New York Times	Deep Pockets, Deeply Political
New York Times	Santorum's Gospel Of Inequality
Chicago Tribune	A Double Dip Recession?
Chicago Tribune	Should We Be Angry At The Rich?
Chicago Tribune	Number Of Asset Poor Americans Rising
New York Times	Class Matters. Why Won't We Admit It?
Washington Post	OECD Report Cites Rising Income Inequality
New York Times	Newt's War On Poor Children
New York Times	The Middle Class Agenda
New York Times	For Jobless, Little Hope Of Restoring Better Days

A HUD Letter to Dubuque, Findings of NonCompliance Http: //bit.ly/190Wxl2

SUBJECT	DATE
US economy is in freefall	3/2/2009
Job situation is dire	4/7/2010
	12/19/2011
"There always has been and, hopefully, and I do say that, there always will be"	2/17/2012
	10/10/2011
	10/11/2011
	1/31/2012
	12/11/2011
Social Contract is unraveling In many countries	12/19/2011
Said in Iowa of really poor children- "they have no habit of 'I do this and you give me cash' unless it's illegal"	12/2/2011
Real median income of working age households has declined from $61,600 into 2000 to $55,300 in 2010	12/19/2011
	12/1/2011

INDEX

100 Best Communities for Young People 194

20/20 News Magazine 43, 107

Al Green 176

Albert Ellis 204

Aldi's 131

All American City .... Back Cover

Anthony Quinn 195

Aristotle 55

Auschwitz 181

Bain Capital 142

Barbara Walters 182

Ben Franklin 98

Betty Jane 107

Biden 182

Billy Jack 58

Bishop Bomber 41,46,57,237

Bob Dylan 57

Bobby Seale 180

Book of Judges 166

Bread For the World 161

Canaan 11,24

Canfield Hotel 66

Carl Sandburg 36

Carpenter's Union Hall 3

Cedar Rapids .. iii, iv, xiii, 180, 184, 229

Chad Parker 68

Charlton Heston 37

Chicago Black Hawks 41,84

Chief Joseph 174

Christmas 56, 65, 132, 133

Chuck Berry 123

Clinton, Iowa 29, 30

Community Days of Caring 185

Corinthians 179

Crazy Horse 38

Crusoe 63

Custer 37, 39

Dachau .... xv, xviii, 181

Dale Earnhardt Jr 127

Dave Smith 164

David Beckmann 161

David Dukes 108

Des Moines v

Des Moines Register .... iii, iv

Detroit 14

Dracula 105

Dubuqueland Storage 53

Eagle Grocery 89, 117, 120

East Dubuque 189

Ecclesiates 3:1 .... 5, 18

Edward Albee 12

Edward Conrad 142

Eldridge Cleaver 180

Elijah 79

Ezekiel 79

F. I. S. T. 154

Family Dollar 52, 150

Farmers' Market 4, 5

Forbes .... vii, 130

Francis Bacon 177

Frontier Dubuque Survey 232

Gaddafi 148

Gene Autry 23

George Kennedy............................ 38
Geromey Gilliand 105, 109
Gibson Guitar 127
Grimm's... 105
Harry Stack Sullivan........................ 13
Henry Fonda.................................. 195
Hillcrest 89
HUD............................ 5, 13, 54, 57, 77,
    104, 111, 229, 234, 238
Huey Newton 180
Human Organization....................... 53
Hyundai... 144
HyVee...................................... 113, 114
IBM 63, 103
Iowa Bystander 54
Iowa City.........48, 61, 63, 90, 118, 121
Iowa City Hospital......................... 121
Iowa Human Rights
    Commission............................ 181
Iowa Public Radio.................... 54, 229
IRCNA 90
J Edgar Hoover 180
Jackson Street.......................... 51, 163
James Brown 178
James Loewen................................. 55
Jellystone Park................................. 76
Jimmy Carter.................................. 148
John Berger 27
John Carlos.................................... 180
John Deere................80, 81, 151, 187
John G Neihardt "Twilight of
    the Sioux" 116
John Kass .... iii, v, xiii, 5, 104
Jonathan Narcisse........................... 54
Joyce Conners............................... 103
Joyce Russell 54
KANT 92
Kelly Larson .... v, 1, 12
KKK 5, 105, 108, 182
K-Mart... 42

Kendrick Lamar "good kid,
    m.A.A.d city" 46
Kris Kristofferson 99
Lenz Monument............................. 91
Let It Rise 200
Maquoketa 87, 88
Marilyn Manson.............................. 85
Martin Buber 114
Martin Luther King......................... 176
Marvin Gaye
    "What's Goin' On"................. 233
Maslow 148
Matthew (bible) ....vii, 28
Matthew Modine......................iii, 145
Mel Gibson 202
Mercy Hospital 19, 163
Mike VanderMillen 104, 105
Mike VanMilligen..................... 54, 103
Minuchin 56
Mozart 175
MS 189
Muscatine, Ia.................................. 89
Myrtle Beach 33
NA (Narcotics Anonymous) 90
NAACP 42, 43, 181, 182, 194
Nashville 72, 74, 75, 76, 77
National Barn Dancce.................... 23
Nintendo 85, 159, 160
Noah... 199
Noonan's 3, 27, 80
Northeast Iowa Community
    College......................xiv, 193, 194
Numbers 30:1.................................. 77
Obama 182
Old Wooden Cross 6, 200
Papillon... 58
Pat Butram..................................... 23
Paul Krugman............................ 56, 92
Peosta, Ia 163
Peter Norman................................ 180

Phi Theta Kappa 194
Phil Robinson 139
Pistol Pete Maravich....................... 29
Pizza Hut 86
Players Bar........................... 54, 55, 181
Poe 66
Powerade.. 119
President Bush 142
Preston Daniels.............................. 181
PTSD 181
Ramen Noodles 176
Red Herring...................................... 205
Renfield 105
Rescue Mission 31, 141, 205
Robert Mitchum.............................. 38
Robert Taylor Holmes................. 44, 45
Rocky.. 38
Rorschach.. 206
Safe Community Task Forcee 11
Sam's Club................................. 67, 68
San Diego 101
Scott Baxter 194
Senior High School......................... 107
Silvertone 127
Sitting Bull 86
Soylent Green 37
St Christopher 30
Stephen King 115
Stone Phillips 182
Sundown Laws 54
Sylvester Stallone 163
Take This Job and Shove It.... 154, 163
Taqiyah 44, 45
Telegraph Herald .... iv, xiv, 4,
          41, 43, 82, 104, 194, 234, 236
Terry Tobin 194
Thanksgiving.................. 52, 67, 69, 70

The American Dream.................... 112
The Baptism of Jesse Taylor 60, 61
The Barn Sherrill, Iowa..................... 36
The Black Commentator 55
The Dubuque Community
          Church..................... 191, 199, 204
The Field of Dreams ... viii, 17, 139, 154
The Great Recession ....i, 3, 11, 12,
          14, 41, 56, 65, 67, 103, 126
The Key City .... xiii, 112, 193
The Lady From Dubuque 12
The Man With the Golden Gun
          Roger Moore............................. 38
The Mines of Spain........................... 33
The Ox Bow Incident 195
The Passion 202
The Resurrection 202
The Stones 28, 100
The Tabernacle of Faith 133
Tommie Smith 180
Trayvon Martin................................ 104
Trinity 39
True Value 74, 155, 186
U Haul 180
University of Dubuque.................... 180
University of Vermont...................... 55
Walgreen's....................................... 122
Washington Post 161, 234, 236, 238
Washington Street 122, 185, 186
Welu Printing..................................... 65
William James................................. 191
Wisconsin .... xiii, 156, 219
WLS 23
Woodrow Wilson 30
Woodstock, Il..................................... 33
ZZ Top... 64